"Son Of Wales Award"
For best new author and poet
2016

∽

Interview with Al Cole from CBS Radio Talk Show
People of Distinction for his book Cave Days
2020

Copyright 2015 by Kingsley Ross Hill

Second Edition – 2022

All rights reserved.
Written permission must be secured from the publisher
to use or reproduce any part of this book, except for brief quotations
in critical reviews or article.

ISBN 978-0-9879493-1-8

Published in Swansea, Wales
by King of the Castle Publishing.

Front Cover Artwork by Sylvia Nicholson

To contact Kingsley Hill email at gowerofthehills@gmail.com
www.kingsleyrosshillbooks.com

Printed and bound in Canada by Island Blue Book Printing,
Victoria, BC

Acknowledgments

My deepest thanks to those who have encouraged me to climb this new mountain in the writing of Cave Days, Book 1 of the Gower Peninsula Series.

To my wonderful wife Janais, for her love, devotion and encouragement.

To my son, Jonathan, who walked with me through the time of my great tribulation. A son like you, Champ, a dad can only dream of, but God made my dreams come true when he gave me you.

To my horse family, Great Thunder, Thunder Spring, and Little Thunder, and an old Man whose name I never knew yet became my great friend.

I would also like to thank the many readers who have enjoyed reading my book "Cave Days" and helped it become such a great success. Thank you for the many letters and stories I have received regarding how it has been a blessing in your lives. My hope and prayer is that you will enjoy my whole series equally as much.

With much love and thanksgiving,
Kingsley Ross Hill

Kingsley supports a number of organisations through the proceeds of his books. His favourite is Lluest Horse and Pony Trust in Carmarthenshire, South Wales. The word Lluest means "Haven" in Welsh.

Lluest rescues horses and ponies that have suffered neglect, cruelty, or abandonment. Their wounds can be physical or mental, sometimes both. When the horses are ready, they are rehabilitated and given a second chance of life in carefully selected loving homes. Every horse remains under the ownership of Lluest, and they are visited in their guardian homes. The dedicated people at Lluest, monitor the mountains and commons, and are a presence at local markets to improve conditions for equines going through the sales.

A portion of the sales of this book goes to support the work of Lluest Horse and Pony Trust to help them continue their excellent work in equine rescue in the Brecon Beacons National Park.

THE CLAM DIGGERS

There is a story of two people, Ordinary people. Nay, surely there is no such thing as two ordinary people. Not if their lives have touched, held souls and caressed, built sand castles and danced with the rainbows in the tides. They are washed in as two pieces of driftwood, always surfing on the same tide, and then collected by excited, running, digging children, singing summer songs of mysteries and mermaids and pictures that tell stories in the sky. There are miles of beach but only two different lives, and the clam diggers, they chose not to hide, always playing in the waves of the same tide.

These memories shall not sleep, but sing and dance and shout, as the child that lives in us always. Only when we cease to dig for shells and to collect the heart-shaped rocks, shall the child within us die. Look! You can see that God's pictures are always painted on the skies. Each new morning and evening there is a brand-new surprise. Look! Here come the clam diggers, coming in on the next tide.

© *Kingsley Ross Hill and Janice Marie McQuirter*

Table of Contents

1	October the Eleventh	1
2	Autumn's Last Dance	16
3	November Grey	32
4	Milk Money, Prawns, and a Wet Night	41
5	I'll Be Home for Christmas	55
6	Leathers Hole	76
7	Message in a Bottle	89
8	Gay Tripp	99
9	A Forever Kiss	122
10	The Thunder Child	132
11	King of Gower!	142
12	Sunset Colours of Love	159
13	Waltzing Through Spring	174
14	The Miracle	189
15	Welcome to the World	212
16	Orange and Indigo	228
17	Life Goes On	253
18	Around the World In Five Days	267
19	Good Morning Deborah!	289
20	The Rock at the End of the World	306
21	The Song of the Morning	323
22	Great Thunder	338
23	Thou Art Mine	359
24	High Tide	398
	About the Author	417

Chapter One

October the Eleventh

I woke to a cool and heavy air that breathed freshly upon my skin, and a strong smell of salt and sea greeted my nostrils. Fully awake, I began to say good morning to the haunting yet soothing sound of the surf that spoke loudly at the entrance. Time to move. I didn't want to get trapped. I climbed to my feet and felt my way along the damp, smooth walls until daylight gave light to my path.

I found the waves already claiming most of the entrance. I was cut off with no time to spare. Stripping to my waist, I put my clothes in my backpack and waded out against the strong tide. The sand was soft beneath my feet, and the water surprisingly warm for the autumn season. I had just got out in time! Another few minutes and I would have had to swim for it. As quickly as I could, I waded around the sandy spit and on to the open beach.

Well, I had just spent my first night in a cave, and the first day of my great adventure was upon me. I walked along the beach collecting thoughts and shells, and listening to the sea gulls' cheers, that seemed to speak louder than my fears.

Cave Days

"What have I done and why am I here?" my soul asks the listening ears. I needed healing and comfort and to make sense of the painful years. Would I find what I was looking for here?

It was the second week of October, I believe. I had just turned 16 in August and I had decided to leave home, or should I say what had once been home. It hadn't been for a long time, not since Mom and Dad had split and then got divorced. Mom had gone away to Canada, and I couldn't get along with my father any more. I blamed him for my mother going away.

∽

As I walked along the sand, I followed the tide lines high up on the beach. The incoming tide looked about three-quarters of the way in, as I compared it with yesterday's tides. It was getting late in the afternoon and the sun was already low in the sky. With the light fading fast, it was time to decide on my shelter, and how I was going to keep warm. I would think about food tomorrow.

The cave that I'd slept in last night was right on the beach, and at high tide the sea claims the whole cave. One could drown being trapped inside. I'd been fortunate that today's tide was a lower one. I hadn't intended falling asleep in the cave, just using it for shelter. There were several caves between Hunts Bay, which was off to the east, and where I was now on Pobbles Beach, a distance of about two miles as the ravens fly, or as a boy could roam. These caves were well above sea level, some high up on the cliffs.

October the Eleventh

I decided to head eastward to my favourite cave, Bacon Hole. I first discovered Bacon Hole on a school outing in the spring of 1969. I was the hero that day, because I found the tooth of the saber toothed cat, and none of my classmates found anything. It sits in Swansea Museum to this day. I had a good history teacher in my middle school years by the name of Mr. Richards. He took us on regular field trips to the different caves in the area, and he had an interest in archaeology and finding prehistoric remains. He made learning interesting and fun. I would leave his classroom believing I could go and discover anything! And that's what I did on weekends – I went on digs and explored all the caves on the Gower Peninsula where I lived. I found many wonderful things, from cavemen and animal bones to flints used for hunting. My favourite find was a stone arrowhead that had been used as the tip of a spear. I imagined myself using that one, and thrusting it into the belly of a wild animal or enemy caveman.

And now I was on my way to live in a cave myself at 16. "You must move forward," my high school teachers told me, "and concentrate on your school work or you will be left behind." I guess they were right on that one. I was going to be left behind alright, 60 million years behind, living in Bacon Hole. So much for modern man with his colour TV's and fancy electronics. I would be back to basic instincts, but I would have a fresh start in life. That's the way I was looking at it anyway. Besides, how do you move ahead in your life if you can't make sense of the past? You stare it in the eyes and say, "I'm not scared of you and you're not going to determine my future." Isn't that why teens run away from home? Do they think their future is going to be as bad and confusing as their past? They didn't teach me the answer to that one at school.

Cave Days

  I continued my way along Pobbles Beach towards Bacon Hole. At the eastern end of Pobbles, the beach becomes Heather Slade Bay, which is a rocky beach with deep pools and gullies. When we were boys, my father would take my brother Fraser and I prawning there. He made big nets for us and taught us how to use them. I would have to make some nets for myself now that I'd be living off the land and the sea. Heather Slade Bay is also good for bass fishing, and I hoped that it would become one of my regular fishing areas where I could catch a good supply of fish. The rocky beach is only exposed at low tide, and you have to time it right or you get cut off by the incoming tide. The area of water around the Gower Peninsula is part of the Bristol Channel, which, next to the Bay of Fundy in Canada, has the second-highest rise and fall of tides in the world. More than once when I was a boy crabbing and fishing with my father, we had to climb a sheer cliff face rather than risk drowning below.

  At low tide, you can walk all the way from Heather Slade to my destination at Hunts Bay, but you have to walk over slippery seaweed rocks, jump over small gullies, and even climb over large boulders to get there. It's not for the faint of heart, but for those who walk the adventure, there can be great rewards. There are lobster holes and edible crab crevices to find and explore.

  The best tool to get lobsters and crabs out of their holes is a wire clothes hanger attached to the end of a broom handle. It is good to have two or three different lengths of sticks so you can reach the various depths of the holes and crevices. You can bend the clothes hanger and fit the shape of the hole and wrestle the creature out.

  I was eight years old when my father first took me on this adventure. After laughing and crying and once or twice

October the Eleventh

believing I was dying, we arrived at Hunts Bay, and with my scraped and bleeding knees and a sore elbow, I held my big red crab up high, and I was a happy boy.

No, I wasn't a boy anymore. "I'm the man now!" I proclaimed. "I caught the biggest crab." Thanks dad.

I continued my walk, but when I reached Heather Slade Bay, the tide was far too high for me to walk the adventure over the rocks, so I climbed up from the beach and walked along the cliff tops. I stopped several times along the way to reminisce about my boyhood years, for each cliff and cave seemed to have a happy memory attached to it.

When I arrived at Hunts Bay, I climbed down from the cliff top on a narrow path through the wild Gorse. It was a seldom used path, one I had memories of as a boy, and it led me right to the entrance of Bacon Hole. There was only enough light to see into the entrance of the cave, and I decided I wouldn't venture further in until the morning.

My cave faced southeast and looked straight out across the Bristol Channel to Devonshire, England. On a clear day you could see all the way to Ilfracombe in North Devonshire, a distance of about 20 miles. The ground at the entrance of Bacon Hole was very rocky, with a few patches of hard clay between the stones. I only had my sleeping bag, and as I kicked the stones from the clay, I thought of the comfort of a mattress. Sometime I would return to my father's house and get the rest of my camping gear. That wouldn't help me tonight, though.

I wriggled around in my sleeping bag, trying not to feel the hard ground under my back. I used my backpack for a pillow and finally I drifted off to sleep.

Cave Days

In spite of the hard ground, I had a good night's sleep. It must have been the healthy sea air, and the absence of tension and strife that I experienced at the house. I was welcomed to the new day by the dawn chorus of the birds. It started about an hour before first light, with the quiet and intermittent squeaks of the rock pipits that dwelt in and around the entrance of the cave. Rock pipits are rare, and even roaming the cliffs as a boy, I rarely saw one.

There are many different bird species on Pennard Cliffs: yellow hammers with their beautiful yellow and green plumage, blue tits and black caps, chit chats and warblers. My favourite is the male bullfinch with his brilliant red front and black head, and a song that makes most people stop during their walk and give praise to the morning. These birds, along with the more common sparrows and finches, haunt the tall grasses and Gorse bushes that grow on the steep slopes of the cliffs.

The next to perform their part in the dawn chorus were the rock doves that dwelt in the heart of the cave. I lay still, listening intently and wondering how many doves were in there and what they were saying. Their song was sweet, and I thought they sounded excited. They must be making their plans for the new day, I thought, and I hoped that my day would be as exciting as theirs. Well, what do you know, I think I can speak fluent Dove. Did you hear that, Mr. Davies, Sir? I may not be able to speak Welsh very well, but I can speak and understand native Dove. What do you think of that, old man? You couldn't teach me that in school, could you?

As a young boy, it had been a treasure to find rock dove nests. They nested far back in the caves and high up on the

October the Eleventh

rocky ledges. Finding their nests required real exploring and often dangerous climbs to reach them.

Suddenly the Gulls woke me from my daydream as they squabbled on the rocks below. I stretched one more time and then crawled out of my sleeping bag. I took some deep breaths—oh the sea air—so fresh and clean, and then on the gentle breeze came the sweet coconut smell of the wild Gorse flower. It thrilled my soul, and I danced a jig. It's wonderful how the sense of smell can make the minutes into years, and the years into minutes.

For a moment, I was walking with my grandmother along East Cliff Road. She stopped and showed me the flowers, and we smelled them all in those happy hours, walking and dodging the spring showers. And then I was dreaming of my lover. Oh how I wished she were here. She smells of the wild Gorse flower, and in the purple, bee-buzzing heather, we are making our cheer, a story told only by the skylarks and a magpie always near.

It was time to start my day, and with my morning jig I claimed this cave as my own. As the sun rose higher, I could see further into my cave and I ventured in to re-explore Bacon Hole.

The entrance has a wonderful overhanging limestone roof that protrudes out about 40 feet, giving the entrance a natural shelter from the wind and rain. When one approaches the cave from the west, along a narrow path through the Gorse, it gives the grandest view of the entrance and overhanging roof. Viewed from this angle, the roof has a splendid triangular v-shape to it, which would have been a symbol of social status, I think, in caveman days. I bet the man who lived in here wore the finest of furs.

Cave Days

There are several large stones at the entrance, one of which I would choose to be my lookout seat, the place where I would greet each new day. I sat on them all until one felt right. I chose the largest one, not because of its size, but for its shape and view. My stone had a nice smooth top to it. It was slightly angled forward, but not uncomfortable.

I sat and thought about what it would have been like to live here thousands of years ago. What would life have been like as a caveman? This seat would be my throne, and I would sit as a king, guarding my home. Inside would be my family, my woman and children—probably several women in those days. And sons; I'd have sons and I would teach them how to hunt and fish, and protect our family from wild animals and enemy clans. But at this moment in time, I felt lonely and I wished I had a cave woman who would be my companion and friend.

I stood now at the entrance of the cave. I didn't have to go inside to realize that this was a very lonely place. It had a heavy air to it, and its silence spoke loud, giving me the feeling that I wasn't alone but rather an uninvited guest. Why was it suddenly so quiet? Had the birds finished their morning song? Did they want me to listen to something, to hear the silent song—the song sung by this lonely place and by cavemen's souls, now gone? I listened and heard stories of the family that had lived in Bacon Hole.

I heard what happened when they got sick or injured, or attacked by wild animals and other cave clans. So many of them died from their wounds, and from sicknesses that could easily be cured today. I thought about having a wife that I loved, and having to watch her die, and one of my little children, seeing the spirit leave her eyes. Oh, what a harsh and desperate time.

October the Eleventh

"But there has to be something more to their lives than this; tell me," I shouted out to a spirit nearby.

"Yes, it's the simplicity," he said, "and being so connected to one's fellow man and woman, working together as a family and clan, having to rely on one another to survive, and each member knowing their role and having —a respected and honored place in the family."

"This is wealth," he said, compared to today's idle and selfish hand." I thought of the love between a man and a woman, in the family clan. It would be that much stronger, wouldn't it, compared to today's modern man? The spirit didn't answer. He didn't need to. For I knew that was the way it was. And standing here peering into the cave, I envied the caveman whose loving woman and children waited around the fire for him to return home with food and animal skins.

Suddenly the spirit spoke again, saying, "Come on inside. Didn't you live here before? Why do you stand like a stranger outside your own door?" Shivers ran up my spine as I remembered so much more, and deep in my soul I wondered: could I have lived here before?

My family dwelt in the heart of the cave. We had animal furs to sleep on, and my woman was making clothes. Our children played and painted pictures on the walls, as the flames of the fire danced and flickered, giving warmth and light, and telling the stories of our lives. We all sat and ate together in love's orange glow. I love my woman and children, and I am a rich man, you know!

"Well, spirit, I'm coming in now. What's your name anyway?"

"I can't answer that, but one day you will know," answered the spirit.

The cave was much as I remembered. It went deep into the cliff and was broadest in the middle. This had been the cave family's living area, and it would also be mine. There were still some rocks where I had built a fireplace as a boy. Kneeling down, I started to dig in the dry hard clay. There was still some charcoal in the ground; it was the remains of my very own fire. The years melted away, and I was sitting at my fire with my three best friends. We spent hours that night sharing our secret stories, or what we *wished* were our stories. Like the mysteries of French kissing with Heather Swanson, a wonderful experience that we all claimed to know so well. And then, of course, we shared what we were going to be when we grew up. Each of us in turn puffed on a tobacco pipe, borrowed from my friend Mitch's father, just for the occasion.

Then it was my turn to take the pipe. Puffed up with pride and smoke, I told of my plans to be a great explorer, and one day set foot where no one else had ever been. "There are places in the mountains of Canada, lads, that have yet to be discovered. There are wild animals—wolves, bears, and mountain lions, and I want to hunt them all. There are lakes and rivers teaming with fish, so thick you could walk across them, and I'm going to find myself a pure-blooded native woman, as wild as the land I'm going to claim! There are many tribes of Indians, and I'm going to choose a beautiful woman, who can teach me much about the land. We will live a life of freedom in a log cabin in the wilderness. I'll fish and hunt for a living, a life that people can only dream of or imagine in this country. I'm going to live that life."

October the Eleventh

My friends nodded their heads and grunted in approval, for none of us dared to argue that we could be anything less than what we had shared.

Suddenly the fluttering wings of a rock dove at the back of the cave brought me back to the present. For a few minutes I felt at a loss – for there would be no one to tell stories to; only the spirits of the cave family long gone. I stood up and ventured further into the cave, following its dark recesses deep under the Pennard Cliffs above. The roof remained high, and continued at about the same height until you reached the heart of the cave. It then lowered considerably and the light faded fast.

It gave me an eerie claustrophobic feeling, added to the initial fear that the whole cave could collapse at any moment. I remembered a time in my primary school years when I was out in the playground with my classmates. All of a sudden we heard this terrific crash like loud thunder and felt the ground shake. It only lasted a few seconds, and it couldn't have been thunder. The sky was clear and blue. Later that day Mr. Richards, our art and history teacher, announced that one of the caves had collapsed at Pobbles Beach. "That's what the noise and ground shaking was, boys and girls."

Suddenly I heard a distant roar and a swoosh noise. I bolted like a rabbit back to the entrance, only to hear the same sound again. It was the large swells of the tide crashing into the rocks and gully below the cave. Gosh, I was nervous. I was going to have to get used to these noises if I was going to live in Bacon Hole. Come on Kings! Pull yourself together. This cave has been here for thousands of years, surviving two ice ages. It's not going to fall now.

Cave Days

I picked up my courage and went back into the heart of the cave. I stood again at my fireplace and then I knelt down and started to reshape the rock circle. Once I had put all the stones together, my fireplace looked small, so I decided to bring in some more rocks from outside.

There were lots around and the perfect size. I brought in several loads, one rock in each hand, and soon I had a large circle of them. Now I would have a large fire, big enough to chase away the spirits. I would collect a good supply of wood, and store it against the far wall.

I began to get a vision of my home, and I marked out an area in the clay with a sharp stone where I would have my bed, about six to eight feet away from the fire, that would give me enough warmth and light, and be far enough away so I wouldn't catch a hot cinder in my sleep.

With my fireplace finished, I decided to spend the next few hours collecting wood. The weather had been unusually dry for September and October—an Indian summer, my father called it. (But there were no Indians; I would have to wait until I went to Canada to see one.) I needed to take full advantage of finding dry wood, for the rains would come any day now, as it was almost the middle of October. I could remember some years when it was rainy and damp from mid-August to the end of March. Add April showers to that, and you wonder if you will ever see the sun again.

East of my cave is the cove of Hunts Bay. There above the tide line, I collected a fair supply of driftwood that had spent the summer months drying in the sun. I was doing well. After several trips back and forth to my cave, I climbed to the cliff top and collected some dead Gorse bush, which would be great as a fire starter. One strike of the match and it would burn instantly.

My hands were soon pricked and cut from the Gorse however. I needed an ax, as well as a camping mattress and blankets for my bed. Much as I didn't want to return to my father's house, I would have to make a trip back for essential supplies....

It was getting late in the afternoon now, and I had about two hours at most before it would be dark. I decided to go to my father's house right away and get it over with, although the thought of going back there caused me to feel troubled inside.

Before I left my cave, I built up a nice fire in my new fireplace. I climbed back to the cliff top and over to Hunts farm. From there, I cut across the fields to get to my father's house. When I arrived, I was relieved to find that my father and my brother Fraser were out, probably still at work. I went right to the garden shed and got my ax. My fishing gear was there too, and also a camping lantern and flashlight. "They will come in handy," I said aloud, putting them in my backpack. My camping mattress was in one of the storage areas inside the house. I quickly tried the door and it wasn't locked, so I went inside and found the mattress.

"I'm out of here!" I carried the mattress and my fishing box under one arm, and the backpack and fishing rods over my other shoulder, and soon I was on my way back to the Cliffs. By the time I got back to the cave, it was dark, and I couldn't see anything inside.

I got out my flashlight and held it high, dancing its beam back and forth from one wall to the other, as only the light would chase away my fears. I reached the heart of the cave and my fire. The darkness was heavy, and even with my beam of light, I felt like something was going to reach out and grab me at any moment.

"What was that?!" The flapping of wings brushed past my head. I fumbled for my matches and struck one, then put it to the Gorse, which burned instantly. I began to breathe easier as the flames of the fire got bigger and bigger. I picked up some small rocks and threw them to the back of the cave. Suddenly, several birds—I could see that they were rock doves—came flying past my head.

"No more surprises!" I shouted, throwing another few rocks. This time nothing came out. That must have been all of them. Wait, what about bats? No, they would be gone by now; every creature was out of the cave. Everything that could be seen, that is.

But it was the unseen that I was afraid of, dark spirits in the heavy silence of this place. I could hear them shouting loudly above the crackling fire. They told stories of the terrifying spirit beings who lived in the back of the cave. Was I imagining them? Were they real? I threw several large logs on the fire now, and it wasn't long before the whole heart of the cave lit up as if in daylight, chasing the spirits to the back of the cave, to the place where my fears would always dwell. Even standing in the light and warmth of the fire, as I looked back at those dark recesses, I knew that so long as I lived in this cave they would always remain my "hell."

I blew up my air mattress and laid it out on the area that I'd marked out on the clay, about eight feet from the fire. I put two more logs on—they should last till morning—and then I got into my sleeping bag and faced away from the fire. I could feel its warmth on my back, and its light wrestled with the shadows on the wall. I would try to fall asleep while the fire was big and giving off the most light. I battled for a few minutes with my fears, and with the most frightening thoughts of all, which focused on the dark corner at the end of the cave. Could it be the place where the past still lived? ... where the ghosts still screamed and shouted?

The battle in my mind became severe, for in my soul I could hear them. There seemed to be a place in my awareness where I was stuck, and struggling to get out. It was a place somewhere between reality and my imagination, where my dreams reached out and danced with my fears. I wished I knew where it was, and what it was!

If the spirits were real, it would be less frightening than this state of not knowing. I would have to choose which was real, and then I would be able to sleep. I decided it was my imagination, at least for tonight, but the silent screams told me otherwise. Come on Kings! Think of something else. The spring comes after the winter; think of that, and try to get some sleep.

Suddenly I awoke, or had I even been asleep? A log had moved on the fire. My fears were awakened again. I climbed out of my sleeping bag, picked up some more rocks and ran shouting towards the dark corner. I threw the rocks. "Is anyone here?"

Only my fears answered, and they shouted, "Oh yes, we are all here." Defeated, I walked to the entrance of the cave. It was too dark and dangerous to go anywhere else, and where could I go, with the laughing demons behind me and the cruel sea before me? I tried to think of a sunny day, with all the shadows gone away. It was a long time until summer, but tomorrow is another day. And you know what? The sun will come up anyway.... and I fell asleep.

Chapter Two

Autumn's Last Dance

OH SWEET MORNING SONG

How sweet your song this morning,
oh bright and golden morning.
Your sun rose,
and you kissed me.
I listen, and sing to your words,
With skylark and robin and all the other birds.
Our song sends the night shadows along.
And though summer be long away,
each new morning you bring a brand new day.
I will sing and celebrate all day long,
for I have heard your sweet morning song.
I will dance and shout,
because the darkness has gone,
And your light shines again upon the earth.
Black has become green,
and the sea is blue again,
and I can hold hands and dance with you.

Autumn's Last Dance

> Oh, my sweet morning song,
> you warm my face,
> and touch me,
> and my life is born again.
> Bluebell, Heather and Daisy all shout out your name.
> Your song is sung in the field,
> and on the hills,
> and in the gentle rain.
> It is morning,
> and life begins again.
> Oh sweet morning song.
> You came anyway.

I woke up hungry and thought of food. I had managed to save a hundred pounds before I left home, and that would be enough money to live on for a few months, if I was careful. What then? I thought, as I climbed up onto my throne and looked out across the Bristol Channel.

The sea is emerald green today, my favourite colour. I would go into the village and buy some food and then explore the cliffs and beaches this afternoon, and decide where I was going to hunt and fish. If I was going to live in the wild, then hunting and fishing is how I would survive. At least I had shelter already, even if I was too afraid to sleep in the heart of the cave. I would sleep at the entrance for now, and with the caves overhanging roof, I would keep dry.

Before leaving for the village, I went back into my cave—no, 'the cave'. I couldn't call it "my cave" until I conquered my fear of sleeping inside. I checked my fireplace. All the wood had burned, and only the hot ash remained inside my circle of stones. It was sure different here in the light of day. Gone was the frightening night, but as I stared into the dark at the back of the cave, it said, "I will see you again tonight."

"I know that you will, Fear," I replied, "but not until tonight. I'm going to say goodbye now because I'm going out into the light."

I walked along the cliff tops to Southgate village. Southgate village is at the end of the main but narrow road that winds through Pennard's lanes and on through the little village of Pennard, my home village. The road continues until it ends at a roundabout and green in front of Pennard stores, my destination to buy food. At the roundabout, the main road branches off into three small roads, Southgate Road and the East Cliff and West Cliff roads. Just a stone's throw from both East Cliff and West Cliff roads are spectacular cliff top walks.

These walks boast some of the most beautiful scenery in the Gower Peninsula. As you walk westward, the direction in which I was walking today, you have the sea to your left with views of high cliff headlands and rocky crags that jut out into the foaming surf 200 feet below. Often, you can see ravens and kestrels riding the thermal air currents overhead. And occasionally a buzzard or two can be seen circling high above as they hunt for their prey.

What would it be today? It was a kestrel hovering with its body almost still as it looked for a mouse or a small bird. I watched its hovering wings close as it dropped like a brick on its prey. Then suddenly, out of the bracken, it reappeared carrying what looked like a mouse or vole.

The view to the right is of Cefn Bryn, which in the Welsh language means a hill. Cefn Bryn is one of the highest hills on

Autumn's Last Dance

the Gower Peninsula. During the spring and summer months, the Bryn is arrayed in his purple heather garment that he wears like a king on high, the purple heather is contrast to the deep green ferns and brown bracken that grows on the lower slopes of the mighty hill. Add a clear blue sky and the song of the skylarks, and your soul can only soar on high with the wind. When you walk amongst the bluebells and daffodils, here and there, the wild primroses smile at you. And the smell—oh, the sweet smell of the fragrant flowers, as they are blown gently on the sea breeze.

But the greatest reward of all is when you come to the glorious beaches of Pobbles and Three Cliff Bays, and in the distance, beyond the storytelling river, is the great Tor and the Bell Rock. The Bell Rock rings in my heart, and my spirit leaves my body and flies to Oxwich Bay, and I am lifted higher and higher over beaches and memories, and the songs of the Seagull Singing Bay, where girls and kisses, and wild horses come to play, until I land on the golden sands holding life in my hands.

I arrived at the village and went into the Pennard stores. I bought the basics: bread and butter, some cold cereal, some tinfoil and food I could heat up over a fire. Beans, beans, and more beans. Maybe that will frighten the spirits away. Oh, and I would need some milk, and a bottle of pop for a treat. I also bought some throwaway dishes and cutlery. There would be no washing dishes in my cave, unless the spirits wanted to clean up. I doubt it, they don't like camping.

That was enough food for one trip, or I wouldn't be able to carry it all. I was ravishingly hungry now as I walked back, and I couldn't wait to wolf down a bowl of cereal, and some bread and jam. Oh no, I'd forgotten the jam! Oh well, I wasn't walking back now. Bread and butter would have to do.

As I make my breakfast, I sit upon my throne and look out across the Bristol Channel. The morning mist has lifted, and I can see the rolling hills of North Devonshire, 20 miles away. I stop and think for a few minutes about my grandparents living in Devonshire. It has been a long time since I've seen them. I imagine them cozy and warm in their little cottage on the other side of the rolling hills.

Well, with food in my stomach, it's time to start my day. I climbed down from my throne and walked to the edge of the cliff. It's a sheer drop of 150 feet to the gully below, no place for a sleepwalker. I stepped back quickly as a gust of wind blew on my back.

I could tell by the rocks now exposed above the waves that the tide was going out. It would be a good time to go and re-explore the beaches, and decide where to start fishing. I took my fishing gear and climbed to the top of the cliff. I decided to walk the East Cliff path until I reached the village again, and from there would take the West Cliff path to Pobbles and Three Cliff Bay. By the time I reach Pobbles Beach, the tide should be far enough out for me to walk across the sand to Three Cliffs Point and fish where the river joins the sea.

As I walked, I recalled fond memories of fishing in the river as a boy. The bass fishing can be good there all year round. Then I remembered something that I had always wanted to try.

Several years ago, I had watched a man spearing skate in the river in the late summer. I'd only ever watched someone else do it, and I had always wanted to try it myself. Well, this would be the day to try, I thought. It wasn't late summer any more though; we were well into the autumn, but I remembered a friend saying that the skate or "thorn back rays" as he called them, went up the river as late as Christmas. By the time I reached the river, I was excited to try my luck.

The Three Cliffs River has another name by which she is called, a name I first heard when I was about nine years old.

"That be the Killy Willy, boy."

"The Killy Willy, Sir?"

"Yes boy, you're standing in it, the wandering river. Caught anything boy?"

"Yes sir! Two eels and a rainbow trout."

"Well done, boy."

"She has many secrets, boy, does Killy Willy, yes sir."

When the Killy Willy reaches the Three Cliffs Valley, she is called the Three Cliffs River. She goes by that name all the way to the sea as she rolls and winds, and sings like a happy serpent laughing all the way to the waves. She has other names too, from where she starts at Ilston Churchyard, where the gravestones are too old for names. She wanders beside the fir woods, where the fairy world plays, and then on under the stone bridge to old Park Mill School, where I was once kissed by Susan Smith.

Like the old man said, she has many secrets.

I would start my fishing adventures where the Killy Willy joined the sea, at Three Cliffs Point. The man had used a spear gun with a sharp stainless steel spear, but I would have no such tool. I would have to make spears by cutting branches from trees and sharpening them with my knife. So that's what I did. I sharpened my knife with a fishing hook sharpener that was in my fishing box, and then walked along the river bank towards Three Cliffs Woods, where I would cut my spear. As I walked, my eyes searched the sandy bottom of the river bed. The water was clear and the bottom easy to see.

Sometimes the wild horses would walk in the river upstream to have a drink, and the water would be murky until they moved on. I continued to scan the river until I came to one of Killy Willy's twisting corners. Here the water was deeper, and the current much slower.

What was that in the sand? I could see fins in the shape of a fish, and two eyes on the top of the head. It was a skate, it had to be! It was far too big for a flounder or place, both of which were known to travel up the river. My heart began to race. I dropped my fishing box and rods on the bank and ran into the woods to make my spear. Would it still be there when I got back?

I looked at several trees, trying to find the right branch, and finally found one the perfect size—long and not too wide. I quickly started hacking off the branch with my knife. Having stopped to sharpen it really paid off as it cut through the branch easily. My spear was about 6 feet in length and 1 inch thick, perfect for stabbing or throwing. I sharpened the end, getting it ready for my throw. The bank was high and the water deep where I'd seen the skate. I would have to stand quietly on the bank and throw the spear hard into the flesh and then jump into the water to retrieve it. I needed to make a good barb too, so the skate wouldn't be able to wriggle off the spear. I carved it about 6 inches away from the point. It was time to head back to the river, and I ran holding my spear like a proud warrior.

Autumn's Last Dance

I slowed when I reached the bank, and snuck up on my hands and knees to look over the edge to see if he was still there. He was, and his whole body was on the top of the sand now. He was a lot bigger than I first thought. I stood up slowly, adrenaline pumping through my veins. I needed to throw my spear hard and make it count, there would be no second chance.

As I threw my spear, my grip was good and I was able to get a lot of power behind it. It was a great throw, going right through the skate, which turned on to its side and wriggled gently. For a few fleeting moments, I felt sorry for the poor creature, but soon my excitement took over. Wow, that was great! What a thrill!

I waded into the pool and reached for the end of the spear. The skate flapped harder as I lifted him out of the water and onto the bank. Wow, he was sure a big one, and look at that white meat! The spear had gone right through him, right below his head.

I cut off his wings, and also sliced off some thick meat along his spine, working from the neck to the tail. The seagulls that had watched me from a distance now flew overhead, circling and squawking as if flying over a fishing trawler. "Don't you crap on me," I shouted, picking up the frame of the skate and throwing it back in the water.

I walked back down to the river and washed the meat in the faster flowing water. Well, that was enough adventure for one day. As I walked back along the beach, I felt proud of my success. It certainly gave me some confidence in what I hoped to be the start of being able to live off the land and sea. I didn't want to just survive at it, half starving. I wanted to be a success at being self-sufficient and having plenty to eat, both fish and game. If I could just get through the winter and learn what I needed to, living in the spring and summer would be easier.

When I arrived back at the cave, I quickly made a fire. I was so hungry I could hardly wait to try the skate. Once the fire was at a good heat, I put the skate wings, wrapped in tinfoil, on a large flat stone in the middle of the fire. I called this my cooking stone because it was the perfect shape for pots and pans. I tried to regulate the heat of the fire, with the different shapes and sizes of the pieces of driftwood, almost burning my hands several times. This was primitive cooking alright, and I wondered how the cavemen had done it. "How did you guys do it?" I shouted. I half expected the spirits to laugh or shout out at any moment, or at least say, "What the heck are you doing, man?"

Soon the juices began to flow out of the foil, and the smell of the fish filled the still air. "Mmmmm, can you smell that?" I said aloud, looking to the back of the cave. "You can smell it, but you can't eat it, can you, because you're a spirit. How do you like that then!"

It was time to check the fish. I didn't want to burn it. With two flat pieces of wood, I lifted it to the edge of the fireplace, resting it on a flat stone. I opened the tinfoil and the smell was scrumptious. Yes! The meat was soft and white, and perfectly cooked. It melted in my mouth, and I soon devoured a whole wing of skate. I wrapped the rest up in fresh foil. That would do for tomorrow's supper, I figured. It was cold enough in the cave for cooked fish to keep for one night.

What now? I'd had my supper, and the sun would soon go down. I know, I'll set some rabbit snares. I've just got

Autumn's Last Dance

enough time before they start coming out of their burrows. I had found six snares in my fishing box earlier. I couldn't remember having put them there, but I was sure glad to see them. There were only two ways to catch rabbits here on the cliffs, shooting them or snaring them, but wait, there was another way, come to think of it. Suddenly my mind was flooded with wonderful memories of my hunting ferret that I had named Ripper.

When I was 10 years old, I saved my pocket money and sent away to Norfolk, England for a ferret to hunt rabbits with. My father had shown me that the rabbits on Pennard Cliffs lived in rabbit warrens, and depending on the size of the warren, there could be many rabbit burrows, a series of tunnels dug underground where the rabbits lived and raised their young. Some of the big warrens had hundreds of burrows in them; others were small and had less than 10.

My father and I picked the ferret up from the railway station, where it had travelled hundreds of miles to reach us in Swansea. My father warned me to wait until we got home before I opened his box to have a look at him. "He will be frightened, Kings, after his journey, and hungry too." But I thought I knew better, and the ferret ripped a large gash in my finger, and that's how Ripper got his name. We were off to a painful start, but things would get better.

On the way home my father stopped off at the sporting goods store and bought me six purse nets, as they were called. The next day, with my bandaged finger and a thick pair of motorcycle gloves, I headed over to the nearest rabbit warren with my dad. We spent about half an hour setting the nets over the front of the rabbit burrows.

Cave Days

"Now Son," Dad said, "I want you to stand over the rabbit nets with a good-sized stick in your hand. I'm going to put the ferret down one of the burrows. The rabbits are going to smell the ferret coming after them, and they'll come bolting out of their holes into the nets. Now, you bonk them good and hard on the head, and knock them out before they escape from those nets. I'll keep an eye out for the ferret."

I'll never forget that weekend with my father, it was like he was a boy again and we were best friends. He put Ripper down one of the burrows, and I stood over those nets like I was guarding the Crown Jewels. For 10 minutes there was nothing. "What's wrong, Dad?" I asked.

"Just you wait," he said.

Suddenly, there were rabbits everywhere. Two were in one net at the same time. By the time I'd knocked them over the head, there was another one in a net 10 feet away. "Quick, Kings, he's getting away!" Dad shouted.

I got to the net just in time. The rabbit had escaped the net except for one of its hind legs. "Take that!" I said, and hit it on the head. My father had fallen over with laughter, and then we sat and waited for half an hour before Ripper came back out of the burrow.

"I'm glad he's out," Dad said. "If the ferret catches a rabbit in a burrow, then he'll stay in the burrow and eat it, and fall asleep. Then you have to go and dig the ferret out of the burrow, and that can take hours, even all day."

That night, my father taught me how to skin and gut a rabbit. We had one for supper. It tasted like chicken.

"Hunting rabbits with a ferret was cruel," my mother said.

"It's a good thing for our Kings to learn," was Dad's reply. "You never know, one day our Kings may be living off the land." Little did my dad know he was speaking prophecy that day.

I was sure glad for all he had taught me, and even though I didn't have a ferret and nets now, I knew a lot about catching rabbits. To set up a snare, you find what is known as a rabbit run. Rabbits are creatures of habit, and if undisturbed, they'll walk or run the same path each day and usually around the same time. I climbed down the grass bank that was to the left of the cave's entrance. I counted 10 burrows. This was a small warren, but it would do me fine for a while.

The runs I found close to the cave were coming out of bramble bushes. I could see where the rabbits had worn patches through the thickets, and in front of the runs were fresh droppings where they had been sitting. I quickly set up three snares.

A snare is very easy to set up. It consists of a choke wire, shaped to a loop and set big enough for the head and neck of the rabbit. The snare is held by a stick or twig to one side of the wire. The other side is pegged into the ground so the rabbit doesn't run away. You want it to look as natural as possible to the rabbit, and you want to make sure the snare is right on the run's path. The rabbit sticks his head through the loop of wire and the wire tightens around its neck in a slip knot. The harder the rabbit pulls to try and get away, the tighter the wire gets around its neck, and you have yourself a rabbit. Unless a fox or badger gets to it first, that is, and then you're left with just skin and fur, or nothing at all. For that reason, it's best to check the snares at early dawn.

Cave Days

I headed back up the grass bank and across to my cave. I would have to wait until first light before I could check and see if I'd caught a rabbit. It was going to be a long night. It always was in the cave.

With my wood supply dwindling, I sat around a small fire with my usual companions—Fear and Darkness—and waited for the morning. Eventually, my tiredness won the fight with Fear, and I lay down to sleep. At least I was sleeping inside the heart of my cave now, and only ran to the entrance when Fear made its most frightening sounds.

I woke to the flapping wings of the rock doves that were now getting used to me being in the Cave. I could hear the seagulls but no wind. I hurried to the entrance and then climbed up on my throne to do the weather report. It was cloudy but dry, with only a light breeze on the water. It was about half tide, and it looked to be coming in, as the rocks were dry in front of a gentle swell.

Suddenly, in excitement, I remembered my snares! I jumped down from my throne and ran to the rabbit burrows. My first two snares were empty, but there was a furry grey animal in the third. It was a rabbit alright, and a mature one. It was still warm and must have been snared at early dawn. I would gut it and skin it, whether I felt like it or not. I couldn't let it go to waste, besides, it was my first rabbit that I'd caught living in the wild. It was something to celebrate! I would keep the fur pelt too, and when I had enough of them, I'd make a jacket or a blanket. Hmm, I think I'll just stick to a blanket, unless I can find a cave woman.

After getting my knife from the cave, I took the rabbit down to Hunts Beach to gut it. There I used the salt water

Autumn's Last Dance

to clean and purify the skin, and to wash the blood from the meat. I felt proud of myself as I returned to my cave. I caught a skate yesterday, and the rabbit today. I was moving up in caveman status!

To celebrate, I decided to go into the village and buy a Cornish pasty, a custard slice, and a bottle of cider—which I will say is for my father. It did mean dipping into my money that I was saving for emergencies, but I was doing well. I deserved this.

For the next few weeks, I continued to re-explore the haunts of my great boyhood adventures. When the skate had completely gone from the river, I learned to fish off the rocks, and the rabbits remained plentiful. As long as I kept myself busy, I didn't get bored. I spent long hours in search of driftwood. Some pieces I carried for miles, as I soon used up all the wood from the beaches that were near my cave. I built up a new supply and I hoped I could make it last.

With each new day, I expected the rains to come. But for a little while longer, they didn't, and I was able to walk in the golden fall and be part of autumn's last dance.

It is interesting that the seasons of the year seem to be different for us all, in the way they come and go. At least, it is for me. Although the calendar records the beginning and the end of the seasons, it is in the fabric of our individual makeup, where we see, feel and taste, when they begin and end. They reach out and touch us, caressing our souls, with a knowing of life, death and rebirth, and this awareness is created within us as human beings. When one dwells in a cave, and so many of the other distractions of life are gone, you can see that even the days have seasons, and the hours and minutes too…if you don't run from the silence, for it can shout so loud.

The seasons of the hours and the minutes can be felt in the wind and seen on the sea, and in the light and warmth of the sun, which is influenced by the shape and size of the clouds as they cast their long shadow pictures upon the deep waters and the meadows.

If you look carefully, watching the different seasons of the day, it can be far more exciting than watching TV or a movie. For the seasons have a story to tell you. But what I like most is that if you listen and understand, they only tell their stories to you, or to one who is walking closely with you, sharing the same mind and heart as a friend or lover.

When the wind is but a gentle breeze upon the sea, there are ripples, and if the sun is smiling in a clear noon sky, then the sea shimmers and sparkles, having put on her silent fancy dress. Then soon after, the east wind blows, too hard for ripples, even though the sun's smile is still so warm. And the clouds cause the sea to become angry, so she puts on her dress of grey; and after the wind has blown and wrestled with the clouds most of the day, he is tired and still, and then the sun smiles again;, and underneath the mists, the sea paints her nails and puts on her best shoes ready to spend her jealous day.

After finishing my day collecting wood, I sat at my fireplace and wrote a poem about autumn. I named it Autumn's Last Dance after watching some leaves that seemed to be stuck on a tree. As I watched them, they seemed to be shouting, wanting someone to hear their stories. Then a big gust of wind blew them dancing from the tree. This poem is about their dance and what they said to me.

AUTUMN'S LAST DANCE

Autumn leaves passed by the entrance of my cave.
I watched them dance and swirl
around the barren branches of the old sycamore tree.
Their dance was silent,
yet their music played so loud.
But why were they dancing and was I the only crowd?
Then I saw four leaves stuck on the tree and shouting out loud.
Why are they shouting,
I asked two leaves
blown into my cave,
gold and proud.
Haven't you heard, you and that bird?
It is Autumn's last dance and
those leaves,
they want a chance.
Then I understood what I'd heard,
me and the bird,
A chance to sing and dance and
tell our summer stories to the listening
souls of previous years.
Suddenly, the North Wind sneezed,
sending the four leaves dancing from the tree.
I jumped out from the entrance of my cave and
started to dance,
and the bird sang and fluttered in joyous trance.
For we were all part of Autumn's last dance.
© *Kingsley Ross Hill*

Chapter Three

November Grey

I carved another notch on the sycamore branch, my calendar by the sea. It was November 3rd. Just another day, but today the rains came.

♪❋

NOVEMBER GREY

You started raining in the late afternoon and rained for three weeks straight, only stopping for brief pockets of time when I looked into blue sky windows of summer stories, and drank all of autumn's last wine.

Then you blinked and the blinds were drawn, and I was drunk from all that was mine, and when I awoke, only grey—no more sunshine. The days went by, and then the weeks, and then forever and a day, and I could not find the blue sky. My stories went away. The sea was the same colour as the sky, and the cool mists came to stay. The bird sang only one song. Only grey, only grey, only grey; welcome to November Grey.

© *Kingsley Ross Hill*

November Grey

"Tell me, Fear, how long is November Grey?"

"Oh, not long", he said, "only forever and a day. Why don't you run home? There's not going to be another sunny day. Tell me, wild boy, why is it that you stay?"

My days now consisted of trying to keep warm and dry, and having enough food. I ventured out for short periods of time to fish, and check my rabbit snares, but with the rains so torrential, I was soaked to the skin within minutes. I would build up the fire, strip off my clothes and hang them on some branches I'd made into a clothes hanger. Then I would sit naked by the fire for what seemed like an eternity, until my clothes were damp dry. I don't think I ever got them completely dry without catching them on fire. I burned two holes in one of my pairs of jeans, and they actually looked quite cool. I think I'll put a patent on them and sell them at Woolworths, under the brand name, Smoky Hole Jeans! Gosh, it gets boring living in a cave.

When a day came that it stopped raining, even for an hour, I would go for a walk to the village and buy some food. Just to have something different from fish and rabbit was such a treat, but my money was running out, and the song of spring was a long way off.

Sometimes, in the dark of the night, I would dream of hearing the first call of the cuckoo bird. This was no ordinary bird, but one that came from a faraway land, and that held the keys of spring in his hand. He arrived at the same time every year, on that first day of spring. He announced to all the birds the new chorus they would sing.

Cave Days

CUCKOO'S SONG

Cuckoo-cuckoo is his song, as he turns the key of the new spring gong, and my soul hears, and knows that the winter has gone. Soon I will dance in spring's gay song, and tell summer stories of yesterdays gone, that come alive again as new hopes and dreams that are born of girls and ice cream and summer dresses, and painted toes, all the sunny days long. Could I have some more ice cream, please, before all the strawberries are gone?

© *Kingsley Ross Hill*

The next dry day I vowed I would return to my father's house and pick up my winter clothes and an umbrella, if I could find one. At least, I would have a change of clothes and wouldn't have to sit around the fire for hours, waiting for my wet ones to dry. I would have other options, like changing into dry clothes and taking a grand tour of my cave which would take all of about four minutes, maybe six, if I went to the very back of the cave and stared into the dark abyss. But then I might meet Fear. I didn't want to visit him unless I had to.

With my fire burning bright, and my clothes only damp, I counted my rabbit pelts, and reckoned I would soon have enough for a blanket. I would have to go into the village and buy a needle and thread. I had visions of sitting on my throne, robed in my fur blanket. I'd be 'the cave man of Bacon Hole'!

The nights remained the loneliest time, and Fear continued to prowl the cave. I looked at my woodpile. It was diminishing fast, but there was still a bit there. I was sure glad that I had collected some more in those last days of autumn, before the rain set in. All the wood outside was soaked through now, and wouldn't dry out until the summer. I had tried to burn wet wood before, and it was far too smokey for my cave. I would have to ration my remaining wood again if I had any hope of it lasting until the spring. But what about the night time? And what about Fear? I needed a big fire if I was going to stay in here.

November Grey joined forces with the cold winds of December, and I shivered some more. My loneliness and isolation became desperate, and I became aware more than in any other time of my life of my need for companionship with another human being. Oh, to just say hello to someone, to shake their hand and look into their face and have a conversation. One can only talk to animals and birds for so long. Even if I named a seagull Charle, our relationship doesn't cut it and I haven't heard anything back from her either; not even flowers, just some empty shellfish dropped outside my cave. That's it for you, Miss Sylvia Gull! Our relationship is over; we are not dating any more, and you know what? You've got really bad breath!

Living in the cave was showing me what I looked like on the inside, and what I needed in my life to keep my soul warm and alive. I am a man, a wonderful man, and I'm not meant to be alone in my soul. I need a friend and a lover, someone to love me for just who I am. Was it God that I needed ... or the love of a woman?

I had grown to believe, for the first time in my life, that it was God that I needed. I had an inner life, a soul and a spirit, and a knowledge that no other human being could fully know or understand my deepest needs and longings. Surely, only God could, he was my creator!

On the outside, I was losing sight of what I looked like. I needed to look into a mirror, or at my reflection in a rock pool. But when you have an identity on the inside, you don't need to keep looking at yourself, because you know who you are. That's what I was learning, and it was a painful lesson. I was lonely and desperate, that was the truth of it.

I decided that the next morning, I would venture out, no matter how bad the rain was, and seek out company with my fellow man. I put another piece of wood on the fire and thought about the coming morning. It seemed so far away. I spent much of the night awake now, going in and out of dreams and restless sleep. I think I kept going to bed too early. It was dark at 4:30, and there was nothing else to do, except dream of the springtime, and wonder if last night's dreams were real. Or were they awake thoughts while I was trying to fall asleep? Who knows. Everything seems the same. One long night, and my awake times, my reality, seems like a dream.

The morning finally came, but almost without a song. And then I saw Robin. He sat on the highest branch of the leafless sycamore, the only tree near the entrance of my cave. I'd given up carving my calendar notches on its lower branch. Even my tree had become a stranger to me. It had once spoken loudly, and laughed green leaves, and told me yellow stories, but now it was silent. "Oh, Mr. Robin bird, sing me a song! Tell me something please! I'm lonely, you see."

Suddenly he sang, holding his head up high as if pointing to heaven, and his song was the sweetest song I've ever heard.

I wept for several minutes as he sang of the springtime and of summer warmth. His songs touched my cold and barren soul. I remembered some stories, and I dared to dream of new ones, even if it was just for a few minutes. I was alive again.

I climbed down from my cave entrance to the narrow cliff path that led down to Hunts Bay. It was low tide, and the rain was a gentle mist upon my skin. I walked along the rocky shore and thought again of my prawning and crabbing days with my father, and I wondered if life would ever be fun again.

I climbed up the steep path from the beach to East Cliff Road. From there, I cut across the fields of Hunt's Farm, and on to my father's house, about two miles away. The backyard of the house joins a field which is part of another farm, called Down's Farm.

I hid out in the field and watched the house for a while, before climbing over the fence. I didn't know what date it was, whether it was a weekend or a weekday. I hoped it was a weekday because then my father would have left for work and my brother for school. They both left the house at about 7:30 a.m.

Not seeing my father's car, I thought I would chance it and climb over the fence. As I peered in through the kitchen window, all seemed quiet. I turned the door handle slowly. It was locked. Good, that meant they were out for sure. I checked under the doormat and found the key. I was rather surprised to find it was still there. I thought that with me having left home, and living in the wild, my father would have moved it, not wanting me to come into the house.

Maybe he wanted me to come home? No, I was too angry and hurting to come home. Besides, it wasn't a home any more ever since Mum had left. I opened the door and went inside.

Cave Days

"Dad? Fraser?" I called out, just in case. There was no answer. Only the cold silent voice of sadness that I could not live with. It was worse than Fear.

I noticed the calendar on the fridge door. It had some appointments written on it and days crossed off. My gosh, it was December 18, almost Christmas. For a few moments I just stood there, stunned. It was almost Christmas and I was alone. There would be food, joy – or at least, the pretending of joy. We had all gotten very good at that. Would Mum come home for Christmas? She did during the first few years of leaving us. Then we could all pretend to be happy again, at least for a little while.

I opened the fridge. Wow, food! This was Christmas for me already. There were eggs, sausages and bacon. I looked around the kitchen for a bag, and then started stuffing it with food. Merry Christmas everyone! Quick, check the cupboards. There were beans, corned beef, and soup, and I'll take that bag of cookies.

I stuffed the bag full, and then went upstairs to my room. I was half expecting my clothes to have gone as I wasn't living here anymore, and my father had been so angry with me on the day I'd left. But everything was still there, just the way I'd left it almost three months ago. For a few minutes, I was overcome with emotions. This was my room, and this house had been my home since I was five years old. Was my dad trying to tell me that he loved me by leaving everything the way it was? My heart wanted to believe that.

Come on, Kings, no time for this. Remember how angry he was with you. Pull yourself together man. Yes, pride, just give me a few minutes and I'll be right with you.

November Grey

I filled my sports bag with clothes, making sure I put in all my jean pants, sweaters, and two winter coats. Oh yes, and my socks and hiking boots. There would be no more sitting around the fire waiting for my clothes to dry. I had at least three pairs of everything now, but I couldn't find an umbrella. Oh well, I'd have to make do without one.

The clock in the hallway read 11:30 a.m. I felt nervous being in the house now, in case Dad or Fraser came home early. It was time to leave. On my way out I stopped in the kitchen and scribbled my father a note, telling him I was hungry and needed the food. "Try not to worry, Dad, I'm doing all right."

As I locked the door behind me and put the key back under the mat, I felt that in some way I was showing my father some sort of respect, even though I'd robbed the fridge. Maybe he would understand. Oh yes, I must check the garden shed and see if one of Dad's old prawning nets is there.

I couldn't see anything at first, only tools and his model aeroplanes hanging from the roof. Then I saw it, my dad's big prawning net. It was the one he only let my brother Fraser and me use when we had been on our best behaviour. Gosh, it must be eight years old. I checked the netting and it was still good and strong. I closed the shed door behind me, threw my sports bag and the net over the fence into the field, took one more look back at the house, and I was on my way across the fields to Hunts Bay.

As I walked, my bag of food was heavy, and I stopped every so often to change shoulders with my sports bag. I tried to think of something else, other than the distance I had to go. I looked to the sky and saw the sun was now westering, and the afternoon shadows danced with the fears in my heart, as once again I would enter the darkness of my cave.

Cave Days

Dropping my bags and net at the entrance, I climbed up onto my lookout stone. At least it wasn't raining, and there were some breaks in the clouds over the bay. Who knows? Maybe tomorrow will be a brighter day.

Well, better get a fire started before it's too dark to see. As I went to my woodpile, I realised that even with the rationing I had done, there was only enough left for a few more small fires, or one big one. I did still have a small pile for emergencies, enough for cooking food once a day for about another week, but there was no touching that, other than for cooking.

With Fear attacking my heart, and shadows and shapes taunting me, I chose to have one big fire. "Did you hear that, you spooks?" I shouted out. "I'm going to have one **BIG** fire, and chase you out of my cave forever!"

Except for my emergency supply, I put every last piece of wood onto the fire, and with the flames leaping high in the air, I danced around the fire. After all, I had something to celebrate. I had my winter clothes, and lots of new food, and bacon and eggs too, and I believed my father still loved me. My room was just the way I'd left it, like he was waiting for me to come home. The light filled the cave, and darkness fled away, lifting my soul to sing and shout. The heat on my body felt wonderful, and I imagined it as the kiss of a woman—hot, hot, like the burning sun, and I shouted out my stories to the listening everyone.

Chapter Four

Milk Money, Prawns, and a Wet Night

It was morning, December 19th, and I decided again to keep a calendar by notching the branch of the sycamore tree. I told myself that every day now it would be closer to spring – although the shortest day wouldn't be until tomorrow the 20th, or was it the day after?

Now, let's see.... How long is it until spring? There is the rest of this month and then it will be January, and then February, and then March. Then comes April, and we quite often get some of the most beautiful weather of the whole year in April. It's also the month when the Cuckoo announces the official start of the season. That was three months, and about 10 days away. My spirits sank. But then I remembered the food I had taken from the house. I had sausages, eggs and bacon! It was going to be a great breakfast! And I wouldn't have to fish or catch rabbits for a few days! What a treat!

I decided to declare today, December 19 and the next few days a public holiday, calling them "Bacon and Eggs days." I could do that, couldn't I? Declare a public holiday, I mean.

Cave Days

Of course I could, after all, I am The Man, the caveman of Bacon Hole.

Somehow, I didn't think the general public would celebrate the holiday with me. I think it might have something to do with my only subjects being spooks. Oh well, they can all keep their Christmas, and I'll keep my bacon and egg days. Bah humbug to you, 'Fear'. Do you guys keep Christmas around here? That's right. Don't answer. You guys are just jealous because you can't have Christmas turkey, and you can smell my bacon and eggs cooking on the fire. Get a whiff of that, you spooks, and guess what? I don't share. So get out of my cave, 'Fear'! How is that for Christmas spirit? Christmas spirit, get it??? Christmas spirit! Ha ha ha! Oh, the sausages taste so good, and the bacon and eggs!! Mmmmmm... Oh, you have to taste it, 'Fear' to believe it. It's soooooo good. Mmmmm...

My new food lasted me for three days, and it was indeed like having a holiday. Not having to hunt and fish was such a treat, and as I finished my last bacon and egg breakfast, I vowed to eat like this more often. How was I going to be able to go back to fish and rabbits again?

Oh, what's the matter, cave boy? Is your holiday over? It's back to fish and rabbits for you.

"Oh, shut up 'Fear', and leave me alone. You too darkness and loneliness."

If you don't like it, why don't you run home to daddy then, or run to mommy! Oh yes, you can't, can you, because she ran away from you and is thousands of miles away in Canada.

"Oh, shut up and leave me alone!"

You are alone.

"No, I'm not! I believe in God. He's with me."

Milk Money, Prawns, and a Wet Night

God?! What a joke! He must love you a whole lot to have you living in a cave.

"Shut up!"

I decided to take a walk along Hunts Beach, and plan how I was going to hold out in the wild until spring. With a troubled mind, but a satisfied stomach, I climbed down the steep cliff path, which was muddy and slippery from the rain and roaming sheep. I slipped and fell twice on my way to the beach, but as well as a wet arse, it had given me an idea for fresh meat.

Where I'd fallen were sheep droppings, and during the winter months when the grass was dormant, the sheep farmers would allow their sheep to graze the cliff tops, so their fields would not be overgrazed. I would kill myself a sheep, and eat like a king. I would keep a lookout for one that had gone astray.

As I reached Hunts Bay, the tide was a fair way out, so I walked out onto the rocks. Fond memories flooded my heart and mind as I remembered childhood days, prawning and crabbing with my father. I felt in my heart something I had not felt for a long time. Love... love from my father, and I had his prawning net now. I would try it out on tomorrow's low tide.

As I walked the beach, visiting pools and jumping over gullies, I began to experience a distinct feeling of pride. I'd lived on the cliffs now for nearly three months, and I was living off the land and the sea. Well done, Kings, old boy. Jolly good show.

I went back to my cave and opened the little pocket on my backpack. It's where I kept my money, what was left of it. There was enough to buy a big cigar and a bottle of beer in the village, if they'd sell them to me, that is. I know, I'll say they're for my father if they question me. And besides, it will give me the opportunity to converse with my fellow man. I was still feeling such a need for connection with another human being.

I went into Pennard Store and bought my cigar and beer, and they did not ask any questions, although the lady in the store had a twinkle in her eye as she handed me my change.

I would make the most of the dry weather and walk along the west cliff path, my favourite of the Pennard cliff walks. I said hello to two men and a lady who were out walking their dogs. The lady even stopped and said, "Good morning... do you have a day off school?"

And I replied, "I do indeed, madam," as cocky as a peacock. How wonderful to say good morning and have a conversation with another human being. I wasn't as invisible or as unwanted as Fear had said. But then he is a liar anyway, isn't he?

Yes, I am a wanted and sought after man. Even the woman's dog liked me. I walked tall, puffing on my cigar, and taking the odd swig of beer – I wanted to make it last.

What now? I was out of wood and out of money, except for two shillings and sixpence, and I wasn't going back to eating only rabbits and fish again. Come on, Kings, there must be something you can think of, and I looked around for a stray sheep. There didn't seem to be any around. When you weren't looking for them they were all over the place.

Suddenly I had a wonderful idea. I had worked for the local milkman when I was a boy, delivering milk and eggs from Down's farm. We travelled in a truck and went door-to-door delivering the milk and picking up the empty milk bottles as we went along. Now, on the West Cliff Road where I was

Milk Money, Prawns, and a Wet Night

walking, the houses had long driveways, and people would leave the money for their milk and eggs in envelopes, and put them under the empty milk bottles every Friday, rather than have Mr. James or myself have to open the gate and walk or drive the long driveway to the house. It had been three years since I delivered milk, and I wondered if things could still be the same? Could it be that easy?

Yesterday, when I'd gone back to the house to get supplies, the date on the calendar had read, Thursday the 18th. So today was Friday. It was the day to pay the milkman. My heart raced with excitement as I checked at the top of the first driveway. I could hardly believe my eyes. There was a brown envelope under the empty milk bottles and I quickly opened it to find a crisp 10-pound note. I hurried to the next driveway. There was a five-pound note rolled up in the neck of the milk bottle, and also three pounds of small change on the floor. Each swig of beer became a celebration now, as I continued on up the road until I'd visited the last driveway. I counted my earnings and I had 35 pounds. That was serious money for a cave dweller.

I had started about halfway along West Cliff Road. There was a whole half of the road I hadn't checked yet. That would do for another Friday, I decided. And besides, it would be too obvious to Mr. James, that he'd been robbed, if I continued. I re-lit my cigar, swigged down my last gulp of beer, and swanked down the road with a new spring in my steps. Well done, Kings. Jolly good show, old man.

Suddenly, a familiar truck turned the corner. It was Mr. James, the milkman. Quickly I left the road and followed a bramble path, which led me back to the cliff top where I continued my way back to my cave. I'd timed that just right.

Cave Days

I hadn't always called the milkman **Mr. James**. He had once been my friend Philip, as well as the man who gave me my first job. But the day he shot my pet magpie, Jerry, he became my enemy.

Jerry was my great boyhood friend. He rode on the handlebars of my bike, and slept on the headboard of my bed. He banged on the window of my classroom when it was time for me to finish, or sometimes just when he wanted to play. Once he had the whole class write an essay about him. I felt extra special that day, and all the other children looked at me like a hero as Jerry rode home with me, sitting on my shoulders. He made my enemies jealous and filled my days with more fun and adventure than a boy could ever dream of. Jerry, the magpie, changed my life forever, but that is another story.

But Philip James shot my magpie, and now he was beginning to pay. I'd get one more robbery out of James' milk round one of these Fridays. I'll wait for a while, though, as people will be on the lookout after today.

Reaching my cave, I sat on my throne and looked out over the bay. "I'm the man," I shouted out on the wind. "The man of Bacon Hole!"

The holes in the grey sky grew smaller, and I shivered in the damp air. I thought of the night without any fire. Cold and darkness would be my lot, but now it was only early in the day. There had to be something to look forward to between now and the dark night. I had £35 in my pocket, and I had started to avenge the shooting of my magpie. They were positive things, weren't they?? My conscience argued with me. Oh shut up and leave me alone.

Suddenly the two blue holes in the sky were only eyes, and then they blinked closed. They reminded me of God watching me. "He sees everything that we do," my grandma told me as a child. "And that feeling we get when we do something wrong, that's him looking inside."

"Was that you, God?" I shouted, looking through the holes in the sky. "What did you see, then? And how was your day? Would you like to hear about mine? It's grey, glorious grey, for the rest of the bloody well day. Goodbye God, have a nice day."

I climbed down from my throne and stood at the entrance of my cave. Well, to heck with this; I'm not sitting around here with you spooks all day. You can haunt me during the night, but not during the day. Did you hear that, Fear?

"I heard," he said. "Go and enjoy your day, but remember I'll be here waiting for you."

"Screw you. I'm outta here!" I quickly went into my cave and grabbed my father's prawning net. I had seen from my throne that it was low tide. I would do some prawning in the rock pools and gullies, and it would help to pass the day.

I climbed up the path beside my cave to the clifftop and walked westwards to Heatherslade Bay. Several times along the way, I thought it would pour down with rain. The sky was as dark as evening, and the atmosphere was heavy. Surprisingly it didn't rain. When I reached Heatherslade, I began walking along the sides of the very large rock pool, and I remembered my father saying, "You will have to fish this one from the sides, because it's too deep to wade in." I walked briskly, holding the net deep in the water and pushing it through the thick weeds along the side of the pool. It was heavy work, and about every six feet I lifted the net to inspect the catch.

Cave Days

I walked the whole length of one side of the pool and caught nothing. Not even one for all that effort. What was wrong? Did I have the net too deep? I would try the other side of the pool, although I was now remembering that it was summer time when I had prawned with my father. Would there be any here in the winter?

There was. The second time I lifted the net, I had caught eight prawns. "Yes!" I shouted to a passing gull who was hoping to share my catch. "No such luck for you, Mr. Gull! These are all mine."

I caught another 12 prawns from the big pool and continued on across the rocks, keeping an eye on the tide behind me which seemed to be staying still. I must have caught it right on the low. It would stay out for an hour, and then start coming in fast. There wasn't a wind yet, just a cool breath on my face. I continued to net each pool, moving quickly while I had the time. The prawns were coming in abundance now. I had about 100 already.

What was that? A freak wave? No, it was too calm and there was no wind. I stopped for a moment and looked out to the grey sea. It was the same colour as the sky, and I could not tell where the sea ended and the sky started. It was a day where they walked together.

Suddenly, I saw a flash of lightning and then heard a crash of thunder. It was far out at sea. There were a few swells now, and the sea was breathing again, not coming in and not going out, just deciding what it was going to do, like a large mysterious creature. I can remember standing on Pobbles Beach as a boy and being fascinated by this. When the sea was coming in and going out, I saw it move, but when it was still, it was thinking

Milk Money, Prawns, and a Wet Night

and contemplating like a real sea monster, and my father would whisper in my ear, "it's alive." And it was, and after being still, it would swell and pulsate and then decide to come in. It was a decision made a long time ago, I decided, when God had set its boundaries and told it to come in, but only so far, and then it was to go out again. God's voice is always upon the sea. You just have to listen and you can hear him speak.

I decided to prawn in a few more rock pools and then make my way back to where I could climb up the rocks and on up to the cliff top. There were only a few places from Heatherslade Bay where you could climb up the rocks and find a pathway up, otherwise you were cut off by the tide.

I made it back to the path with time to spare. The tide still had a ways to come in. I took a rest halfway up the cliff and counted my catch – 153 prawns. I would eat well tonight. Then I remembered I was out of wood, except for my small emergency supply, and I had no more matches. I would have to stop at the village store if I wanted to eat my prawns tonight. I had money, though, thanks to James' milk round. I would buy a few treats along with my matches – but what was I going to do about wood? I know, I'll buy a box of those fire starter blocks and light the whole box underneath my frying pan of prawns!

I was hungry already and I walked quickly along the cliff top toward the village. The thunder and lightning was moving in fast now from out at sea. There were great crackles of fork lightning stretching across the sky, almost overhead, and loud thunder crashes followed. The sky became almost black and then down poured the rain. I ran the last quarter mile to Pennard Stores and I was soaked through by the time I got there.

"You wet, boy?" said Mr. Skittle, who owned the store. "I'm afraid we don't sell dry clothes in here boy, just food. You have some nice prawns there. Where did you catch all those? What is it you need, boy? I'm going to close up shop. There is no one going to be coming in tonight, not in this storm. You better get home, boy, and be careful not to be struck by lightning. We don't often get a storm like this. I don't like it."

"Before you close the store, Mr. Skittle, Sir, could I please have a box of matches and some fire starter blocks?"

"What on earth do you want fire starter blocks for on a night like this, boy? Wait a minute, is your name Kingsley Hill? If you are, your grandparents were in the store earlier asking if anyone knew where you were. You're not the wild boy, are you?"

"No sir, I'm not. I've never heard of Kingsley Hill. Now can I please have some matches and fire blocks?"

"I'll tell you what, lad, you can have this last lot of kindling wood for 50p, if you need to make a fire."

"Thank you sir, that would be great!"

"And one more thing, boy. If you are him, I'd go home. You have people who love you."

I carried the kindling wrapped in newspaper under my coat, which was already soaked through. But with my fire starter blocks, it would burn, even if it did get wet. As I continued my way to the cave, the rain was torrential. Thunder crashed and lightning crackled, right over my head. I walked faster and then ran; the flashes were so bright. I closed my eyes and shouted out a prayer in panic. Please God, don't let me be struck by lightning, please just let me get back to the cave.

Milk Money, Prawns, and a Wet Night

Suddenly, I tripped and fell, grazing my hands and wrists badly on the sharp stones. My bag had burst, spewing out my fire starter and matches, and my kindling lay in a wet puddle. I huddled over my box of matches and it was, as I feared, soaked through. There would be no fire tonight. The rain stung as it got into the cuts in my hands. I stood up and kicked the remaining kindling that was still in newspaper across the path. God, what a night! What had my life come to?

I continued on like a drowned rat. My prawns, my prawns! I raced back and found them still in the bag and not damaged, and I ran all the way to the cave. I arrived at the entrance with some sense of accomplishment. At least I hadn't been struck by lightning, and I still had my prawns and net. I stood at my fireplace shivering, and trembling with the shock of my fall. Then there was a loud clap of thunder so powerful it seemed to shake the whole cave. I raced back to the entrance, fearing it would collapse at the next clout of thunder. The lightning crackled and flashed, blindingly bright. I sat behind my lookout throne and closed my eyes. I was soaked to the bone.

Slowly the storm passed over and seemed to concentrate in one area over the bay. I went back into the cave only being able to see for a few seconds at a time when the lightning flashed. I'll wait for the next flash, I decided, and then look around for my clothes. I found them, but they were cold and damp, and I could feel the chill in my body. Stripping off the clothes I was wearing, I climbed into my sleeping bag naked. It was cold, but at least I was dry. I curled up into a ball and shivered.

Slowly the storm moved further and further away, out across the Bristol Channel, and the lightning stopped, leaving me in complete darkness. The darkness in the cave tonight was unlike any other darkness I'd ever experienced. This darkness I could feel in the marrow of my soul, and I was so afraid. "Is that you, Fear? You must be here, for all I can feel is you."

♪☼

LIGHT UPON MY DARKNESS

There was now only one glimmer of hope left in my dying soul. And it was the flicker of a lone candle that burned in the coldest and darkest night. I was alone, and so afraid, and I was shivering cold, and oh, the terrible darkness! It was so dark I could feel it touching my face. Like a thick, wet web of blinding fog, it slowly chilled me through to my bones. Oh God, please help me, I'm so afraid!

I wandered aimlessly, stumbling and falling, lost in an endless night of pitch black darkness, searching and searching for the light. In my desperate state, I stumbled toward the candle. But when I reached it, it was no longer just a flicker of light. It was a dazzling brilliance of light, such as my eyes had never seen! Its awesome brightness shined as far as I could see, more brilliant than the Sun. I couldn't bear to look at it, and I turned and looked away.

And when I looked around, there was no more darkness! All I could see was brilliant radiating light, which shone from the candle in every direction. I wanted to run, but there was nowhere to run to; its beam of light shone on everything at the same time. I now felt more afraid of the candle's light than I did of the darkness in my own life. I couldn't bear to stand in its presence.

The light was searching, shining its penetrating gaze into my innermost being, illuminating me for what I really was. I realised then why I was so afraid of the light; the light was God's searching grace, looking into my heart and my being. I was so afraid I fell to the ground and covered my face. Suddenly there was a hand on my shoulder and a strong but gentle voice said, Kingsley, don't be afraid.

© Kingsley Ross Hill

I woke up crying. Was I dead? Where had the light gone, and the gentle voice that said my name and told me not to be afraid? It was pitch black and I felt only the loneliness of my soul. I pinched myself to see if I was alive. I felt my pinch and I pinched harder. I spoke and I heard myself speak. Could other people hear me and see me? Was I dead and didn't know it? I cried out. "God, help me! I feel dead and I want to be alive!"

There was no light to see where I was. If I was alive, then I lived in a cave, but I'd lost my sense of direction. Only cold walls and darkness surrounded me. Was I in hell? I lay in my nightmare, waiting for the light. "Can someone see me? Can you hear me?" I screamed. "I want to be in the light, not the darkness!" The spirits were all laughing at me. "Is this a dream? Are you real spirits?"

Cave Days

Fear answered for them all, and said, "Yes, we are real. Welcome to darkness and death."

"I'm not dead! I'm alive! I'm alive!" I shouted, as I scrambled to my feet and felt my way along the cold walls. Suddenly there was a ray of light. It was the entrance of my cave. There was light out across the bay. I'm alive! I'm alive!" I shouted at the dawn.

It was a long time before the dawn answered me back through the cry of a herring gull, and he said, "Yes, you're alive, but did you listen to God? Did you hear what he said?"

Chapter Five

I'll Be Home for Christmas

I waited at the entrance of my cave for the dawn to become morning. Today, the morning seemed to be coming so slowly. Was it even coming at all? It was so dark and the night had been so long, and my dream, it was so real. I felt like God was looking through me, right into my heart. And the voice that said, "Don't be afraid, it is I." I heard it! A gentle, and yet strong, voice spoke to me so clearly. Was God really seeking me? Did he really care about my life, and what I was going through?

As I meditated upon the events of the night, I was sure of two things; one was that God was trying to get my attention, and the other was that I was too lonely and isolated in this cave. I was tired of the darkness and cold, and I needed to be around people. I want to be cared about, I wanted to matter to someone, to matter whether I lived or died. And I also wanted to care about someone.

This morning, something had changed in my soul. The dawn chorus had started and finished, and I hadn't even heard

Cave Days

it. The birds were singing their morning songs, and I couldn't sing along. The music in my soul was gone. It was almost Christmas, and I wanted to hear a Christmas song.

I decided to go back to my father's house and check out what was going on. Mr. Skittle had said that Grandma and Grandpa had been in the store asking if anyone knew of my whereabouts, so I knew they were at the house.

I felt nervous as I walked across the fields. What would my father say? Would he be angry and turn me away? No, not at Christmas. Grandma and Grandpa would welcome me, that's for sure.

I watched the house from behind the hedge, and through the kitchen window I saw Grandma and Grandpa. Just then, I heard some Christmas music coming from our neighbour's house next door. It was that old classic Christmas song "I'll be home for Christmas" by Bing Crosby. As I listened to the words, I wept.

I was trying to come home for Christmas, but where was my home? Mum wasn't at the house, so it couldn't be home, not without her. I felt my heart tug, and then tear again. I missed her so much! Why did she have to go away? She would be spending Christmas with her family in Canada, she had said. I thought my brother Fraser and I were her family, even if she didn't get on with my father. One thing I knew, she had left a big hole in my heart.

Suddenly, I saw my father come into the kitchen. I shivered and I thought of a nice Christmas dinner and all the wonderful food and love that was part of Christmas day, and presents. I wondered if I would have any this year. I didn't think I deserved any. I had left home and become a thief. Oh yes, and I'd stolen from the fridge, and I hadn't seen my father

I'll Be Home for Christmas

and brother for so long What do I say? Hello everyone, I'm home … let's jingle all the way, shall we?

I continued to peer into the house from the other side of the hedge. I was wrestling with so much inside myself. I wanted to go in so badly, but I didn't want to be rejected. Suddenly, I was looking right into my father's eyes. He beckoned me to come in. "Come in," he was saying, gesturing with his hands. It was almost as if he knew I was there. Maybe he did.

With a smile in my heart and guilt on my face, I climbed over the hedge and knocked on the back door. My father answered the door and said, "Come in, Kings. You're just in time, Grandma and Grandpa are down for Christmas."

I couldn't believe it! I was welcome. I went into the living room, and there were Grandma and Grandpa.

"Oh, King!" Grandma said, "Where on earth have you been? We have all been so worried!"

"You have been gone for months." Grandpa added. "Your father didn't tell Grandma and I until Wednesday when we arrived. He didn't want to worry us. Now, this has got to stop, Kingsley. You can't go on like this, living like a wild man! You have a place to live and people who love you! Anyway, Kingsley, you and I and your father have to talk. We will talk about things tomorrow evening after Christmas dinner."

Christmas dinner, I thought, not really hearing what Grandpa had said. That means it's Christmas Eve. Wow. It's Christmas Eve, and I'm home for Christmas. I timed that right, but I knew in my heart it was no coincidence. No, it was God bringing me home for Christmas. He'd heard the cry of my heart. "I still hate you God," I said under my breath. "Damn you for taking away my mother."

Cave Days

Just then, my brother Fraser came into the room. "Kings! Where have you been? It's so good to see you. Grandma and Grandpa have been so worried since Dad told them you had left home. Dad's been worried too."

That pricked my conscience because my father wasn't one to show his feelings.

"Was he really worried?" I asked.

"Yes, Kings, we've never seen him so stressed. You're living in the wild, Kings. You're a hero in the village, mind. Everyone is talking about it. The police were here yesterday. Mr. Skittle from Pennard stores phoned Dad and the police because you had gone into the store."

"What did Dad say to them?" I asked.

"Nothing really. He just told them that you had run away from home and he didn't know where you were."

"That's good," I said. "I don't want anyone finding out where I live." But really, I was more concerned about whether I'd been found out for stealing James' milk money. Fraser didn't mention anything about that, so I was obviously alright.

It was good to be home for Christmas. There would be food and warmth, and a roof over my head. And there would be people to talk to, other than the spooks in the cave. I guess I can say, "Thank you, God ... thanks for letting me come home for Christmas, but this doesn't mean we are friends though. It just means that you have done something nice for once in my life."

"Oh, King." Grandma said. "We are all so thankful that you are home safe. Grandpa and I have said a special prayer each day for you since your Dad told us you were away from home."

"That's nice." I said, pushing her away as she continued to try and hug me.

"Oh, don't push your old grandma away, King. I am just so happy you are safe."

Just then, Grandpa came to my rescue with a call for all of us to come into the dining room for supper. Another few minutes with Grandma hugging me, and I think I would have broken down and cried. I was feeling so vulnerable.

We all sat down at the table. It was a strange feeling to sit with people again, even my own family. The isolation of the cave and the cliffs had pierced my soul, and I wondered if I would get used to being around people again. Lonely in my cave, I needed them. But here, sitting with my own family, I was uncomfortable. Maybe a lot of what I was feeling was guilt, knowing I had worried them so. But there was also a strong feeling that they didn't understand me, even though they tried.

Grandma and Grandpa passed the bowls of food around the table. Oh, the smell of the food and the abundance of it. We had roast chicken and gravy, roast potatoes and sweet corn, peas and carrots. I looked across at Dad, who looked like he was holding back tears. There was a silence around the table as we ate, which was made louder by the Christmas music from next door, which we could hear from the kitchen window. At first, I put the silence down to everyone enjoying the food. But after we finished eating, the silence was still there, and it was getting louder. Somebody say something. What could I say? Hello everyone. Lovely to see you. I live in a cave and I just robbed James, the milkman.

Cave Days

Grandpa broke the silence. "A lovely meal, dear." This was echoed by my father, and then Fraser, and I said, "Thank you, Grandma." And that was the depth of our conversation. I'm sure we could have won an Oscar with that performance. Well, it was obviously me. Dad and Grandma and Grandpa didn't know what to say, or they were saving it for tomorrow's talk after Christmas dinner. Anyway, I was glad when Grandma brought in the dessert, Bird's custard on treacle pudding. Now that was worth being silent about. Gosh, it was good. I was stuffed with good food.

Suddenly, Grandma spoke up: "You are going to stay aren't you, Kings? Tonight's Christmas Eve."

"Yes Grandma, of course. It's Christmas." What else was I going to say? No, I must go back to my cave because Fear and the other spooks are going to miss me?

"Your room is just the way you left it," Dad added. "Only Fraser has been using the top bunk."

"Yeah, that's great, Dad. I'll sleep in my room tonight."

I couldn't stand the heaviness around the table, so I said to Fraser, "Shall we go up to my room? I want to talk." Fraser quickly followed me upstairs. I think he was excited to hear about my adventures. I, however, was feeling quite emotional and didn't want to say much, other than finding out how he was doing.

"I hope you don't mind, Kings, me using your room while you have been away. I didn't sleep in your bunk. I slept in the top one like when we were kids."

"No, that's cool," I said. "I don't mind you in my room. It's yours now anyway, because I'm not coming back."

I'll Be Home for Christmas

As Fraser excused himself to go to the bathroom, I looked around my room. My old jeans and red leather jacket were still in the corner. I hadn't taken them with me when I'd come back to get my winter clothes. It was as if everything was still waiting for me to come back, even my father. Maybe that's why he hadn't moved anything. He hadn't said anything to me at the dinner table, but in his eyes I saw love and sadness. I jumped onto my bunk bed. Suddenly, so many memories flooded the pages of my mind, and I had to fight back the tears before Fraser came back and saw me crying.

He returned, still hoping I would share some of my adventures with him. Well, this was better than facing the music that I'm sure would be playing if I were downstairs. It's a song called, "I can only imagine what they will say."

Maybe I will take off back to the cave tonight when everyone is asleep. No, I couldn't do that. That would hurt my brother. Look how excited he is that I've come home. And besides, this is probably the last Christmas that we'll spend together in our family home. And Dad, angry as I am with him, I do love him, and he's tried hard to be a good dad since Mum left. He looks so strained and sad. I guess I'm the problem around here, aren't I? Well, I'll stay until tomorrow night, or Boxing Day if the weather is bad. I must admit, to have a full stomach of good food, other than rabbits and fish, and to be in the warm, is really nice.

"Okay, Fraser, so you want to hear about some of my adventures? Tell you what, why don't you climb up to the top bunk and I'll keep lying here and we can talk for a bit, because I'm tired."

"Yeah, that's fine, Kings, it will be like old times. The Hill brothers together again."

Cave Days

"Yeah, we had some good times, didn't we, Fraser?"

"So, where do you live, Kings? Are you camping out, or staying with friends? Dad thinks you're camping, because you have the gear that was in the garden shed."

"I would be camping if it was still summer, but it's wet and cold. It's too damp to be in a tent. So I live in a cave, and it's dark and scary as hell. I try to keep a fire going all the time for light and warmth. Sometimes, you wake up in the middle of the night and the fire is out, and you don't know where you are, and it's so freaking dark, there's no light at all because you're underground. There is no light from the night sky because you can't see the moon and stars. It's absolutely pitch black. It's so thick you can touch it. The other night I woke up and thought I was dead. I was pinching myself to make sure I was alive."

"Bloody hell, Kings. That's amazing. I'd never live in a cave. I'd rather be in a tent, no matter how cold it was, and I bet that place is haunted, Kings."

"You're bloody right it is! There are moving shadows and dark figures moving across the walls. Sometimes you see dark shapes in the form of people moving around from the corner of your eye. I'm sure they are spirits, and they don't show themselves completely to you."

"Shit, Kings! Let's sleep with the light on!"

"They won't hurt you here, Fraser. The cave is where the past and present live together. They were there first, thousands of years ago. I'm sure some of the spirits are from the Ice Age and Bronze Age periods. There's even a cave family that once lived there, and I got talking to one of the spirits who told me what life was like living as a caveman. That was cool. He was a good spirit, and then there's Fear. He is evil and haunts me every night. And in the cave you don't know if all this is reality or imagination."

"Shit, Kings! What are you on, man. That's crazy."

"I'm not on anything, Fraser. You have got to be there to experience it. I'm telling you, I've heard and seen things that are life changing. It's an awareness really, that there is a spiritual realm as well as a physical realm, and sometimes they collide. That's what it's like in the cave. Do you remember when we were boys, and Grandma and Grandpa would take us to their chapel? And Grandpa would preach one of his hell and brimstone sermons, and tell us that unless we believed in Jesus to save us, we were lost and going to hell?"

"Yes, I remember, Kings."

"You know what is so scary, Fraser? I believe what Grandpa says. There is a spiritual world, and it can be pretty dark. The other night, I had this dream or vision. I was lost and alone in this terrible dark place. It seemed like Hell. Then, suddenly, there was this radiating light that seemed to be looking through me. I was so afraid and I covered my eyes. I felt like God was looking right into my heart. And then, all of a sudden, I felt a hand on my shoulder, and I heard a strong but gentle voice. And it said, "Do not be afraid."

"You better not tell Grandma and Grandpa about the spirits, Kings. You know what they are like. They only believe in God, and any contact with spirits is of the Devil."

"Yes, you're right there, Fraser. I know one thing, though. If they say anything to me about their loving God, they can stick him up their arse! I am so angry with God. As far as I'm concerned, it's his fault that Mum took off and left us." I took a deep breath. "Anyway, it's Christmas Eve, so let's talk about some things that are happy. We have each other, right?"

"Yes, Kings, and I'm glad you're my brother."

"Thanks Fraser," I said, fighting back the tears. "You're my brother and I love you."

"I'm glad you're okay, Kings. Thanks for coming home for Christmas. Oh, and we got you a Christmas present. It's under the tree. You can open it tomorrow."

"Thanks, I'll look forward to that."

We spent the rest of our time awake, remembering Christmases gone by, and to my brother and me, they all seemed to mingle into one. Sweet and wonderful memories – two brothers waking up on Christmas mornings and pulling our stockings up onto our beds in the early hours of those happy dancing mornings, when our world was innocent, and at peace, when birds sang their songs, sweeter than on any other day of the year. And presents glistened, wrapped in love, and shining brighter than the tinsel on the tree.

After the stockings were opened, and I had eaten half of all my chocolate, just short of being sick, and having already traded one of my toys for half my brother's candy, we headed quickly, shouting and tumbling, down the stairs to sit and watch the presents under the tree. We weren't allowed to open them yet, not until Mum and Dad came down, and if Grandma and Grandpa were down for Christmas, then the wait was even longer. Grandma had to get her corset on. Why did she have to be so fat? I would say to Fraser. And he would say, Grandma calls it plump, and all grandmas are plump, aren't they, Kings? And I would say, all the good ones are, and they give the best presents. It was always worth the wait, even the year Grandma blocked the toilet, it was still worth the wait. We both got a brand new leather football.

Fraser and I talked well into the night. Next thing I knew, it was morning, and Fraser was still asleep. The clock read 5:15 a.m. I was used to waking up at dawn on the cliffs. For a few minutes, I just lay in bed thinking. I know, I said to myself, for old times' sake, I'll wake Fraser and we can go down to the tree.

He was glad that I woke him up, and just like we did when we were kids, we hurried down the stairs. To my surprise, there were lots of presents under the tree, several with my name on them. I was glad I had stayed. Fraser and I sat talking for what seemed like a long time, until Grandma appeared on the scene.

"Good morning, you two boys. Merry Christmas, Kingsley and Fraser. I'm so glad that I have my two grandsons together on Christmas morning. This is the best Christmas present Grandpa and I and your father could have asked for. I'm so glad that you have come home, King."

She didn't mention my mother. I guess Mum had turned into a word not spoken of anymore, but in the hole in my heart, I felt her. I answered my grandmother. "It's good to see you too, Grandma," and Fraser joined me in saying Merry Christmas.

There was nothing I could say about being home. If they knew I was taking off again, it would spoil the whole day.

"Now, we must wait for Grandpa and your dad before we start opening the presents, and try not to eat too big a breakfast boys, because I'm going to cook a nice turkey dinner for this afternoon."

Fraser and I had cereal for breakfast and waited for Grandpa and Dad. Grandpa brought his Bible and read part of the Christmas story to us. Then he said, "Let's pray and give thanks for Christmas day." He said, "Please help us remember that Jesus, God's son, was the reason for the season, and that he is the greatest gift of all, and through him we can have eternal life."

"Yeah, right. Quit preaching, Grandpa. I don't want to hear it. Let's just get on with it and open the presents." But he wasn't done yet.

"And please help Kingsley to come to the understanding that you are seeking him right now in his life, and to not be afraid."

Now I felt afraid. I wasn't expecting this. Those were the same words the voice had said to me in the cave. Grandpa stopped praying. Whoa, that was too close for comfort. It was like Grandpa knew what was going on in my heart.

"Now we can open the presents." Grandma announced.

Suddenly, I could feel Mum in my heart, and I wanted to shout out loud, "It's not Christmas without Mum," but I decided not to. That would spoil everyone's day. I would do my shouting on the inside.

I buried my pain and I thought, it's all your fault, God. As soon as this bullshit is over, I'm off back to the cliffs. Did you hear that, God? Screw you and your gift to the world. What's he ever done for me? Tell me that, if you can! Thought so. Silent again, are we? Why don't you speak up and say something?

Before Grandma started to hand out the presents, I remembered that Fraser had gotten me a gift. I quickly asked Grandma for an envelope, and I put in a £10 note that I had stolen from James. I wrote "Fraser" on the envelope and put it under the tree. It was my turn to open a gift, Grandma said, handing me a present.

"It's from your dad, King, and don't forget to read the card. You boys need to read the cards, not just tear open the presents without knowing who they are from." For sure we'd heard that before.

My card read:

> *Dear Kings,*
> *I found these in the sporting goods store. Thought you could use them out in the wild.*
> *Love,*
> *Your dad*

I couldn't bring myself to read the card out loud. I felt myself choking up with emotion. I opened the present to find a beautiful Bowie knife with a carved bone handle, and as sharp as a razor. There was also a throwing knife. I'd try that out on the rabbits and put them out of their misery when they were caught in the snares.

"Thanks Dad." I said, my voice now excited. Where was Dad?

"He's gone into the kitchen," Grandma said.

I followed him, only to find him standing in front of the window, weeping. I went over and put my arms around him. "Thanks, Dad. The knives are just what I need. How did you know?"

"I'm glad you like them, old son. You be careful with that big one. I sharpened the blade myself." Dad stayed in the kitchen to compose himself, I think, and I went back into the living room. I felt touched by his gift. Even with everything going on, he knew my heart, and he had given me the perfect gift. I would be that much braver now, with a knife on each side of me when I lay down to sleep, and I would be able to skin my rabbits better and quicker.

Dad returned to the room and we finished opening the presents. Dad had also bought a real bow and arrow set each for Fraser and me. We spent the whole afternoon target practising in the back field. By the end of the afternoon, Fraser and I were getting really good with our aim. I figured if I kept on like this, I'd be able to shoot rabbits instead of snaring them.

"You can also shoot at the spirits in the cave," Fraser said, with a smile on his face.

"You've got that right, Fraser. If only I could kill 'Fear', my life would be a lot easier."

Grandma called from the back garden. "Come on, you two boys! It's dinner time. Your dad and Grandpa are waiting."

I felt a lump in my throat as we climbed back over the garden hedge. I was looking forward to Christmas dinner, but not the conversation with Grandpa and my father that would follow. What was I going to say?

I'll just listen and let them ask the questions. There is no way I'm coming back to this house to live. It's not a home any more, and I don't like the neighbours asking me questions about where my mother is. It's bad enough with her having taken off, without feeling I have to make excuses as to why she's not here. And I'm not going to stay with my grandparents either, and listen to their religious threats! I would get so tired of listening to what a bad boy I was, having run away from home and worrying everyone. I was a 'sinner', they called it, and needed to be saved. I called it being a young man just trying to make some sense of this painful thing called life that I find myself in, and especially trying to understand all this pain in my heart. I needed to discover some meaning and purpose for my life, and not to be told that God was going to punish me unless I lived my life differently.

'Hey God, if you were a god of mercy and love, like you claim to be, then you would know and understand that what I've been through in my life is enough punishment for anyone. Screw you, God, and you too, Grandma and Grandpa, and if that's all your loving God can say – that I'm a sinner, and that he's going to send me to hell when I die – then I want nothing to do with him!'

Grandpa and Dad were already sitting at the table when Fraser and I came in. And Grandma was bringing the food in from the kitchen. The large turkey sat in the middle of the table. Oh, the sweet smell of the meat and gravy, and yes, that was Grandma's homemade gravy, and there would be one of her famous treacle puddings and custard for dessert. My taste buds were exploding. Grandpa gave thanks, and we were soon into the food. It was delicious and I ate until I hurt.

After our praises to Grandma for our meal, it was silent again. There seemed to be a heavy tension in the air around Grandpa. Maybe he was gearing up to read me the riot act. It was always hard to read Grandpa. Most often he seemed to be a serious man. Though he did have a sense of humour, and a good one at that. But today would not be a day for humour for my grandfather, more likely, a hell-and-brimstone sermon aimed at me, big sinner that I was. The longer the silence remained, the more uncomfortable I became. If you preach to me, old man, I'll tell you where to go. I'm not taking any of this bullshit from anyone.

Cave Days

After dessert was finished, Grandma asked Fraser to help with the dishes in the kitchen. Grandpa asked if Dad and I would follow him into the living room for our talk. I felt my whole body tensing up, as I expected only condemnation. Dad and I sat on the couch, and my grandpa in my father's chair.

"Now Kingsley, you can't go on living like this, out there somewhere in the wild, without your father, or anyone else for that matter, knowing where you are."

"Why not?" I said. "What's wrong with living in the wild?"

"It's just not done, that's why. You can't possibly go on living like a wild man, roaming the neighbourhood."

"Grandpa's right," my father added, "You're going to end up with pneumonia or getting into trouble with the police."

"Now wait a minute here. I'm not doing anything wrong. I'm living off the land and sea, and there is no law that says I can't do that. It's something you guys couldn't do if you tried. And I'm not roaming around the neighbourhood getting into trouble."

"There is a law against it, Kingsley. You are still under your father's care."

"Well, that's just too bad, isn't it! Because I'm not coming back here, Grandpa."

"And why not, Kingsley? You will have a roof over your head, food in your stomach, and people who love you."

"It's not enough. I'm not happy here, and you can't make me stay."

"We will see about that, Kingsley, and there's one other law that you're breaking."

"And what's that? Tell me. No, let me guess! It's that God of yours, isn't it? Well, I don't give a damn about him, and why don't you stop threatening me with him."

"I'm not threatening you, Kingsley, and don't speak to me so rudely. It will be your own conscience that condemns you, and that is God speaking to you, not me."

"Is there anything else you want me for, Grandpa? Can I go now?"

"No, not yet. There is something your father and I want you to consider."

"And what's that?"

"Your father has agreed with Grandma and I that it would be best for you to come and live with us for a while, until you're stable and can get a job." I looked at Dad.

"I think it would be the best thing for you, old son, until you feel stable enough in your life to come back and live with Fraser and I. This is a good opportunity for you, and Grandpa has said he will help you find a job. If I were you, I'd take it."

"Look, we can try it for six months," Grandpa added, "and if you're not happy, you can come back to your father."

"No Grandpa, I'm happy where I am."

"Don't be stupid, Kingsley. You can't possibly be happy where you're living – living without a roof over your head, and warmth, and proper food. Don't be so foolhardy."

"The answer is no, Grandpa."

I got up and went upstairs to my bedroom. Dad soon followed me up. "Come on, Kings. I think you're making a big mistake. This is a real opportunity for you, old son. Just try it for six months. You've got nothing to lose, and you might really enjoy it. It can be like having a fresh start. Look, it's not that I don't want you here. I just can't give you the love and care you need. Fraser is at school. I have to work all day, and there's no one here. There's still a month or two of winter to go through yet. It's going to be cold on the cliffs."

"I'll survive dad. I'm managing alright."

"I know you will survive, old son. There are not too many people who could live off the land and sea like you have been doing, but it's time now to get a job and start building a life for yourself, and with a stable, loving home with Grandma and Grandpa, there's no reason why you can't do really well. Look, nobody is going to force you to do anything. Just think about what Grandpa and I said."

"Okay, I'll think about it, but I'm not making any promises."

Grandma now appeared on the scene. "Oh King," she pleaded, "please see sense and give things a try with Grandpa and me. I know it won't be the same as having your mother, but we will do our best to give you a stable and loving home."

"I told dad I would think it over, Grandma. Now can you please leave me alone."

Grandma started sobbing and went downstairs. I sat alone in my room for the next few hours. I did consider Grandma and Grandpa's offer. I was fortunate to have them in my life, and to have been offered the opportunity to go and live with them, but they didn't understand how much pain I was in. It seemed that nobody understood how I felt. I was in too much of a mess to be around people, especially those I loved. At least in the wild I could be myself, and not have to deal with people telling me how I should feel and how I should live my life.

I wasn't ready to face the pain in my heart. I was angry at God and the world, and that's all there was to it. The answer was "no," and early tomorrow morning, I would head back to the cliffs again. That was my home now, and nobody was going to stop me.

While I was alone in my room, I found another sports bag, and I put some more of my clothes in it. I also took another blanket and pillow off my bed. And with my knives and my bow and arrows packed, I was ready to leave in the morning.

I didn't go back downstairs. I'd heard enough preaching for the evening. I waited until Fraser came up for the night.

"What have you decided to do, Kings?" he asked. "Are you going to live with Grandma and Grandpa? I'd sure like to go and live in Devonshire, Kings. Just think of all the food, and fishing off Hope's Nose. You could go and catch those massive pollack and mackerel off the rocks, like we used to do on our summer holidays."

"I have thought about it, Fraser, and I'm not going. Now please don't say anything to Grandma and Dad."

"I won't say anything, Kings, as long as you will be alright. I only have one brother, Kings, and I don't want anything to happen to you."

"Don't worry. Nothing is going to happen to me. Nobody understands I have to do this."

"When will I see you again, Kings? Nobody knows where you are."

"I'll tell you what, Fraser. About every two weeks, I'll throw something at the bedroom window at night, and you'll know it's me, and we can have a visit in the back field."

"Is that a promise, Kings?"

"Yes."

"Let's shake hands on it, then," said Fraser.

"Okay, it's a deal," I said, and I shook my brother's hand.

"I'll tell you what, Kings. I'll make up a food parcel for you every time you come, and you won't have to live only on fish and rabbit."

"I'd really appreciate that, Fraser, and don't forget, you mustn't tell anyone that I'm going in the morning, even Dad."

"Okay, Kings."

Fraser and I retired to our bunks. "Will you wake me before you leave Kings?"

"It depends how early it is Fraser. Sometimes I'm up at the crack of dawn. Don't forget, if you don't see me in the morning, I will throw something up at the window in a few weeks."

Fraser didn't say anything more. He was probably wondering what the hell was wrong with me, turning down an offer to go and live with Grandma and Grandpa. It's not like I had a job, or a girlfriend, or anything else going for me here in Wales.

I went to sleep wondering what was wrong with me. There was only one thing that I was acutely aware of, and that was the hole in my heart. I knew that tomorrow morning I'd be gone.

I woke at the crack of dawn. Fraser was still fast asleep and I decided not to wake him. I'd be too emotional if I did. Grabbing my bag, I quickly snuck down the stairs. Good – everyone was still in bed. Wait...there was an envelope on the kitchen table with my name on it. I would open it when I was clear of the house. I sensed that Grandpa would also be up early, wanting to talk to me.

Halfway across the field and out of sight of the house, I opened the letter. It was from dad, and there was a £50 note in it.

The letter read:

> *Dear Kings, I was hoping that you would take the opportunity to have a home with Grandma and Grandpa because I can't give you what you need. Regardless of your decision, I want you to have this money. Think of it as an extra Christmas present, and be careful with those knives. Remember, your room is waiting for you any time.*
> *Love, Dad.*

I began to weep. What was I doing? Dad loves me and misses me. Grandma and Grandpa have offered me a home with them in Devonshire. I could have a fresh start. I'm running away from love and belonging, food and warmth, and a roof over my head….but I still kept walking. Was I punishing myself by turning down Grandma and Grandpa's offer? I felt so confused. As I walked across the fields, the dawn grew into a beautiful morning. And with the chorus of the bird's morning song, I felt in my soul a renewed hope and strength. Being at home for Christmas and being around my family had done me good, and I was continuing on my journey, whatever that might be. It was now fully light, and there wasn't a cloud in the sky.

Chapter Six

Leathers Hole

When I arrived back at the cave, I dropped off my bag and then decided to go for a walk on the beach. It was the sort of day that makes one feel that it's a new beginning, and I decided that this day would be a new beginning for me. I would move from Bacon Hole and leave its darkness and ghosts behind, and I would find a brighter place to live. There were many caves on the Gower Peninsula, and I would choose a new one to be my home.

As I walked along Pobbles Beach, little did I know that today would be the start of one of the greatest adventures of my life.

Suddenly, the ground beneath me began to shake and I heard the thunder of hooves behind me. I turned to see galloping towards me, the biggest stallion I'd ever seen. I ran to the surf, hoping he would pass me by. He slowed to a trot and then stopped right in front of me. Reddish brown in colour, he looked massive and angry. Waving my arms, I shouted, "be gone with you!"

Then he charged me, chasing me into the sea. I stood there up to my waist amidst the waves and watched as he went

Leathers Hole

up on his hind legs and then slammed his front hooves into the sand. All the time he kept looking at me, making an angry grunting noise and showing his teeth. I backed up even more. I'd soon be swimming. Suddenly, to my relief, he backed off and continued his gallop along the beach. I stayed in the waves until I'd watched him go a long way away, almost out of sight. Then I made a run for it, back to the beach and on up to the high rocks where I had played 'King of the Castle' as a boy. The stallion was now out of sight, but I wasn't king of the castle any more, he was! What a magnificent animal.

That was enough adventure for one morning. I returned to my cave and made plans to move my home. It was still early in the day, so I had plenty of time to explore and decide on a new cave.

Well, good morning, 'Fear', and all you other spooks. Or should I say, Bah, humbug? You guys don't keep Christmas around here, do you? How can you! You're a bunch of spooks, but don't worry, I've got a present for you anyway. Guess what? I'm moving out of this dark hole and finding a new place to live. How's that for a Christmas present? You can have the whole cave to yourselves again. Hey, Fear! Don't be upset. I know you will miss me, not having anyone to haunt and scare at night, but keep your chin up, old man. I'm sure that in a few thousand years, someone else will come and live in Bacon Hole.

It continued to be a beautiful day, and I decided to go and re-explore a cave that I had explored as a boy. This cave is known as Leathers Hole, and it's high on a cliff top called the Great Tor. The Great Tor is not called great because of its overall height. It is not the highest of the Gower cliffs, at just under 200 feet, but it is certainly one of the most impressive.

It goes soaring up from the sands in a series of bold rounded slabs. Ravens nest high up towards the summit, and on a foggy day, or when the morning mists rest low, the crown of the mighty rock is hidden like a king in hiding, and it is far more mysterious.

I first explored Leathers Hole with my father and brother when I was about 10 years old. I have a vivid memory of my father tying a rope around his waist and telling my brother and me to hold on tightly as we walked the narrow and slippery path to the cave's entrance.

The cliff top area around the Great Tor is known as Penmaen Burrows. My father had also taken my brother and I ferreting on the burrows with my pet ferret, Ripper, and we had caught lots of rabbits thereo, so it should be a good area for me to continue hunting rabbits. I felt excited at the thought of using my throwing knives, and my bow and arrows. I had a big Bowie knife now, to skin my rabbits with, instead of having to use my fishing knife, which was getting blunt. The beach below the Great Tor is called Tor Bay, and the fishing there is good, so if Leathers Hole was comfortable enough to live in, then I would make it my new home.

I was still shaken up from my experience with the stallion, so I decided to walk along the cliff tops for as much of the way to the Great Tor as I could, rather than walking along the beach, which would have been the easiest and quickest way there. I did, however, have to come down from the cliff top at one place along the way. That was at the entrance to Three Cliffs Valley. There, I had to cross the Killy Willy River, not far from where I'd speared my big skate. After crossing the river, I would then climb up the sand dunes and on up to Penmaen Burrows.

Leathers Hole

As I continued my way along, the birds were singing their morning songs, and the yellow sun kissed the side of my face as it travelled on its own journey across the sky. Oh, to feel its warmth, and hear the birds sing. Surely my soul was hearing the promise that spring was not too far away.

From the cliff tops, my eyes searched the sands below for the stallion. I wanted to know where he was before I climbed down to the beach in the valley. I didn't want to be chased into the sea again. That had been too close a call.

There seemed to be no sign of the stallion as I arrived at the valley. I crossed the Killy Willy, looking all around me. He was still nowhere to be seen. Once through the river, I climbed the dunes and on up to Penmaen Burrows.

If I remembered correctly, Leathers Hole was on the eastern side of the Great Tor, and one had to climb down to the entrance from the top of the cliff. Wow! The view was stunning in every direction from where I stood at the top of the Tor. This had to be one of the reasons it was called Great.

I hereby claim this place as my new throne! Before me is the emerald green Bristol Channel, and I can see all the way to the rolling hills of Devonshire. To the east is the breathtaking view of Three Cliffs and Pobbles Bay, with the Bell Rock standing like a lonely, mysterious island in the middle of the sands. Also, from here is surely the grandest view of the low grasslands where the wild horses roam and graze. And there on the hill stands Pennard Castle, shouting loudly of ages past, its precious memories calling out to me from its crumbling walls. Yesterday walks with today, always hand-in-hand.

Cave Days

PENNARD CASTLE

Summers of children run barefoot
down your golden slopes,
And you watch them running, running,
as fast as legs will carry.
Look, Mr Blackbird, I can fly,
and fall always softly as into a mother's arms.
I stand up again, and feel the dew soaked grass as
it sticks like velvet slippers to my feet.
I walk to the still flowing river,
where children's secrets keep
A gentle splash, and my feet are clean again,
And I climb back up your golden slopes,
just to run down again
Oh please, Mr. Pennard Castle,
turn back your Time Machine.
For I still hope and I still dream, that I,
the Prince will find my Princess,
That from behind your ancient walls
you have seen that this is not a dream!
© *Kingsley Ross Hill*

Behind me is the majestic hill of Cefn Bryn, not yet arrayed in its spring glory. Today, two buzzards soar in the clear skies above its shining crown. And to the west is the ever changing picture of Oxwich Bay, one of the Gower Peninsula's most beautiful stretches of sand. During the low spring tides, there is a golden circle that stretches all the way around from

Leathers Hole

Pobbles Beach to the old Oxwich church, a distance of about four miles, and along this magnificent circle are quiet coves where one can be alone, even in the summer months. There are sand dunes with wild flowers and dancing grasses from whence the wind whispers secrets. There are beautiful woods, and the marshland with many rare birds, and the Crawley stream flows out from the woods and shakes hands with the lonely sea. Surely, where I stand now overlooks one of the most beautiful places on earth. No, it is the most beautiful place on earth, of this I am sure.

It is all in the eye of the beholder, it is said. Ahh, but one's *soul* must know the place. You must touch and caress one another so that *the place* knows *you*. Only then does it become sacred, and the most beautiful place on earth, and one day I will bring my Princess here, and look deep into her eyes. If I see that her soul is as beautiful as this place, I will know that she is the one that from behind the castle walls has waited for her Prince, and we shall stand here, hand in hand until the setting of the sun.

It was time to climb down from my lookout and find the cave. I remembered the slippery narrowing path, which I now followed as it led me out to the highest rock from the landward side of the Tor. I recalled my father's words: "when you pass over a camel's hump, you are on the right track and will soon see the entrance." I was on the camel's hump alright, so I should see the entrance any time. And there it was, Leathers Hole!

Leathers Hole is one of the most inaccessible of the Gower caves. One has to be careful not to slip and fall on the treacherous narrow path, especially during these winter months.

As I stood at the entrance, there was a sound of silence similar to the one that had first greeted me at Bacon Hole, but then there was less sound of wind and sea, compared to here on the Great Tor. I kneeled at the entrance and listened, and the silence grew louder. It was as if this cave was waiting ... expecting me to enter and be part of its history. For indeed, that was what I was doing.

"How long have you been waiting?" I asked. There was no answer, only the still silence. Then a breeze blew gently and answered, 'a long time.' I thought of those ancient animal remains that had been found in this cave; those beasts that roamed this land when Britain was still attached to mainland Europe, on what was now sea – the Bristol Channel (my teacher Mr. Richards had said). History began to cry out louder and louder from this place that had waited for my arrival.

The early explorers had found the remains of mammoth, woolly rhinoceros, hyena, and many other species in this cave. These animals had lived thousands of years ago, and now, I, Kingsley Hill, modern caveman extraordinaire, was about to enter into its history. This place was timeless, and my time here would be like a vapour, vanishing like the morning mists. Even if I was to live here for the rest of my life, it would be nothing compared to the thousands of years that this cave had seen. Nonetheless, this would be my time in its history, and I was going to make the most of it.

I went inside. "Fear, are you here?" I shouted. I heard nothing, only the ravens on the heights. Good, maybe he had stayed at Bacon Hole. Maybe only animals had lived here, and no caveman family. The cave consisted of a long passage going deep into the rock. I could remember my father crawling into

Leathers Hole

a short tunnel, while my brother Fraser and I stood where I was standing now. On that day, there was no way that we were going to follow our father into that creepy tunnel. Then we heard a shout "Boys, it opens up into a roomy cavern," but for now, I would set up my camp in the light of the entrance.

It was now early afternoon, and I decided to make one trip back to Bacon Hole. By the time I had brought one load back to my new home, it would be getting dark, so I'd have to do the rest tomorrow.

I walked back to Bacon Hole the same way I'd come, along the cliff tops. The stallion seemed to have disappeared as I scanned the sands below. But I had a strong feeling that our paths would meet again soon.

By the time I reached Pobbles, my blue sky was disappearing fast. A massive dark cloud filled the sky above the Three Cliffs Valley and spots of rain were in the air. It got darker and darker, and I moved quickly across the cliffs. I felt fortunate to reach Bacon Hole before it poured down with rain. So much for taking a load to my new cave today. I'd wait until tomorrow and hope for a dry day.

How was I going to pass the time during the night? There was no firewood, and there would be no going to the Pennard stores. I was sure Mr. Skittle would call the police again, or Grandma and Grandpa. They would be upset enough, having realised that I had left this morning. Their sad faces haunted my mind. Dad would be upset too, and Fraser, my only brother. It had been so good to see him. I must keep my promise and go and see him every few weeks.

As the rain continued, I shivered and wished I had a fire, and thoughts of the comfort of the house filled my mind. There it was warm and sheltered, and my stomach felt hungry as I thought of Grandma's home cooked meals. Then I had an idea, a wonderful idea. I still had a good amount of money thanks to James' milk round and Dad's £50 note. Thanks, Dad. It's going to come in real handy on these cold wet nights. I'll go to the pub tonight in the village. It will be warm and I'll pass the time and have a nice cooked meal. Yes, I'll celebrate my new home at Leathers Hole. 'Did you hear that, Fear? I'm going to the pub to celebrate finding my new home. Don't wait up, because I'll be there until closing time." Just think, this will be the last night he would be able to haunt me. "So you better make the most of it, because tomorrow is moving day. See you spooks later." I'm sure they will have a real fright night waiting for me when I get back.

The rain had stopped just in time as I climbed up the Cliff path and walked along East Cliff Road to the village. From the village it was about another half a mile to the Southgate Pub, so I would arrive in perfect time for an evening meal. But with every step I grew hungrier, picturing Grandma's Christmas dinner in my mind. How was I going to live on fish and rabbits again? I would just have to make regular visits to the village to buy food while my money lasted, and when it ran out, I would rob James again. He owed me big time for what he did to my magpie.

I could see the pub now as I turned the corner, and I felt good. I had clean clothes and money in my pocket. Maybe I would meet a nice girl tonight. Hey, you never know. I opened the heavy door and went inside. The place was almost deserted, apart from an old couple playing cards in the corner, but then what could I expect, it was boxing day night. Only people

Leathers Hole

who were lonely, or didn't have any family came to the pub on boxing day night. I started singing, 'Only the Lonely', by Roy Orbison. And do you know what? I felt less lonely singing.

"What would you like, boy?" shouted a man from behind the bar. "We only have bangers and mash, or fish and chips, that's all we're cooking tonight."

"I'll have bangers and mash!" I shouted back. I couldn't bear the thought of fish, at least not for another hundred years.

"And to drink, boy?"

"I'll have a pint of cider, please." I sat at a table near the window and waited for my food. So much for my hopes of meeting a pretty waitress that I could ask to be my cave woman. Oh well, at least I would have a hot meal and it would help pass the time. It was sure better than hanging around the cave with Fear and his friends.

Just then my friend Mitch's mother and father walked in. "Look Muriel," Glen said, "it's Kingsley! What are you doing, boy? The whole village has been worried about you."

"Our Mitch told us you had run away from home," Muriel added. "Are you alright, Kings? We haven't seen you for so long!"

"I'm doing fine," I said. "I'm living off the land and the sea."

"Aye, you are. They are calling you the 'wild boy'. You have always been a bit wild, haven't you Kings?" Muriel said, as she gave me a big hug.

"A bit wild," Glen said with a smile and a wink.

"You heard him, he is living off the land and the sea, but we love him all the same, don't we Glen?"

"Like a son," Glen echoed. "And our Mitch said you're the best friend he's ever had, Kings."

"Thank you," I said. "I regard Mitch as my best friend too."

Glen and Muriel stayed and joined me for supper. I was sure glad of their company. We talked of old times, and Glen still remembered when Mitch took his pipe for us boys to smoke around the fire in Bacon Hole. Gosh, where had the years gone. Mitch was still in school and planning to go to college, Muriel told me.

"What about you, Kings?" She asked.

Yes, what about me. My school of learning was living in caves and being chased by wild horses. It's the only school of its kind, I was tempted to say.

Instead I said, "right now, I'm deciding what I'm going to do. My grandparents were down for Christmas, and they offered me a home with them in Devonshire, so I might go and work In Devon."

What else was I going to say? I'm going to tame the stallion, and ride around the countryside robbing perfect strangers like Jesse James did? No, I had James' milk round instead of that sort of thing.

My time with Glen and Muriel was the perfect social follow-up after being at home for Christmas. It reaffirmed my need for connection with people. I decided I would come to the pub every few weeks for that reason, and of course for a nice hot meal.

"Take care Kings, and don't be a stranger."

"I won't," I said, as they left the pub for home. What now? It was 11:30 pm and the last guests were leaving the pub. It closed at midnight, so I would have to leave too.

"Good night, everyone." said the man behind the bar.

"Good night," I echoed, putting on my jacket.

Leathers Hole

As I walked back through the village, the streets were dark and lonely. I welcomed each street lamp as if it were another person. When I reached East Cliff road, there were no more streetlamps. The only light came from the occasional house or cottage. As I walked, Mitch's mother's words kept ringing in my head: "Mitch is going to college." And where was I going? I asked my soul.

It's interesting that some words we remember all our lives; they penetrate deep into our being. Even if they are just a sentence, they can have the power to affect our whole life. I can remember the words of my grandmother speaking to me as a boy: "Kingsley, I know that God has a special plan for your life. He has allowed you to suffer for a reason, and one day you will understand that your suffering with asthma has turned into a gift, and that it wasn't a curse after all."

When I was around my friends and peers, I rarely mentioned God, and if I did, it was only to take his name in vain. But in my quiet hours, I often thought of Grandma's words, that God had a plan, and I dared to wonder tonight if God really did have a plan for my life…. There was no one around, only an owl on a nearby post, so I decided to talk to God.

"God, I know you are there. I've known of your existence all my life, through the things you have made, of this I am sure. But do you really have a plan for my life? And if you do, will you tell me, and show me that you do?" The moment I finished talking to God, the owl flew away, as if going to deliver my message to God. "It's a long way to heaven!" I shouted at the owl.

Grandma's words echoed again in my heart. "The very moment we call out to God, he hears us, King, and answers our prayers. We just have to believe he has heard us, and he has."

Cave Days

I arrived at the cliff top above Bacon Hole. It was going to be a challenge to climb down to the entrance through the narrow Gorse path. I was sure glad I had brought my flashlight. It gave off just enough light for me to see the path ahead of me. I stumbled a few times, pricking my hands and knees on the thorns of the Gorse, but I made it down to the entrance. The cave seemed to be darker than usual tonight. Maybe it was just the way I was feeling, having been around people and light at the pub, and then coming back to darkness. There was no way I was going to sleep in the heart of the cave tonight, not without the fire. Holding my flashlight above my head, I ventured in and quickly grabbed my air mattress and blankets.

"I'm not sleeping near you spooks tonight!" I shouted. I set up my bed at the entrance and put out my flashlight. There was nothing else to do now except wait for the dawn and try to get some sleep.

Chapter Seven

Message in a Bottle

I woke to the gentle stir of the wind, and I was warm in my sleeping bag. I had slept well, and for a while I lay listening to the sounds of the morning. The gulls were awake, but I could barely hear the sea. It was still sleeping. The tide lay low, and there was only a gentle swell on the water.

I sat on my throne for the last time as 'the Caveman of Bacon Hole'. "Today is moving day," I announced, as I looked out across the Emerald Sea, and what better way to end my time here than a last walk on Hunts Beach?

I climbed down the narrow path and onto the rocky shore. It was the lowest tide I'd seen since coming to the cave to live, and I was able to walk out to the only sandy part of the beach. Everywhere else there were rocks and gullies.

What was that bobbing in the water? It was an old bottle, and there was something in it. I moved to the edge of the rocks to take a closer look. It was a message in a bottle. The gentle swell of the tide moved the bottle back and forth in the gully and I began to get excited – what could it be? A letter from a beautiful girl looking for her Prince? Or was it from some sailor lost at sea and marooned on an island? I couldn't wait to find out, so I ran back to the cave to get my prawning net; I could reach it with that. But by the time I got back, there was no need for the net, as the tide had brought the bottle up the gully to the shore. It dragged back and forth making a hollow scraping noise on the small pebbles. I picked it up and sat on the rock to inspect it.

It was a green glass bottle with the label long worn off. On one side it had several barnacles on it. This told me that it had been at sea for some time. It was sealed with a cork well into its neck, and the top part of the cork had worn off, so I couldn't pry it out, and I had no corkscrew, so I would have to break the bottle to read what was inside. Holding the bottle like a piece of treasure, I climbed back up the cliff to my throne. I would open it there.

On a small rock, I smashed the neck of the bottle. The note was tied up with a brown piece of string, and slowly I unravelled the tight scroll. It wasn't a treasure map or a letter from a girl as I had hoped. Instead it was a bible verse. Great, what next!

The verse read: "For I know the plans I have for you," declares the Lord, "plans to prosper you and not to harm you, plans to give you hope and a future."

As I read these words, my initial disappointment of it being a Bible verse was shattered. The words spoke deep into my heart like two arms were being put around me, and I knew that these words were a message for me. Wow!

How long had this bottle been drifting at sea? Months? A year? Maybe longer, there were barnacles on it. What were the chances of me finding it? Even of me going down to the beach on this day and at this very time that the bottle came into the shore. There it was just floating on the tide.

Message in a Bottle

God knows me well, I thought, utterly and completely. My talk with Him the night before was in my heart as I remembered asking Him to tell me if he really did have a plan for my life. This experience told me that He did, which I found both exciting and frightening at the same time.

I thought of my dream in the cave, and the gentle voice that spoke those same words. All of a sudden things were starting to make sense, like they were all connected. My heart was opening to the possibilities. Just then the same owl I'd seen on the post when I was praying last night, landed on the ground outside the cave. "Your message was delivered," he said with his eyes and a turn of his head.

Well, it was time to start my day. It was moving day, I reminded myself, and I would have plenty of time to think about these mysterious events. I went into the cave to get my first load of gear. I would take my fishing and hunting equipment first, and as it was low tide I'd walk along the beach from Pobbles instead of along the cliff tops. What about the stallion? I pondered for a few minutes. Would he still be there? No, I hadn't seen him again, he's probably moved to a different area.

I arrived at Pobbles with my first load of gear, and started making my way along the beach. This was much easier than walking the cliff tops all the way.

He seemed to come from nowhere, like a whirlwind he was on me! Dropping my fishing gear I tried to make a run for it, but I tripped and fell. Going up on his hind legs he slammed his front hooves into the sand beside my head, missing me by inches. I lay there frozen, expecting only death. What was the delay I wondered? I moved my hands away from my face and opened my eyes. To my surprise he lowered his head and nudged me on the face with his nose. As I stared into his wild brown eyes, he seemed to look right into my soul and said, "I'm the King around here, what are you doing in my territory?"

I wasn't going to argue! He just stood there for what seemed like an eternity, towering over me and sniffing and smelling, and continuing to nudge me with his warm wet nose. I could feel his warm breath pushing and blowing against my face.

Eventually he lifted his head, and with a grunt and a shake of his head he was on his way. I continued to lay there in fear he would come back. Turning on my side I watched him gallop westward towards Oxwich Bay. Getting up slowly and still trembling, I picked up my gear and ran up the beach. I crossed the Killy Willy and then headed on up the dunes to Penmaen Burrows. I sat exhausted at the entrance of my new cave, and rested for a few hours. Well, that was the end of my walking along the beach, it was only the cliff tops from now on.

It took me the rest of the day to finish my move, but I had done it, and survived the attack from the stallion. I sat and watched the sunset. This would be my first night at Leathers Hole. After inflating my air mattress I lay down to sleep at the entrance. It would take some time before I slept inside the cave, just like at Bacon Hole. The feeling at Leathers hole was different in the fact that it didn't have a heavy air to it, like Bacon Hole did. Even though the entrance was a lot smaller and the inside more enclosed, the atmosphere felt more open.

I drifted off to sleep thinking about the stallion, and how I was going to be able to share his territory with him? There was no way I could go on like this, living in fear of him. How was I going to be able to fish with him around? On the morrow I would seek him out from the cliff tops and observe him. There had to be a way we could live in peace together. Otherwise my adventures in the wild would have to come to an end. The stallion could have killed me, but for some reason he didn't.

"Well God, you protected me all right! Thank you for saving me from the stallion. When he went up on his back legs, I thought it was all over."

I slept well in the sea breeze air, and lay listening to the sounds of the morning. I missed the squeaks of the rock pipits, and there was no sound of rock doves coming from Leathers Hole. But I could still look out over the Bristol Channel, and my view of the beaches was fantastic. I had cereal for breakfast and finished up the last of the milk. Sometime today I would go and explore Penmaen village, and pick up some more food. If I remembered rightly, there was only one store in the village and it was a general store and post office. There was also a farm, and a pub called the King Arthur, at the foot of Cefn Bryn.

I felt excited about going to explore a new territory, but first I would go and search for the stallion. The Gower Peninsula has a wonderful and long history of horses and ponies. It is said that some of the wild horses that roam the area of Cefn Bryn descend from the herds of King Arthur and his Knights of the Round Table. Many historians will tell you otherwise, but I believe they do. An old man told me years ago on the bridge over the Killy Willy, by old Park Mill School, that Arthur got his horses from the wild herds of Gower.

"Tis true, boy."

"Yes Sir, I believe you."

I have told the story ever since. The old man also told me that there was a special lineage of stallions that Arthur and his knights rode, and they were stronger and faster than any other line of horses in all of Britain.

"The lineage is still going to this day, boy."

"Yes Sir."

"And one day, boy, if you seek hard enough, the stallion will show himself to you."

"How will I know that he is the one?"

"You will know him because he will be the wildest horse you have ever seen, and if he doesn't kill you, then he has chosen you. He will know if you are a true son of Gower, boy, a modern day knight.

"Yes Sir," I said excitedly. "I like the sound of that!"

"Do you want to be a knight, boy?"

"Yes Sir, I do."

"Then one day, when you're older, you must search for him."

Shivers ran up my spine as I thought of the stallion. Could he be the special one? How strange that I would remember the old man's words all these years later. I was only about nine when he told me all this. They laughed at me in the village when I told them of the old man's words. "Stay away from that old man, Kingsley. He is very strange, and he lives in another time and place."

I didn't care what they said. I liked the old man and we grew to be great friends. He taught me things that nobody else could.

It was time to go and look for the stallion. The best place to start would be out on top of the Great Tor. From there I could see the full length of the Sands in both directions. I started looking westwards towards Oxwich point. That was the direction I'd seen him go after our last encounter. I'd watched him gallop out of sight. There seemed to be no sign of him this morning, but that didn't mean much. I remembered how quickly he was on me when I'd started walking across the beach. I needed to stay watching for some time, as he might be making his way back and still be out of sight.

From time to time, I turned my head eastwards to Three Cliffs and Pobbles Bay. This was the shorter stretch of sand, and with the tide being low, I could see all the way to the far side of Pobbles and on to the rocks of Heatherslade Bay. There was no sign of him. He could, however, have turned northwards up the Three Cliffs Valley towards Pennard Castle. I could see the castle and part of the valley from where I stood. But there is another area where the horses go to graze and drink from the river that can't be seen from up here on the Tor.

My instincts told me that he would be coming from the west, having travelled along the sands to Oxwich. In both my encounters he had headed west.

A herd of horses were now making their way down the valley towards the beach. I watched them cross the Killy Willy, and come right up to the foot of the dunes. They stopped right at the area where I climbed up the dunes to the Burrows to get to the Tor. There were eight horses in all and they looked to be mares. My stallion certainly wasn't with them. He was reddish brown and a lot bigger. Where was the stallion? I wondered if he had a hideout, away from the other horses, as he was such a wild horse, and he had been alone on both the occasions he had chased me.

I had been up here for a while and there was still no sign of him. I'd give it a few more minutes, and then climb down from the Tor and head along West Cliff to Pobbles. Maybe he was in close to the rocks where I couldn't see him? He had to be somewhere, and there was no way I was going to walk on the beach again. At least not until I knew where he was and felt that I would have enough warning if he was heading in my direction.

Suddenly, a dark speck appeared in the distance. Just a little dark spot in the middle of the Sands towards Oxwich. There were no rocks out in the middle of the Sands in that direction; it had to be an animal. As the minutes went by, the shape was getting bigger and seemed to be coming this way. Maybe it was a horse and rider? People quite often rode horses along this stretch of the beach. I'd seen the riding schools down on the Sands, but not at this time of the year.

I could see now that it was a horse with no rider, and it was making good speed. In fact, it was the fastest I'd ever seen a horse run, and I've seen hundreds of them, having grown up on Gower. It was the stallion alright. Gosh, look at him go! He ran like the wind, thundering past the Tor, and onward toward Pobbles. He splashed across the Killy Willy, but didn't turn northwards to the Valley. He kept on toward Pobbles, until he slowed to a trot and then headed inland towards the rocks. I couldn't see him now. Where could he be going? He hadn't gone far enough along the beach to reach the cove of Pobbles Bay. What was he doing? There were only rocks and tidal caves in that area of the beach. I would go and investigate. At least I knew approximately where he was, and I'd be safe going down the dunes and crossing the river. I'd look for him from the cliff top.

My legs felt heavy as I climbed down the dunes and took off my shoes and socks to cross the Killy Willy. I'd sure done a

Message in a Bottle

lot of walking the last few days. Especially with my move from Bacon Hole. Tired and hungry I reached the cliffs at Pobbles, but my journey was not without reward. There standing in front of one of the caves was the stallion. Gosh, he looked big, even from up here. And why was he just standing there in front of the cave? He looked as though he was standing guard over something. One day when he wasn't around I would have to go and explore and see what was in there. For now, however, I was tired and hungry, too tired to go all the way to the Penmaen village.

Much as I didn't want to go back into Pennard stores again, they were a lot closer than Penmaen. As I continued to walk along the cliff tops, I was concerned that Grandma and Grandpa might have called the police on me, just because they were worried. I hoped that my father would talk them out of doing something stupid like that, and reassure them that I was all right out here in the wild.

What if Mr. Skittle is in the store? Even if he is there, I'm going in to buy some food. I'll get two Cornish pasties and a drink of pop, and if old man Skittle questions me, I'll tell him I'm home again wit^h my family and doing well. I'll even thank him for caring enough the first time and calling the police. "I've seen sense, Mr. Skittle." That would be the perfect cover-up, wouldn't it? He'd appreciate a thank you. No, that would be overdoing it, and besides, even if he doesn't believe me and calls Grandpa or the police, I'll be long gone. They won't find me.

To my relief, Mr. Skittle wasn't in the store. It was a lady that didn't know me. "Can I help you?" she said.

"Yes please, I'd like two Cornish pasties and a bottle of beer for my father." I thought I'd take full advantage of the stranger in the store.

"Would you like your pasties heated up?" She asked.

"Yes please."

"And are you sure this beer is for your father?"

"Oh yes, I often pick one up for him."

She put the beer and pasties in a bag, and I was soon on my way back along the cliff tops.

When I got to Pobbles, I stopped and looked over where I'd seen the stallion. To my surprise he was still there. I sat down on the cliff top and watched him while I ate my pasties. He didn't move for about half an hour, and then all of a sudden he galloped off towards Oxwich.

I remembered that it was 11:30 a.m. when I was in the store, and it had taken me about half an hour to get back here. I had been sitting here for about half an hour, so that would make it about 12:30 p.m. I noted the time. Was the stallion a creature of habit? I wondered, as I walked along the cliffs swigging my beer.

By the time I got back to Leathers Hole, I was exhausted and decided to call it a day. I crawled into my sleeping bag and closed my eyes. I had found the stallion, I had food in my stomach, and the beer had given me a nice buzz. All in all, it had been a pretty good day.

Chapter Eight

Gay Tripp

I woke to the sound of the gulls and the fresh sea air stirring gently through my hair. My sleep had been deep and sweet, and I felt refreshed from yesterday's long day. It was time to greet the new day. I climbed up to my new lookout seat on top of the Tor and gave my weather report to the listening birds. Today would be cloudy, with a light mist coming in from the sea, and there would be wind but no rain, and you birds don't forget to sing, because this afternoon we might see the sun shine again.

I'm going to explore Penmaen village this morning, and you birds are welcome to come with me if you please. You can sing me a new song, called "the darkness has gone," so I shall be happy and sing all the day long. Now let's hear you sing the chorus: "Hooray, hooray, Fear and darkness have gone away!"

There was nothing left for breakfast this morning, so I visited Grandma's Christmas table in my mind, with all the plenty that I could eat. And as I walked over the Burrows towards the village, I thought of all the food they might sell in the Little General Store. I imagined them having anything I wanted to eat. Shreddies with hot milk and brown sugar,

Cave Days

Sourdough bread, still warm with melting butter and red currant jam, Cornish pasties with crisp flaking pastry on the outside and piping hot meat, potato and vegetables on the inside, and lemon meringue pie for dessert. Oh, I can taste the strong, zippy lemon underneath that puffy sweet meringue. And wait a moment, Mrs. Storekeeper, please, don't forget the dandelion and burdock.

Gosh, I'm hungry. But reality is, Kings, it's only a little store and you can't expect too much. There would be eggs and milk, and produce from the local farmers. But freshly made bread? That might be too much to ask. Hey, food is food, and whatever they had would taste wonderful to a hungry caveman, and food always tastes better outside, doesn't it?

Along the Burrows, I saw rabbits coming out of their holes in search of their breakfast. 'No, no, not you,' I shouted. 'I don't want to eat you guys anymore.' They weren't hanging around to find out. They skipped away as soon as they saw me. Maybe it's the way I look, I thought, rubbing my whiskers. When I get to the store, I have to look in the mirror and hopefully not crack it, or I'll have seven years bad luck, according to Mad Jean, our local witch lady in Pennard village.

The morning was turning out just the way I'd predicted. Cloudy, but with no rain. It was just as well, because my only clean clothes were on my back. Suddenly I remembered that I'd left some other clothes hanging on branches at Bacon Hole. Oh well, I wasn't going all the way back for them. I'd leave them for Fear and friends, but I wondered how I was going to dry my clothes at Leathers Hole. There wasn't the ventilation there for me to have a good-sized fire inside the cave. Maybe I could have a small one in the inner chamber just for warmth?

But I hadn't been in to explore it yet. When I got back from the village, I'd try to pluck up the courage to go inside. Any fire big enough to dry my clothes, though, would have to be made outside the entrance.

Maybe I could get modern and make a clothesline! It would work well in the spring and summer air. I could take a bar of soap and do my washing in the Killy Willy, but the air was too damp and cold this time of year. I know...I told Fraser that I'd come and visit him every few weeks, so I'll bring my laundry with me and do it there. Good thinking, King's old boy, you're a blimin' genius.

As I arrived at the village, it was much as I remembered, with just one road, or lane as we local Gower folk call it, going through it. There were a few rows of houses and the general store on one side of the lane. There was a farm and King Arthur's pub on the other, and there were sheep everywhere, in the lane, in the fields, and there were three of them right outside the store.

"Good morning boys, how're things? Oh pardon me, you're girls, aren't you. Excuse me, please, and 'bah bah' to you too. I don't have anything for you today, now out of my way."

Two of them moved, but one stood fast, right in front of the door. "Get out," I shouted, giving it a kick. "If you stand in my way again, I'll come and eat you. Hmmm, that gives me an idea, fresh mutton."

With Bah-bah out of the way, I opened the door and went inside. Wow, I wasn't ready for this! There in front of me was the most beautiful hair I'd ever seen. Long and flowing like a horse's tail, chestnut curls going all the way to her waist, and I could smell perfume. Oh her sweet scent, it was like lavender on a summer breeze. Moving closer, I stood right behind her as she paid for the groceries. Her voice was soft and gentle, and she wore stretch pants and riding boots that clung to her beautiful figure. I lost all sense of what I came into the store for. This was so unexpected and wonderful. Longing and desire flowed through my veins. I hadn't even seen her face, and I wanted to touch her hair and smell her neck. What would I say when she turned around? With my heart pounding, I backed off, thinking she would walk right into me.

She said goodbye to the storekeeper and turned around. She was more beautiful than I'd imagined, and what's more, she said my name.

"Kingsley!" She exclaimed, as I looked into her purple eyes. I loved her before I could even speak any words.

"Gay, " I replied, still looking into her eyes.

"We were in school together, Kingsley, do you remember?"

"Yes, I remember, and we used to travel in Mr. Gibbon's minibus together on our way to school."

We left the store and sat on a picnic table and talked some more. "I got on the bus at Pennard, where most of the kids got on," I said, "and then we'd stop on Clyne Common and picked you up on the way to Swansea."

We talked for a while, catching up on all Gower news, and recalled all the people and places we knew. Where had the time gone? Gay and I had gone to Dumbarton House School for about three years. We rarely saw much of each other at school. We were in different classes, and I was a year older. We saw each other on sports days, and during the morning assembly, before the headmaster sent us all off to class. Mr. Allen was his name, and no one wanted to get on the bad side of him. We both laughed at that.

"Well, Kingsley, I must be going now," she announced, and to my surprise she kissed me. "By the way, would you like to come and watch me ride my horse? I have him at the stables at Penmaen farm. I come and ride him every Saturday. Why don't you come?"

"I will!" I said, still glowing from her kiss. "See you Saturday." I shouted out, as she turned and walked away.

"10 o'clock," she called back.

"I'll be there," I shouted. "Bye, Gay."

"Bye, Kingsley." As she said it, her smile made me warm all over.

∽

Going back into the store, I looked around. What had I come in for? Oh yes, food, glorious food. Feeling my hunger again, I was tempted to fill as many bags as I could carry, but I had a long walk back to Leathers Hole. I'd get the basics and come back a few times during the week as I needed things. I bought some Cornish pasties, which were quickly becoming my favourite food, as I could eat them warm or cold, and not having to cook my food had become a treat. I also got milk and cereal, and a small bundle of kindling for a fire. I looked forward to sitting in front of the fire with its light and warmth, only this time without Fear and his friends.

Mmm, what was that smell? The Baker had arrived. What perfect timing – "Thank you." I picked up two loaves, still warm, and one was a raisin loaf. Now, I mustn't forget butter. Oh, and one more thing, a bottle of pop to celebrate having met Gay.

With my bag of groceries, I decided to walk up the path from the village onto Cefn Bryn and have my lunch on top of King Arthur's stone. Legend has it that there was once a great contest in the days of the knights, where an invitation went out inviting all the knights and nobles, from all over Britain, to come and try to remove a sword from the stone. The sword was no ordinary sword. It was called Excalibur, and it had special powers, believed to have been given from God himself. Whoever was able to pull the sword from the stone would be given the title of "King!"

The knights and other so-called mighty men watched on, as one after the other failed to have the strength to pull the sword from the stone. Eventually, a young boy, no older than 12 years old, begged to have a try at pulling the sword. The knights and nobles laughed at the thought of such a young boy even having a try. "Why, he is only a shepherd boy," they exclaimed. "Go back to your father's farm and milk the cows with the maids," they taunted. But one knight spoke up: "The boy has come a long way to try his luck, let him alone and give the lad a chance." To the amazement of all those present, the young boy pulled the sword from the stone and became a King that day.

Sitting on top of the stone, I ate my pasties and made a toast to Gay with my pop. I was so excited about meeting up with her again after all these years, and I vowed not to wash my cheek until she kissed me again. I was glad she hadn't asked me where I lived. Telling her that I lived in a cave would probably not be the best start to what I hoped would be a love forever more. I wanted to make her my Princess, and I would be her Prince. I might not have a fancy house, only a humble cave, but I could live off the land and the sea, and show her things that few men could. I was growing in my confidence, and that was good. For no faint-hearted man ever won the love of a fair maiden. She can stand with me, hand-in-hand, on top of the Great Tor, and from there I can show her my kingdom, as the Prince of Leathers Hole. And the stallion, I can tell her all about the stallion. Gay knows a lot about horses.

I couldn't wait for Saturday. What day was it? I'd forgotten to get the newspaper. It's Tuesday, that's right, I remember Gay saying she rode her horse most Tuesdays and every Saturday. Well, it was going to be a long wait until Saturday, but that would give me time to learn more about the stallion, and get my home ready for a lady. If she would come and visit me in a cave, that is. As I sat upon King Arthur's stone, I felt the warmth of the sun on my shoulders, and the songs of the skylarks filled the air. The wide open space of the moorland makes one feel free. One is surrounded by the past, and the stories of King Arthur and the knights are still told on the gentle winds. Kestrels still hunt and hover as they did on that day when Arthur pulled the sword from the stone.

I will tell you a secret, dear reader, that I learned as a boy. Anyone can be a King up here, as long as you have courage and a pure heart. I became a Prince when I sat on the stone at age 7, and I am a King sitting here today at 16. Your age or social status matters not, you just have to believe.

"Who told you that you're a Prince?" The old man once asked me.

"It is in the wind," I answered, "and I feel it now when I walk upon the Bryn."

"Then you are a Prince," he exclaimed. And I am!

I sat upon Kingsley's stone until the wild moors became golden, and I looked out across my kingdom as I walked, tall and proud, back down the hill to King Arthur's pub for supper. I am the King, and I will celebrate my reign with a meal.

I looked at the sign on the way in, to see if they had changed it yet to my name.... Word sure gets around slowly up here, ever since the Knights left for the Crusades. I'll give the owner of the pub one week to change the sign, and if it's not done then, I'll bring my sword.

I'll have a pint of cider, bartender, and a steak and kidney pie, if you please. Will that be all, your honour? Yes, only next time you must bow.

My supper was excellent! "Fit for a King if you have the pheasant," the old man had said. Next time, old man, I will try it.

My pie was sufficient, I thought, as I walked down the hill to the Burrows.

Darkness fell just as I arrived back at my cave. Putting down my bag of groceries I made a small fire out of the kindling. I had no large pieces of wood, so it would be a quick blaze. The comforts of being indoors still called out to me, but you just can't listen, not when you're a caveman.

The temperature had dropped sharply and the sky was clear. The kindling burned hot, like a young man's countenance when he asks a girl on a date and she says 'yes'. But it soon burned out, like a face when the answer is 'no'. My face was bright and shining, for Gay had kissed me –and asked me to see her again.

Gay Tripp

I sat as close as I dared to the fire and caught the last of the warmth before climbing into my sleeping bag. I looked up at the night sky, and it spoke of more, and a plan, that I prayed to be a part of. I asked God if he would help me to get to know Gay. I'd never had a real girlfriend before, and I went to sleep thinking of that warm and gentle kiss upon my cheek.

At dawn I woke to the call of the ravens echoing through the still and misty air from the heights of the Tor, announcing the new day. Their calls were determined. They said to me, "You must live your life deliberately."

"I will," I shouted out to the morning, and I climbed to the top of the Tor.

♪☼

BEAUTIFUL DAY

It is a beautiful day!
And there isn't an angry thought
in the mind of **Mr. Blue Sky** today.
Only peace, he says, only peace,
As he puffs on, and then blows away,
the last see-through cloud that he will make today.
The ocean sparkles in conversation with
the light of the rising Sun,
And the sands of Pobbles and Three Cliffs Bay walk
in their white robes as they go to fetch their coffee,
And black-backed gulls fly up and around,
flapping their wings about a Paradise found.
And the Killy Willy River flows like liquid silver,
all the way till it shakes hands with the sea,

Cave Days

And I sing and I dance because
I feel happy and free.
Good morning Mr. Bumblebee.
Have you come for tea?
Or just to see?
Yes, to see, he says,
and he buzzes off to enjoy the beautiful day!
© *Kingsley Ross Hill*

As I looked out across the sands, I could see that it was close to low tide, my favourite time to start fishing. I climbed back down to my cave to get my fishing gear. Wait a moment, I thought, what about the stallion? How can I go fishing with him on the loose? Would he attack me again and chase me into the sea?

I sat at the entrance of my cave and had breakfast. I felt anger towards the stallion this morning. He was disrupting my life. I went back into the cave and got my backpack, and pulled out my Bowie knife that my father had given me for Christmas. I also picked up my spear. It was still sharp from when I'd used it on the skate. With my Bowie knife in one hand, and my spear in the other, I set off along the Burrows and down onto the sands. Just let him charge me now I thought, gripping my spear hard and shaking it in my hand. I'll plunge my spear right into his belly, and finish him off with my knife. I'm sure I looked fierce carrying my weapons across the beach, and I hoped that I wouldn't meet my fellow man or woman along the way. What a different feeling now to want to hide from my fellow man, rather than the craving for contact that I felt when I was lonely.

As I walked along the beach there seemed to be no sign of the stallion, but I would search for him until I found him. No more living in fear of him, Kings, it's time to take your beach back. I hoped I wouldn't have to use my weapons – he was such a beautiful animal, but if he attacked me again, I would defend myself.

As I reached Pobbles beach, there in front of the rocks was the stallion. Suddenly my courage left me, and I felt a knot in my stomach. I gripped my spear hard again and held my knife in front of me. "Come and get me, stallion," I shouted, waving my spear and thrusting my knife back and forth through the air.

Any time now he will charge me, I thought, as I felt my heart racing. To my surprise, he continued to stand still. Why wasn't he charging? He can see me alright. Closer and closer I got, and still he didn't give chase. I could see now that he was standing in front of the same cave as when I had seen him from the cliff top yesterday morning. What was he doing just standing there?

Well, Kings, as long as he stays there, I don't care. Now keep calm and try not to show any fear. I walked right past him now. Surely he was going to charge. Dare I turn around and have a look at him? No, I'll just keep walking. I wanted to look over my shoulders, for I knew he was watching me. I decided to change direction then and I walked down to the sea. Surely if he was going to charge, he would have done so by now. When I reached the waves I turned and faced him. He continued to just stand there. I waited and watched for what seemed like half an hour. Then all of a sudden, he started to move. He walked first and then began to gallop in the direction

Cave Days

of Oxwich Bay. Wow, I've done it! I'd walked the beach and passed right in front of the stallion, and he hadn't attacked me. Does this mean he's accepted me? Or was he preoccupied guarding the cave?

I wanted to see what was in there, but didn't want to risk him coming back and finding me there. I felt that where he had stood was special territory for him. If it wasn't, then why was he standing on guard there? I'd seen him there a few times now, and I knew, from growing up around the wild horses, that they were territorial, and guarded their territory fiercely. I'd been chased several times as a boy by the stallions, and even by the mares when I got too close to their foals. But this stallion wasn't with any other horses. Was he a loner? Or maybe one of the special lineage bloodlines that the old man had told me about? His words spoke again. "He will either kill you or choose you, boy, and he will be the wildest stallion you have ever seen."

"Well, he is that, Sir! The wildest stallion I have ever seen, and do you think he has chosen me? I walked right by him, and he didn't attack me."

"You will soon know, boy. Just keep seeking him and he will teach you many things."

"Yes Sir, I will."

I decided to walk back to the great Tor, along the whole length of the beach. By the time I reached Three Cliffs Bay, the stallion would probably have reached Oxwich, and would be on his way back to his cave. I'd walk close to the sea in case I wasn't met with such a nice welcome on his way back.

Sure enough, just as I was reaching Three Cliffs Point, on this side of the Killy Willy River, I could see him thundering back in my direction.

My gosh, look at that speed. He can run like the wind. Should I run into the sea until he passes by? If he attacks, it's my only escape. No, I will not be afraid!

My heart raced as the stallion changed his line and galloped right towards me. I froze in fear, but he swerved around me and didn't trample me. Realising I was still standing, I breathed out again and then took some deep breaths. Thank you, God! What an amazing animal. I turned around to see where he would stop, and he stopped right in front of his cave and stayed there, standing guard again.

I felt excited. What a rush. He'd come at me like he was going to trample me, but he didn't, and I dared to believe that as time went on, we would make a special connection with each other. A treaty of friendship, maybe?

Well, that was enough excitement for one day. As I walked back along the Sands, the tide continued its way out, and I was able to walk all the way to the Tor. For a while, I walked up the beach to the tide line, and there I found the stallion's hoof prints, and followed them. The Sand was softer up here, making his prints harder to see, but he had then gone back down to the harder sand that was closer to the waves. From there, his footprints disappeared into the distance towards Oxwich Bay. On the low tides, such as today, when one can walk all the way from Pobbles to Oxwich along the Sands, you come to what is known as the Bell Rock. The Bell Rock is a bell-shaped limestone rock that stands in the middle of the sands between Tor Bay and Little Tor Bay, which is the little beach cove to the eastern side of the great Tor, where my cave is.

When the tide comes in, the Bell Rock is cut off, and becomes a true island surrounded by sea. When I was a boy my mother would only allow my brother and I to play on the island when it was an island in the sand, and the sea was still a long way off. I thought she wanted to get rid of us, especially when my brother and I fought like Normans and Saxons. Nay, a mother loves her sons, even when they fight with swords and bow and arrows. Once my brother Fraser and I disobeyed Mum and climbed onto the island when the waves were reaching its front. "We will get off in time," we shouted down in rebellion.

"She's going to give us the wooden spoon anyway," Fraser said, "so we may as well stay up here and earn our spanking."

"I couldn't agree with you more, Fraser," I said, exasperating my mother below.

We ended up getting cut off by the tide and having to wait six hours before we could get off the island again. By that time we didn't need the wooden spoon from Mum to ensure we wouldn't do it again. Once you were marooned upon the island, you had to be a very strong swimmer if you wanted to swim for it and reach the shore. The currents around the Bell Rock can be very strong.

I thought of Gay as I walked past the Bell, and I could feel her ringing in my heart. One day I hoped to take her for a picnic on the rock, and we could watch the sunset together. Maybe I would write her a poem and read it to her there. That wouldn't be until the spring or summer though. The weather would be too cold for a while yet. It seemed so long since Gay had kissed my face – even though it was only yesterday.

As I walked, I played back in my mind the events of yesterday when I had met Gay in the store, reminding myself that it wasn't a dream, and that on Saturday I was going to see her again. Her beautiful scent and long flowing hair, and her kiss, soft and warm on my face, her lovely eyes of purple and promise. How was I going to wait for Saturday? Well, there was only one thing I had to do before I asked her to come to my humble dwelling, and that was to go and explore the inner chamber of Leathers Hole. I couldn't have her see that I was afraid of the inside of my cave. I remembered my dad's words again when he first discovered it, with my brother and I. "Come on, boys, there's a cavern in here. It's like a little room!"

Well, I'm too tired today, and besides, it will soon be dark, but tomorrow afternoon I will go and explore it, after I've been fishing. I felt excited about fishing again. I hadn't realised how much I'd missed it, since my fear of the stallion had kept me away. Maybe he and I could share his territory, I thought. Thank you God for protecting me today. Tomorrow I'll try fishing again and see what the stallion does.

I climbed up the Burrows to the Tor, and into my cave. Good, my food was still there. The crows and ravens hadn't come inside and eaten my fresh bread. I'd put two of my jackets and a rock over the bag, and it seemed to have worked. I decided to have bread, butter and jam for supper while the bread was still fresh. I smelled the bread through the wrapper and squeezed it – yum, it was still fresh alright.

I'd used all the kindling yesterday, so fires were going to be only on special occasions now, since I couldn't find any solid wood that was dry enough to burn. Somewhere, I'd have to find a few dry pieces for when I had a fire with Gay. Meanwhile, I would have to make do with kindling from Penmaen store. If I bought a bundle every time I got some food, I'd build up a supply.

Cave Days

I ate my bread. It tasted so good with its sweet smell in the fresh sea air. So much for saving some for tomorrow, I thought, as I looked out across the Bay, and wolfed down the last piece of a whole loaf. It had been a satisfying day, and the sky was clear. There would be no rain tonight. Any time there is no rain at this time of year, it's a blessing when you're a caveman.

I went to sleep thinking about my adventures with the stallion. I tried to think of a name for him. The name "Thunder" echoed in my mind, but it sounded incomplete on its own. It would be Thunder something.... I rhymed a few words, but they didn't sound right. Oh well, it will come to me sometime.

In my sleep I dreamed of Gay, and the morning came too quickly for once. I hadn't finished my wonderful dream. As I lay in my sleeping bag, the winds howled from the heights of the Tor, and their cold breath upon my face brought me fully awake. I was glad of these dry, blue-sky days, but the cold reminded me that spring was still a long way off. There was frost on the hills this morning and they sparkled as the sun's light woke them. It was as if the hills were singing a song, a winter song, but I wasn't interested in learning it. I wanted to sing "a summer song," about the warm sun, and days that are light and long!

The tide was low again as I looked down from the top of the Tor. I'd make my way across the Sands and start fishing at Three Cliffs Bay, where the Killy Willy joins the sea.

I set off with my fishing gear in one hand and my spear in the other. I felt confident after my experience with the stallion yesterday. If he wanted to harm me, he would have done it yesterday as I replayed in my mind how he had galloped right towards me and then swerved off to miss me. Just relax, Kings, and if he does come, stand your guard and don't show any fear. That brings a whole new meaning to the saying "easier said than done," doesn't it? Oh well, here goes.

I reached the river at Three Cliffs and walked along its banks to the waves. It was time to start fishing. As I set up my gear, I heard the thunder of hooves behind me. No sooner had I turned around to see, when he was right on me. This time he slowed right down in front of me, and still breathing heavily from his gallop, he lifted his head up and down. Then with his big brown eyes fixed upon me, he pushed me into the sea with his nose.

So much for being brave and standing my guard. Here I was again in the ocean waves and I wasn't going to argue. At least this time he didn't charge me. He just walked right up to me and shoved me. "Okay, Thunder," I said, as I felt the chill of the next wave crashing over my back. He continued to stand there with his nose in my face.

"Okay, Thunder, okay, you win." I sat down in the waves. "Now back off will you, I'm freezing here." As if understanding my words, he lifted his head and turned away. Dare I stand up? No, I'll sit here freezing and submit to the King.

Suddenly he was off again, galloping toward Pobbles and his cave.

As I stepped out of the ocean, my skin was numb with the cold, and it was a long way back to Leathers Hole. I took my soaking wet jacket and shirt off, and then poured the water out of my boots. What now, I thought. I mustn't give up.

As I walked towards Pobbles, I stayed close to the sea in case he came back. As the sun rose higher in the sky, I could feel its warmth on my shoulders. My jeans clung to me like a second skin and steamed as I walked along. After walking for about 15 minutes, I began to warm up. I looked inland towards the rocks, and there I saw what was becoming a familiar sight. The stallion was standing in front of his cave. Should I continue or head back? I didn't feel like fishing any more, but I did want to find out more about the stallion's habits. He didn't chase me yesterday when he was standing outside of the cave. He only gave chase when he was on his gallop across the Sands. I would try and walk past him again while he was standing in front of his cave. The tide was still going out, so I left my fishing gear on the sand. I picked up my spear just in case, and I walked up the beach toward the rocks until I was in line with the stallion.

"I must be mad, or my brain has frozen," I muttered, as I walked on towards him. Would he charge me, or stay there? I was about to find out. "Hello, Thunder," I shouted, trying to be bold. "How are you, old boy? Thanks to you, I'm wet and cold, and I didn't get to go fishing. I'm one pissed-off caveman. But you know what, Thunder? You could make it up to me. If you just stay there like you did yesterday and don't chase me, then all is forgiven, okay? I just want to share the beach with you, that's all. I'm not threatening your territory. I know that you're the King around here. Did you hear that, Thunder? I know that you are the King around here! I just want to be your friend, old boy. I continued to talk to him the whole time I was walking past him, and he didn't give chase. He just stood there on guard.

Shivering now as the clouds cloaked the Sun, I needed to get back to my cave and put on some dry clothes. I decided to walk back in front of the stallion to see what he would do.

And this time if he didn't chase me, I would conclude that it was safe to cross the beach as long as he was standing on guard at his cave.

I walked right by, and again he just stood there. "Thank you, Thunder. I can understand you a bit more now."

Once I was about 100 yards past him, I walked back down toward the surf to get my fishing gear, and I just got back in time. The tide had started to come in and had almost reached my tackle box. Picking it up, I made a beeline toward the great Tor. Because I was cold, I tried to run, but the sand was soft and my legs were tired. How I wished I had wood for a fire when I got back to my cave.

When I finally reached the cave, the steep climb up to the Burrows had helped to warm me up. I wriggled out of my wet clothes and crawled into my sleeping bag. Well, it had been quite an adventure, and I'd learned more about the stallion. I still had to find a way to stop him chasing me when he wasn't standing in front of his cave, but that would be for another day.

I thought about how my life was different here than it had been at Bacon Hole. My life was becoming fuller and more exciting now, and it wasn't just the brighter weather. There were other things too, like finding the message in a bottle, and realising that it was a message meant for me. I felt a hope for the future that I didn't have before.

I also have a beautiful girl in my life, and I get to see her on Saturday, and what's more, I'm going to make friends with a wild stallion. Yes, my life is much less lonely now.

I rested in my sleeping bag for a few hours, and then decided to make a start on exploring the inner chamber of my cave.

With only my small flashlight, I followed the narrow tunnel into the heart of the Tor. The air was still and heavy, like it hadn't stirred in 1000 years. It felt claustrophobic and I wanted to turn and run back to the entrance. "Come on Kings, what would Gay think if she thought you were afraid?" Glancing back at the entrance and shaking my flashlight to make sure it wasn't going to go out, I pressed on until I reached the hole in the wall that led to the inner chamber. I stood there for a while, trying to pluck up the courage to go inside. "Come on boys," I heard my father say again. "It's like a room in here."

Well, it's now or never, here goes. I climbed down through the hole, moving my flashlight back and forth, the shadows fleeing from the light beam on one side, only to crowd in again on the other side. Geeze I hate darkness. I wish I could see in the dark and then I wouldn't be afraid.

It was a cavern in there alright, and surprisingly large compared with the small hole where you climbed in. As I looked around on the dry earth, I realised that this cave had had a few visitors, and they weren't cavemen either. There were old Coke cans and candy wrappers, and even some old clothes, and what was that horrible smell? As if I didn't know. It was urine, that's what it was. Great! The place was a piss pit.

I climbed back out and walked to the entrance of my cave, angry at my fellow man.

"How dare people come into my cave and piss up a storm and leave their rubbish." I yelled out to the seagull perched on a rock. "I won't have it, I tell you Mr. Seagull! If I catch anyone pissing in my cave, I'll shoot an arrow up their arse. That's fair, don't you think, Mr. Gull?"

"They did find the cave before you did though, didn't they? Or at least they peed in it and claimed it as their territory before you did."

"That's true, my feathered friend, but *I* wouldn't pee in there. I have some class, you know! Anyway, I'm going to guard this cave from now on and make it my own. Did you hear that, Mr. Gull? It's my cave from now on."

"I heard you," he said, taking to the air.

"Bye, Mr. Gull, see you on the high tide."

"Yeah, see you, Caveman, and in my book, the last person to pee in there owns the place. It's a territorial thing, you know. Spray on it, and you own it."

"Yeah, maybe in the animal kingdom, my feathered friend, but not in the human one. What're you doing around here anyway, Gull? You're a long way from Spain."

"I am, but I'm flying home, and I'll soon be in the warm sun!"

Yes, dear reader, I talk to animals, and if you lived in a cave, you might too!

I spent the rest of the afternoon cleaning out the cavern. I picked up two full bags of rubbish. At least I wasn't afraid of going inside any more. But what was I going to do about the smell? I remembered there had been a children's pail washed up on the beach this morning. If it was still there, I could bring up some salt water and throw it over the smell.

The pail was still there, but it had a hole in it. "There's a hole in my bucket, dear Liza, dear Liza; there's a hole in my bucket, dear Liza, today." Good old song, but I'll have that tune stuck in my head for the rest of the day now.

Cave Days

I sang my song and looked around for something to plug the hole with. It's amazing how handy a piece of bubblegum would be when you're walking along the beach with a hole in your bucket. I sang and sang but nothing....

Finally I found part of an old wine cork. It was still red with the stain of the wine, and it even had a faint aroma left on it. The wine might have been drunk to celebrate something very special. The cork was too big for the little hole in my bucket, so I bit it down to size. Mmm, I don't recommend the taste of cork. Not even in the stir fry – very dry, you know. Finally I made it fit, and I walked down to the sea to fill my bucket.

I'd done quite well; there was only a small leak. Holding my thumb tight against the cork, I could stop the water. I wouldn't be able to hold it and climb at the same time, though, would I?

"No, you wouldn't," squawked a circling gull.

"Well, do you have a better idea?" I shouted back.

There were often pieces of tar amongst the pebbles on the top of the beach, and there were some today. So I blocked the hole with tar by pushing a piece down over the hole from the inside of the bucket, and it held the water well.

So I sang a new version of my song: "There's no hole in my bucket, dear Liza, dear Liza." Yeah, I know, life can get boring on the beach, believe me, but I was happy, happy as a cork in a champagne bottle.

I made three trips back and forth from the sea to my cave, and finally the cavern smelled of salt and sea, not pee. As I looked around, I could see that it would make a good dwelling place, though much smaller an area than Bacon Hole. There was a nice smooth area on the ground, just big enough for me to put my air mattress down. At the back of the cavern there was a large rock in the shape of a seat. "I even have a throne." I exclaimed to myself.

There was one thing it didn't have, though, enough ventilation for a fire. A wood fire would be far too smoky. But maybe I could use some blocks of coal and fire blocks to make a small fire. I'd have to experiment with that.

It was getting late in the day now, and it was Friday. Tomorrow was Saturday, and I'd be seeing Gay. I started to get excited. But wait, look at me, I don't have any clean clothes, and I need a bath. There was only one place to go, I'd go and visit Fraser, and take my best clothes with me to wash. I bagged them up and headed off to my father's house.

Chapter Nine

A Forever Kiss

It was dark as I arrived at the house, and I stood watching from the field for a few minutes. A part of me felt guilty for not having gone with Grandma and Grandpa to live, as my father had asked, but if Dad was home, I knew that he'd be glad to see me.

I noticed a light on in Fraser's bedroom, so I climbed over the hedge and threw some small stones at the window. His face soon appeared and I shouted, "Fraser!"

"Kings!" he called back, opening the window. "I'll come and open the door and let you in."

"Where's dad?" I asked nervously.

"He's out, Kings. It's great to see you. I was wondering if you had forgotten your promise to come and see me."

"No, I hadn't forgotten, Fraser. I'm sorry it's been so long. It's really good to see you too."

"Do you think I can do a wash of my clothes?"

"No worries, Kings, you can put your clothes in the wash, and then we'll hang out."

For a few minutes I felt uncomfortable. I worried that Fraser might think I was only here to do my wash, but I wasn't. I missed him and I wanted to see him. We soon got talking and caught up with all the news. It turned out that Dad was away for the weekend, and that Grandma and Grandpa were back home in Devonshire.

"How's Dad?" I asked.

"Oh, he's just the same, Kings. He seems to live in his own world and not show his feelings most of the time. If you know what I mean?"

"Yes, I know what you mean."

"Although he did cry, Kings, the morning you up and left without them knowing you were going."

Now I felt guilty as I pictured Dad's face. "How were Grandma and Grandpa?" I asked.

"Grandma was upset and crying, and Grandpa was angry. He almost called the police, but Dad told him not to. He said you would come back when you were ready. So how are you doing, Kings? How are things in the wild?"

"Well, I've changed caves, Fraser, and I don't know if you remember a girl named Gay Tripp? Well, I'm going to meet her tomorrow in Penmaen. I met her last weekend, and we're going to spend some time together."

"She's that beautiful girl you used to go to school with at Dumbarton House School, isn't she?"

"Yes, that's right, and she is absolutely stunning now."

"Wow, Kings, you're living the life you want in the wild, *and* you're spending time with Gay Tripp. I'm envious."

"And that's not all, Fraser. I found a 'wild stallion', and he's as wild and crazy as you can imagine. He chased me into the sea, and a few times I thought he was going to kill me, but for some reason he didn't. He slammed down his hooves, missing my head by inches. *And* you are not going to believe this, but I found a message in a bottle – in the ocean – and there was a message in it.

"Wow, you do live an exciting life. I wish mine was," Fraser said, sounding a bit discouraged.

Fraser and I talked well into the night, and he asked if I wanted to stay. "We can raid the fridge, Kings. Dad's just done a big grocery shop. Keep talking, bro, I'm loving this."

"Food, glorious food. A full fridge – that is music to my ears." I replied.

"...and besides," Fraser continued, "you still have to dry your clothes."

Since Dad was away, I agreed. It would have been too hard if he'd been home. "Okay, Fraser, I'll stay until the morning. A full stomach and a hot bath would fit the bill perfectly. I'll have to get up early in the morning, though, as I have to get to Penmaen by 10 o'clock."

"I'll give you a ride there on my motorbike if you like."

"That would be fantastic. That settles it, I'm staying. Thanks so much, Fraser," and off we went to raid the fridge. Dad had sure gone shopping alright. There were sausages, bacon and eggs, and a fresh loaf of bread, and strawberry jam.

"We'll eat well tonight, bro," I said, and we did! The smell of bacon filled the house and we ate until we hurt.

"Well, the morning comes early, Kings, and it's already 1:30 a.m.," said Fraser. "I'm off to bed. Let's leave the house about eight in the morning. That will give you plenty of time to get to Penmaen."

"That will be great. I really appreciate it," I said. Before I retired for the night, I packed my clean clothes and ran myself a bath. I would be looking and smelling good for Gay.

Oh, this is great, I thought to myself, as I lay soaking in the bubbles. I would have to make a habit of visiting more often.

Morning came quickly alright, and after wolfing down a bowl of cereal, I was soon sitting on the back of Fraser's motorcycle heading towards Penmaen.

"Do you want me to drop you off right at the stables where you're meeting Gay?" he asked.

"No, I have to drop my bag of clothes off at the cave first. So just drop me off at the Burrows overlooking Three Cliffs Bay and I can walk down from there."

After I dropped my clothes off at the cave, I headed to the village to meet Gay. "Kings, you're looking good," I said to myself, feeling excited and nervous at the same time, and wondering what it would be like to see her again. Would it be as good as I dreamed it would be?

As I made my way to the stables, I passed the general store and there were fresh cut flowers outside. So I walked back and picked out a bunch for Gay. All that was missing now was a poem, but I'd save that for another day.

As I walked along, I decided I'd read her a poem sometime when there was a sunset, if things worked out between us. I even thought of a name for the poem, 'Behind the Sunset'.

My heart began to beat faster as I reached the riding field.

"Hello Kingsley," Gay shouted, as she rode over to meet me. "I'm so glad you came, and this is Blaze, my horse."

"Hello Blaze," I said, patting the side of his neck. Gay looked beautiful in her riding gear, her long hair up in a bun, with a few curls peeking out behind her riding hat, and her violet eyes bright and sparkling. Her smile was making me melt.

She was obviously excited to see me, and what could I do but smile back and bask in her radiance. Her lips were red with lipstick, contrasting with her creamy white skin, and a blush that made me blush was written on her soft cheeks. Above the smell of horses and fields was the faint scent of lavender. Oh, I felt weak in the legs, and words would not come out of my mouth. I just stared and smiled some more, and just when I thought she couldn't look any more beautiful, she wore this look of wonder, as to why I would look at her that way. And we both tried to say something at the same time and muddled our words, and we both laughed loudly, and Blaze neighed. This must be a new experience for him to.

"It's great to see you, Gay," I said finally, and handed her the flowers.

"Kingsley, they are beautiful!" she exclaimed, and she lifted them up to smell them. Then she climbed down from her horse and kissed me, and she whispered, "I'm so glad you're here. I've been looking forward to seeing you all week."

And I've been looking forward to seeing you before I was born! No I didn't say that. That would be a bit forward, wouldn't it? But that's how I felt. I'd save it for the poem. Maybe I'd title the poem 'Before I Was Born' instead of 'Before The Sunset'. I think they would kind of say the same thing.

I answered Gay back. "I've been looking forward to seeing you all week too." I was trembling and glowing in her presence.

"Can you hold the flowers until I'm finished riding?" she asked. "And how did you know that Irises are my favourite flower?"

"Some things you just know," I exclaimed excitedly.

A Forever Kiss

Gay's smile filled her riding hat, and her blush shone like the sun crossing the sky. "I'll be about half an hour finishing my ride, Kingsley. You can wait for me and watch from the bench over there if you like."

On the bench was a picnic basket. Is this for us I wondered? Are we going for a picnic up on Cefn Bryn? If we are, what a perfect day for it. There wasn't a cloud in the sky, and I could feel the sun warm on my shoulders.

As I watched Gay riding, she looked so graceful. On the far side of the field were some jumps, and she and Blaze made them look easy, as they travelled through the air as light and graceful as a butterfly. Standing up on the bench now, I clapped my hands and shouted, "Well done, Gay."

She cantered back with the biggest smile. "Thanks Kingsley, I'm practising for a show that Blaze and I are competing in up in England next weekend."

"You're going to do well, I know it!"

"Thanks, Kingsley, for your encouragement. I've packed us a picnic, by the way. I thought we could go up on Cefn Bryn."

"It's the perfect day for it Gay," I said excitedly.

Gay went back to the top of the field to continue her practice. So the picnic box was for us…

Gay trotted Blaze back across the field and dismounted, and we walked to the stables together. "Would you like to lead him?" she said, handing me the rope. I took the rope and handed her back the flowers, and as I led Blaze to the stables, I dreamt of leading my stallion across the beach with Gay riding on his back. I can dream, can't I?

"So tell me Kingsley," she said softly. "Why did you choose Irises?"

Cave Days

"They remind me of your eyes, with their beautiful violet colour, and the blue of the sky." I said.

"You only saw my eyes for the first time last week, apart from years ago when we were at school," she said.

"How could I forget?" I replied, and our eyes met and danced with each other.

Yours are green, Kingsley," she said, as tears filled hers. She reached out and took my hand, and then kissed me again. This time gently on my lips, and I would keep this kiss safely with her other's in the jewel box of my heart.

I kissed her back, feeling our tongues meet, and I trembled and glowed in our embrace. I lost thought of everything else, and dropping the rope from Blaze, I held Gay's face in my hands and kissed her again. I kissed as I had never kissed before. All other kisses had been dreams, and it felt like all my dreams had been of this day and this kiss! It was as if I was putting all the years of my life into this one, long, tender kiss. It *was* literally all the years of my life, for I had never kissed a girl before, and we lost time and place, in a kiss that will last a lifetime. Sweet and innocent was our bliss, in this 'forever kiss'.

Suddenly we both smelled horse, and Blaze's wet nose was pressed against my cheek. I opened my eyes to hear Gay's laughter. "I think Blaze watched the whole thing. I'm sure he did." I said, rubbing his head. "You saw the whole thing, didn't you boy."

When we got to the stable, Gay watered and fed Blaze. "Here, Kingsley," she said, handing me a brush. "He loves it when you brush him." I continued to brush Blaze, as Gay checked his shoes. Then Gay took off her riding boots and hung up her hat and jacket.

A Forever Kiss

We headed up the hill to Cefn Bryn with our picnic. As we walked, the sun warmed us while birds sang around us. We crossed a little stream that only runs during the winter months and sometimes in early spring. I jumped to a rock in the middle, and Gay took my hand, and we danced on the rock to the sound of the stream, and then jumped to the other side. Oh, to feel her hand in mine, and her long hair danced in the wind, and here and there our eyes met, and it was only each other we saw. With her gentle touch and sweet scent, I am a King, you see.

We climbed to the top of the hill and looked back across the emerald sea. Wait, what is that? There is something more beautiful to see. I can feel her eyes waiting for me. I look up, and our eyes meet; there is so much to see, where I see you, and you see me, two souls together, innocent and free! For a while, we just held each other, in the gentle wind that is in conversation with the sea. Up here on top of Cefn Bryn, the birds sing of Gay and me. I am a rich man, Mr. Kestrel, you see! From our embrace that could have lasted forever, and said what words could not speak, we walked on to King Arthur's stone. There at 'Kingsley's Stone', as I renamed it this day, we opened our picnic basket and spread our blanket.

"Now you sit down, my Prince, and I'll serve us our picnic," she said. She pulled out a bottle of apple cider and two glasses, and sandwiches already made. There were even Irish linen serviettes and a home-made trifle, oh, and a bar of Cadbury's chocolate. She had taken such time and effort to make this beautiful picnic. "Thank you, Gay, this is wonderful, my Princess, and we have the most beautiful day."

"It is the spring in the middle of winter, Kingsley," she exclaimed.

"Yes it is," I echoed. "Today the spring has come just for us, up here on Cefn Bryn."

I held Gay's face in my hands again. I smelt her hair, and our hands caressed, and I kissed her gently on her cheek. She slowly turned her head to meet my kiss, and again we kissed with all the years of our lives, innocent passion and love. Surely this is how life begins, with the kiss of life. Our kiss was witnessed, only by a secret past of knights and battles, loves that were won and lost. Here on this lonely hill, I, Kingsley, have won the love of Princess Gay.

'Are you there, old man? Can you see me? I am a Prince and a Knight, and I've won a Princess!'

'Yes boy, I can see you, and I'm proud of you. There's one more thing that I want you to know. You have found the special stallion, or to be more precise, he's found you. He has chosen you, Kingsley. You must tame him, and he will be yours.'

'Yes Sir!'

'You don't have to call me 'Sir' any more, Kingsley. You're a knight now, and you must never forget it.'

Gay and I sat upon Cefn Bryn until the warmth of the sun left, leaving the gentle breeze and the cool air to draw us closer. I would have to hunt a sheep, and make Gay a warm wool blanket, I thought, wrapping my arms around her and giving her my jacket to keep warm. Holding her in my embrace kept me warm and excited. To feel my arms around her and to smell her long flowing hair was intoxicating, and my breathing changed as she reclined back to my chest and rested her perfumed head against my cheek. Her long hair was as a blanket upon my face keeping me warm, and her scent was as the promise of the springtime before us.

A Forever Kiss

We shared our hearts, telling of our hopes and dreams, even our fears we trusted to each other. We ended our day by climbing on top of Kingsley's Stone, and as a true king and queen, we beheld our Kingdom before us. There was little light left, and no moon as we walked, yet danced inside, down the Bryn. When we reached the stables, Gay's mother arrived to pick her up.

"I'll be right there, Mum," she shouted, before turning to me again.

She kissed me again, before I could say goodbye, and then said, "Kingsley, I will be away next weekend at the horse show in England, and my parents want to stay up there and make a holiday of it for another week. So I will meet you here in two weeks."

"The same time, 10 o'clock," I said.

"Yes, same time," she echoed back. I'll see you in two Saturdays, Kingsley."

"I'll make the picnic next time, Gay, and I'll show you my cave and the stallion."

"I'll miss you," she said, and with another kiss she was on her way.

The general store was still open in the village, so I bought a bundle of kindling and a bottle of pop to celebrate. Wow, what a day. I wish it could have gone on forever.

I danced my way along the Burrows and back to my cave. Two weeks. Two whole weeks! How was I going to pass the time? I would concentrate on learning more about the stallion... and one day, tame him, and make him mine.

In the meantime, I will get my cave ready for my Princess. I have two weeks to get it ready, plenty of time.

Swigging my pop, I smiled and said to myself again, "What a day, Kings! You're a happy man."

Chapter Ten

The Thunder Child

I woke to find another blue sky day and enjoyed a bowl of cereal on top of the Tor. My mind flashed back to yesterday as I thought about Gay. I replayed our time together in my mind and heart, and wondered again how I was going to manage being away from her for two long weeks…. At least I had nice weather, that would help a lot with the things I'd be able to do. I would resume my observations of the stallion today.

As I climbed down from the Burrows to the sands, I carried my spear and knife, just in case. When the stallion stood guard outside his cave, he didn't give chase; it was only when he went on his gallops from Pobbles to Oxwich and back, and I was on the beach at the same time, that he chased me.

I had no idea where he was today. I looked across the Sands to Oxwich, and then towards Pobbles. There was no sign of him. Was he standing outside his cave again? It was about this time of day when he'd been standing there last time. I would soon find out, walking close to the sea in case he was still on his gallop. I reached three cliffs point and there in the distance was the haunting figure of the stallion. He was standing at his post.

The Thunder Child

I began to relax now, knowing he wasn't thundering across the sands behind me, and I made my way up the beach so I could walk right past him. I wanted to show him that I wasn't afraid, and at the same time respect him. I knew he could trample me into the sand any time if he wanted to. I wanted to look for driftwood high up on the pebbles at Pobbles Cove. The warmer weather would have started to dry out some of the small pieces and I wanted to bring some back to my cave so I could have a fire when I invited Gay to visit.

As I walked past the stallion, he remained still, just as he had the other day. He really was becoming accepting of me, and I called out: "It's good to see you, old boy; thanks for being my friend." When I reached the pebbles at Pobbles, there was quite a lot of driftwood that had been brought in on the high tides and strong winds of the winter season. The large pieces were still very wet, but I found several smaller ones that had started to dry out. I placed them on some rocks facing the sun and planned to pick them up on my way back.

I'd only eaten an hour or so ago, but the walk had made me hungry again. So I decided to walk the West Cliff path to Pennard stores. "Who cares if Mr. Skittle is there." I said to myself. "It won't bother me now. What can he do anyway?" As I walked the cliff tops, there were signs of spring. Daffodils—only a few bunches in flower here and there—but oh, they were so beautiful to me. Shining like little yellow Suns. Oh, and look at the Primroses. How lovely they are, making promises of warm spring days when the sunshine smiles and spring songs fill the air with happy music and lovely fragrance, as life begins again. I saw Crocuses too, with heads of purple and white, and some of the Gorse bushes were partly in flower on their southern sides, as they said good morning to the climbing sun. Their dainty little yellow petals shone like bouquets to be given to the princess fairies who were on their way to the spring ball. And the birds sang such a sweet song, and I sang with them, and I named our song "The Day Between Winter and Spring."

It was a day that could give hope to any barren soul. There were little buds on the hedgerows, just waiting to burst into chorus. The new shoots of the wild fern had pushed their way through Winter's blanket, having dreamed too much in their sleep, and now their shining heads are turning to the Sun. My soul, too, is bursting into life. I have a heart full of love, for a girl named Gay. I am sure that this day is named after her: "Gay, Gay, Gay", and I'm making a friend who is a stallion.

I reached Pennard stores and bought my old favorite: two Cornish pasties and a bottle of beer. "The beer is for your father, isn't it?" the lady asked. "Yes it is," I said, nervously looking around in case Mr. Skittle was there. If he saw me buying beer, he'd soon cut that out.

"Could I have my pasties warmed up, please, and I'll take a newspaper while I'm at it. And how is Mr. Skittle? Well, I hope."

"Oh, he's just in the back if you would like a word with him."

"Oh gosh no. Please don't disturb him, just wondered how he was doing, that's all."

"Here's your pasties and a newspaper, and I'll mention to Mr. Skittle that you asked after him, and who are you?"

"John Smith," I said loudly, and I got the heck out of there.

The Thunder Child

Kings, you idiot, that was a close call. What if old man Skittle had come out? Oh well, he didn't, so no harm done. John Smith— he will have to think about that for a while.

I walked back along West Cliff and ate my lunch overlooking the stallion. Suddenly he was up and gone, galloping towards Oxwich. As I finished my lunch, I opened the newspaper, which said Sunday, February 5th. In its pages the world seemed the same to me as when I'd left it, a lifetime ago. In four months, I had learned that my life was out here now, wild and free. Not in the confused, confined life I'd left behind in society.

One day I would have to return there and take my place in the community, wherever that might be, but not until the end of my journey here. I would return with the wisdom and understanding that I could only have learned from my experiences out here.

Yes, I was beginning to understand my life here on the cliffs. God is stilling my soul, and giving me peace, I thought, instead of restlessness. No more am I afraid of the silence, as I listen to its stories. No longer does the stillness shout too loud, making me afraid. It is healing to me now, and I can hear a silent inner voice, speaking to my heart.

After finishing lunch, I headed back to Pobbles Cove to pick up my driftwood. The smaller pieces I collected had dried out a little more in the warm afternoon sun. I could still see the steam coming off the larger pieces, and I wondered how long the sunshine would last. In the newspaper, the forecast said sunshine for the next four days. A rare and brave report from the weatherman, I thought, for February on the Gower Peninsula. Growing up in grey Wales, the weatherman had one of the worst jobs, I thought, nearly always being wrong when we wanted sunshine. Did he hide in a bunker somewhere, until the sun stayed out for weeks and people smiled? Or was he happy and warm in a cosy cottage, with a wood fire when the skies were grey? If I saw him, I would smile at him for four sunny days. It was important to make the most of the sunshine. I didn't want to go back to "November Grey!"

Fear had said it would last forever and a day. He was wrong about that. I put my driftwood into my backpack and headed back to the Tor. It was time to experiment with making a fire. When Gay got back, I wanted to share with her a blazing fire that we could sit in front of and enjoy the warmth, but I didn't want to smoke us out of the cave. Yes, I'd make a fire tonight and see how it went.

I had made a small fireplace out of stones that I had carried up from the beach. It looked quite sharp actually; a well-shaped circle of light grey limestone rocks. It was the highlight of my living room, I'll have you know, dear reader, along with unusual pieces of driftwood that travelled far and wide to grace the inner chamber of my cave.

During the night hours, while I lie, comfortable, on my rabbit fur blanket, they tell stories of their journeys across the sea. One was once a bench where people sat and had picnics. He told me how he missed hearing their conversations. One piece was once an old man's walking stick and it even had a sculptured bone handle. When the old man died, his wife didn't want the stick because it reminded her of him too much, so she threw it out into the sea at their favourite beach, and that's how it made its way to me. "Made in Ireland," it says on the bone handle.

"You crossed the Irish Sea," I said to it, holding it up in my hand.

"Will you walk with me?" he asked me. "It's been such a long time since anyone took me for a walk."

"Yes, I'll walk with you," I answered back, "especially as you came all the way across the Irish Sea to get to me. We all come from somewhere," I said, "and we all have a story to tell. You're welcome to stay with me, old stick, until one day I'll send you on another journey far across the sea."

The air in the inner chamber of Leathers Hole is still and stale, as if in its heavy presence, it can hold onto time itself. Just like the driftwood that can speak so loud, the silence in the air tells stories of the past. Surely I am a time traveller on my blanket of fur in Leathers Hole. For what is the past if you can't hear it, and feel it, and recognize it in your soul?

When the gentle winds of memory stir, to not feel, to not know when the winds blow is surely to be dead.

It was time to try and light a fire. I lit a large candle for light, saving my flashlight for necessities. The flame burned still and straight, without even a flicker. There were no air currents in here, or even spirits to make the flame dance. I was glad of that. Using the light of the candle, I emptied my driftwood into the fireplace, and I began to organise it, piece by piece. I would have to keep the fire small as there was no airflow that I could feel coming from the main entrance. And the candle's flame remained still, apart from when I brushed past it like a time traveller going back into the past. Rolling up small pieces of paper, I placed them between the wood, which I had placed pointing upwards, as fire loves to climb. I hoped the paper would give off enough energy to at least get the kindling started; and hopefully the driftwood would be dry enough to burn, and not smoke too much.

Cave Days

Well, here goes, I thought, striking a match and lighting the paper in three places. If I can get an even flame all around, then the driftwood will stand a much better chance of burning. The kindling caught quickly, and the flames were soon licking at the driftwood. But the smoke was thick and heavy, and there was nowhere that it wanted to go, so it hung there over the fire, like a floating grey ghost. As the smoke reached the roof, it came billowing back down again, choking out the little air that was left. My eyes began to burn, and then my chest. Holding my breath, I climbed out to the main entrance tunnel, and then on outside the cave. I took some deep breaths to clear my lungs. My eyes soon stopped stinging, but they ran with tears for several minutes after.

Well, that wasn't going to work. If I had stayed in there for just a few more minutes, I'd have been in real trouble. I should have used my common sense, which told me all along that there wasn't enough ventilation to have a fire in the inner chamber of the cave. I'd have to make my fires only outside the entrance. There is a beautiful view from there, looking out across the ocean and up to the stars. Watching the night sky would be romantic, and certainly better than staring at smoky grey walls and coughing.

Wrapping a scarf over my face I went back into the cave to get my sleeping bag and pillow, which stunk of smoke. Yes, I'd sleep here tonight, at the entrance, and maybe by the morning the smoke would have cleared enough for me to go and get my breakfast food.

Over the next few weeks, my adventures with the stallion continued. He chased me into the sea three more times, but I had provoked him by walking on the beach when he was on what I now call his morning territorial gallops. He never once chased me when he was standing in front of his cave, though. Whenever he finished his return gallop from Oxwich to Pobbles, and then stood on guard outside the cave, that was my cue to start my walk, or go fishing. We had come to an understanding. I respected him as King of the Sands, and he respected me as his fellow creature. I mean we are both wild and untameable.

I had started to follow the stallion in the afternoons now, observing him from the cliff tops until it grew too dark to see. I was learning a lot about him and the other horses. Every afternoon at about 3 o'clock, he left his post at the cave and started walking up the three cliffs Valley towards Pennard Castle. There is good grazing grass there in the Valley, below the castle, and there is a herd of horses that live in and around the area. They're known as 'the Three Cliffs Herd' and this herd has been in the Valley since I was a boy. They like feeding on the lush grass and the marshland along the banks of the Pennard Pill, known to me as the Killy Willy. "They have been there for hundreds of years, boy, since Arthur was a boy."

"Yes, Sir."

They usually stayed in the Valley with their foals, from the time they were born in late April and May, to late September or early October when the weather turned cold. Then the herd moved around to different parts of the Gower Peninsula, seeking new grazing areas and shelter from the strong winds and driving rain that came in from the Bristol Channel.

Over the last few days, I had counted nine horses in the Valley. Five of them were mature mares and a few of them looked like they were carrying foals. Another three looked like young mares, probably born in the late spring of the past year.

The ninth horse didn't seem to be around today. He looked to be a young stallion and was probably nearby somewhere. Even the stallions usually stayed close to the main herd, although they often grazed a distance away, so as to have early warning of any danger that might threaten the herd. I had fond memories of watching the foals being born when I was a boy. I had a friend called Debbie James, who was close to my age, and on the weekends we would go and find the horses, and try and get close enough to them to check out their tummies and see which ones were pregnant.

It was great fun roaming around trying to find the different herds, and the greatest reward for our long walks was to see the mares giving birth. We would take turns naming the newborn foals, as we watched them come into the world, full of wonder and surprise. We also had another reason for going to see the horses. We would pretend that they were our own children, and thus their names became beloved to us as we watched the foals grow.

I had also seen two stallions in my adventures watching the Three Cliffs Herd. One was only young, born last spring, but the other was a mature stallion, probably the leader of the herd. It was in my observations of his interaction with my stallion that I learned a lot about life in this herd. Their behaviour taught me things that related to my own life.

Each afternoon I watched my stallion make his journey up to the Valley, and as soon as he reached the grazing area beneath Pennard Castle, he was chased away by the other horses. Two or three of the herd would chase him about half way back down the Valley, and then the mature stallion, who I had named Rain Cloud because of his light grey coat with dark grey spots, would continue to chase my stallion all the way back to the beach, and sometimes a mile or so across the Sands.

I could hear my stallion snorting and grunting, and a few times he turned and fought, but each time he was driven back. He made this screaming and crying noise as he retreated, and that's when I knew what the second part of his name was. "Child", because he cried like a child. Why did he not stand his ground and fight back harder, he was just as big as Rain Cloud?! He reminded me of myself, trying to fit in and be accepted by the crowd. Each day he would try again, but he was always turned away. Didn't he believe in himself anymore? Did he not have the courage to take them on? Was he losing hope? I knew how that felt.

One afternoon he walked only as far as the head of the Valley. He stood there for a while as if contemplating, then he lowered his head and turned away. "No, no," I shouted out from the top of the cliff. "You mustn't give up. You can beat him, I know it!" I cried. "You just have to believe that you can."

For a moment, he stopped and lifted his head, as if having heard my words, but then he lowered his head again to the ground and walked slowly back to his cave. I wept, feeling his sadness. He'd had enough, and I felt pain in my heart as I watched the whip of rejection slowly break the spirit of the King. I felt God was showing me, through the stallion, a reflection of my life; what it had been, and in some ways still was. That was why I'd come to the cliffs to live, because I didn't fit in, and wasn't accepted by the crowd.

Chapter Eleven

King of Gower!

There were only two days to wait now, and Gay would be back from the trip to England. I wondered how she'd done in the horse show. I knew she had been practising her jumps in preparation for the trials for six months. Maybe she had won one of the competitions?

It was time to get my cavern ready. After her riding practice on Saturday, I was planning to invite her for a picnic up on the Tor and show her around my territory, shared, of course, with my stallion. It will be an adventure alright, as I'm sure that Thunder Child will come and introduce himself to her. I had already collected a sufficient amount of driftwood over the last week or so, and on my trips to buy food at Penmaen store, I had brought back four bundles of kindling—enough for Gay and I to enjoy some nice fires outside my cave. I envisioned us sitting at a slow burning fire and watching the sunset together.

That reminds me: I want to write her a poem and read it to her on Saturday night. Wow, only two more nights and she'll be here. I can't wait. Now, what's left to get ready? More candles for the cavern. Especially as I can't even have a small fire in there without getting smoked out. Oh well, I'll make do. As long as I have enough candles for light, and some more blankets to put over the air mattress and the dusty ground around it. There is no smell of pee in there now, not since I washed it away with the sea water. Yes, I'll soon have it fit for a lady— well, certainly for a country lass anyway. I know, I'll burn some scented candles. That will make the whole cave smell lovely, and really impress her.

Suddenly it dawned on me what I should do. I'll go and visit Fraser again at the house. It's been almost two weeks since I've seen him. I can pick up some blankets and wash my clothes. I want to look my best for Gay. Yes, I can have a bath and wash my hair, and there's also some camping equipment in Dad's shed. I'll bring back the lantern and the cooking stove, that way I can cook Gay something nice on the stove, rather than over the fire.

So that was my plan. I'd head over to the house tonight. It would be a win-win situation, and I'd also have the luxury of a night's sleep in my old bed. Yes, my plan was perfect. I would have time to do my wash, bring back the camping gear, and organise my cave the next day. Maybe Fraser would give me a ride back to Penmaen on his motorcycle, like he did last time.

Before I bagged my clothes and headed off to the house, I inspected my cavern with a flashlight. I felt proud that I'd slept in the darkness for almost two weeks now, apart from last night when it was still too smoky from my fire. At least I could show Gay that I wasn't afraid of the dark—which was a far cry from how I'd been at Bacon Hole. Suddenly my flashlight shone on my rabbit pelts, and I had a great idea for how I could further impress Gay. So far I had placed them together on the ground next to my air mattress and called them a blanket. Comfy and warm as they were to lie on, they weren't a real blanket yet. I'd make a real blanket out of them hopefully tomorrow.

I picked them up and took them to the light of the entrance, and I counted 48 pelts. Wow, that was a lot of rabbits. Would that be enough to make a blanket, or a robe? I shaped them together on the ground, and the evening sun made the fur glisten like the orange sky above. There were almost enough pelts; I needed another two or three, and that would be enough to make a great blanket.

Then I thought again. No, I said to myself, each pelt represents a rabbit that I've hunted and used as part of my ability to eat and keep warm and survive out here in the wild. And not just survive, but flourish. So it should be a robe that I make, not merely a blanket hidden away in the dark and obscurity of my cave. I envisioned myself standing on top of the Tor with my glistening robe draped over my shoulders as if I were a King!

Never mind the caveman of Bacon Hole—a title I had worn with courage and pride. Well, okay…with a lot of fear too, but not anymore. I will wear my robe as the King of the Great Tor, and each morning I'll look out over my territory from its heights. I'd sure moved up in title and status since leaving Bacon Hole.

My excitement waned a little as I watched some dark clouds moving in from the Channel, and I could see rain in the sky over Oxwich Point. It was coming this way. Oh well, I couldn't complain. I'd had 11 days of dry weather and most of it was sunshine. I had to remind myself that it wasn't spring yet—but each day we got closer. Before leaving for the house, I set up four rabbit snares. It was time I tried out my new area, and by the amount of rabbit holes and runs, there promised to be a plentiful supply.

As I walked along the fields to the house, I thought about my brother. It was sure going to be good to see him. Although I was coming with my own agenda, I knew he would be pleased to see me. Stopping in Pennard stores to buy candles, I also asked if they had a needle and thread. "We just have these small sewing kits," the lady said. "What are you sewing? I thought you boys only played football and rugby, and left all the mending and sewing to us girls, or did your mother send you to buy a sewing kit?"

"I...yeah, my mother sent me," I replied, not wanting her to think that I was a sissy, buying a needle and thread. "My mother needs to sew two fur blankets together, so she needs a large needle and strong thread!"

"Well then, these small kits will be no good," she replied. "Let me go and look in the back and see what I can find." Well, hurry up, I thought to myself. I didn't want to be in the store too long in case old man Skittle showed up.

She came back with two large glover needles and a roll of thick cotton twine. "These might do," she said. "The eyes on the needles are nice and big, and this cotton is very thick; it's more like twine, only very flexible! It should be strong enough to sew a fur blanket."

"Thank you so much," I said, "I'm sure these will do the trick." My excitement probably gave my secret away, that the needle and thread were actually for me, but the lady didn't say anything more in regards to the sewing. She only asked if there was anything else that she could help me with. "Oh yes, I'll have two Cornish pasties and a bottle of beer," I said.

"For your father," she added, finishing my sentence.
"Aye that's right," I said.

"Be careful," she called out as I left the store. "Don't let the village policeman see you drinking that."

I wanted to call back "I won't," but I just kept walking and shouted back, "Thank you very much."

I sat at the bus stop and ate my pasties, and I swigged down a gulp of beer after each passing car. Well, I'd soon be at the house….

When I was close, I stopped in the back field for a while and observed. All was quiet, so I climbed over into the garden and rang the doorbell. Feeling a bit nervous, I hoped it was Fraser who answered the door, and it was.

"Kings!" he said excitedly, "It's great to see you. You just missed Dad. How are you doing? We were just talking about you. Dad was wondering how you were doing with your knives and bow and arrows. I wouldn't worry, Kings, if he comes back. Dad's cool with you living in the wild now. Grandma and Grandpa phone every few days to see if you're back, and Dad just says you'll be back when you're ready to come back."

"That's great, Fraser. It means a lot to me to know he understands. Would you mind if I wash my clothes again and have a bath?"

"No, that's fine, make yourself at home, it's just great to see you, Kings. So what's been happening … how's life in the wild?"

"I'm doing really well, Fraser, you should see my new cave. I'm living in the inner chamber of Leathers Hole. I've got my very own room in the heart of the Tor."

"Shit, Kings, isn't that haunted in there too?"

King of Gower!

"No, it's really peaceful actually. It's not like Bacon Hole, with all the moving shadows and noises. Unless it's just me who's changed? And I *have* changed."

"I did notice there is something different about you now, Kings. You have this confidence… and peace about you"

"You're right, Fraser, I feel it. There is a presence around me, and I'm not afraid anymore, and it's not just positive thinking or self talk. Now that I'm living in my cave and don't have all the distractions I used to have, I have time to think and feel in a way I never could before, and I can actually sense that I'm not alone any more. Do you remember when Grandma and Grandpa would take us to their chapel, and we would hear those hell and brimstone sermons from the preacher?"

"Yeah, I remember Kings. We would come out of chapel feeling like a second hand dartboard and that we were all going to hell because of the life we were living."

"Yes that's exactly how it felt Fraser, but I'm experiencing something completely different. I don't think God is out to get me, I think he is helping me. At least that is what I am discovering anyway. I know that it's hard to understand, but something is happening to me in my life that I can't explain. At my words Fraser remained silent and didn't say anything. Maybe I sounded crazy to him, I don't know. Sometimes I sounded crazy to myself.

Finally he spoke. "I hope you're not going to turn into one of those Jesus freaks, Kings."

"No never," I replied.

Changing the subject quickly Fraser asked, "So Kings, tell me what happened with Gay, after I dropped you off the other weekend."

"Oh it was great. We went for a picnic up on Cefn Bryn. She is such a beautiful girl, and I can't wait to see her again."

"Are you going out together now or what?"

"Yes, you could say that."

"Wow, I'm jealous, Kings. My brother is going out with Gay Tripp. When are you seeing her next?"

"She's been away for two weeks, up in England at a horse show, but she gets back on the weekend. I'm meeting her on Saturday after her riding practice. I thought I would show her my cave and have a picnic on the Tor."

"Fantastic, Kings, I wish I was going out with her."

"Thanks, Fraser, I'm pretty excited about it."

"How long are you staying, Kings? Can you stay the night? I can give you a ride back to Penmaen in the morning before work."

"That would be great. I was going to suggest that I stay over and spend some time with you."

"I'll tell you, what Kings, if I give you a ride back in the morning, could I come and see your cave? I haven't walked down to the Great Tor in years."

"Sure Fraser, it's a deal. I'll show you around my territory, but please remember not to tell anyone, not even Dad, where I am."

"I won't. You have my word on that."

Fraser and I enjoyed hanging out together, and I got my washing done and had a nice bath. This was luxury, I thought, as I lay in the warmth and bubbles. Then, after raiding the fridge, I headed off to a comfortable bed. Wow, one thing's for sure, you can't beat a comfortable bed. Well, maybe you can … lying on the hot sand dunes with Gay, for example.

King of Gower!

In the morning we found that Dad had come and gone, but there was a note on the table. "Good morning boys. Sorry I missed you last evening. I didn't get home until late, and I had to leave early this morning for West Wales. Glad you came over, Kings. Hopefully, next time we can have a visit. How are the knives and bow and arrow working out? Take care, old son, and remember, you're welcome home any time."

I felt good as I read Dad's letter. He really was accepting of my situation.

After breakfast, Fraser helped me find the camping lantern and stove in the garden shed and I was all set. I climbed on the back of his motorcycle and we were soon on our way to Penmaen.

It was a lovely morning as we rode along the country lanes. No sign of rain, only the promise of a beautiful day ahead, which made my spirit rise with the smiling sun. Fraser banked the bike around some of the narrow corners, as I held on tightly to my bag of clothes and leaned back on the camping gear and blankets that were strapped to the back of the bike.

"I'm travelling in style, Fraser," I shouted out from underneath my helmet.

"Glad you're enjoying it, Kings," he shouted back. "Motorcycling is the only way to fly."

"It sure is," I agreed, but it would come in second compared to riding the stallion.

Fraser parked the bike just off the main road, and we walked across the Burrows and out onto the Tor. Suddenly I remembered my rabbit snares, and I asked Fraser if he'd like to check them for me.

Cave Days

"Yes!" he said excitedly, putting down the camping gear. "I haven't done this since dad took us ferreting, and we used to smack the rabbits on the head ... remember, Kings?"

"Yeah, I remember alright. The first snare is on the bank there, Fraser," I said, pointing down the hill. It was a fair way down from where we were standing, and he ran down to check it.

"There's one in here, there's one in here," I could hear him shouting at the bottom of the hill, and he soon ran back holding a large rabbit by the ears."

"Did you bring the snare back with you?"

"No. Sorry, Kings. I was too excited to get the rabbit."

"No worries, I've got to reset it anyway."

"He's huge, Kings, almost the size of a hare."

"He's definitely a mature one, Fraser."

"What are you going to do with him?"

"I'm gonna skin 'im. I'm making a fur blanket out of the pelts."

"Wow!" How many do you have? Do you have enough to make the blanket yet?"

"I've got 49 now, including this one. I figure I need at least 50 to make a good-size blanket, and there are three more snares to check yet."

"Can I check them, Kings, can I? This is awesome."

It was like watching myself when I first came to the cliffs to live. He was so excited. "Sure," I said, pointing out the other snares.

There was nothing in the next two, but the last one had another rabbit in it.

"You got number 50, Kings," he shouted out.

"That's great, Fraser," I shouted back. "Now I can make my blanket."

"This is great, Kings, living out here in the wild. Living off the land and sea, while the rest of us have to go to work. You are a legend, Kings, and I'm proud to be your brother."

"Thanks," I said, holding back the tears. "Do you want to watch me skin and gut the rabbits? I'm using the knives Dad gave me for Christmas."

"Yes, I'd love to watch."

"Usually I do the skinning down by the river, so I can wash the blood off right away," I said. "That way there's no mess. It's the blood that ruins the fur if you don't clean it in a reasonable amount of time."

After cleaning the pelts in the river, I took them down to the sea and washed them again in the waves. I also used a flat stone to push down on the blood vessels on the skin of the pelt, to make sure all the blood was gone. "The salt water is also a purifier, and once the pelts are stretched and dried, they don't smell like dead rabbits anymore; they smell like nice fur. No wonder the ladies like them," I said, and we both laughed.

We climbed back up through the dunes and on up to the Tor.

"Before you leave for work, Fraser, I want to show you my cave, and don't forget to tell Dad how I'm using my Bowie knife to skin the rabbits."

As we stood outside the entrance of my cave, I noticed a large rabbit sitting outside one of the burrows on the bank below us.

"Stay there, Fraser," I whispered, "and don't make any noise while I go and get my bow and arrow from inside the cave." I crept in slowly and grabbed my bow and two arrows.

"Watch this," I whispered to Fraser, pulling an arrow back on the cord and aiming at the rabbit below us. I let go of the arrow, and with a thud it went right into the fur of the rabbit.

"My gosh, Kings, you just killed a rabbit with a bow and arrow! What a shot! You're lethal man. No one could shoot a rabbit like that from this distance, and hit him with an arrow."

"It's just practice, Fraser. That's what I do when I get bored and have nothing to do. I shoot my bow and arrow and throw my knives. Well, I'm not going all the way down to the river to gut this one. I'll do it here, outside the cave."

Fraser watched intently as I made a bloody mess, not having the water to wash the meat and skin. "Look at my hands!" I said, holding them up. "I look like Jack the Ripper after his latest murder!" Fraser laughed.

I went into the cave and Fraser followed. "I'll show you where I live," I said, "in the little cavern in the heart of the Tor."

Giving Fraser the flashlight, I said, "Go on ahead and I'll follow behind you."

"Shit, Kings. It's dark in here."

"It's all right," I assured him. "There is nothing in here, other than my fishing gear and the other pelts."

"Gosh, you're right; it's just like a room in here, Kings. I vaguely remember Dad bringing us here when we were boys. What an awesome hideout, man. If you light the lantern, and burn those candles, it will be just like a cosy den."

King of Gower!

"That's what I'm hoping for. I'm going to bring Gay here on Saturday."

"I'd love to see her face, Kings, when she sees this, it will either turn her on, or she'll run for the hills. The Hill brothers, that is."

We laughed and laughed, and I said, "I hope it turns her on."

"I have to leave for work now, Kings, but you have to let me know how it goes on Saturday."

"I will, and I'll drop by in a few weeks for a visit. Or you can drop by and see me here, but don't bring anyone else, okay?"

Okay, Kings, I won't, and don't forget the camping stove on the bank."

"I won't. Bye for now, and give my love to Dad."

"I will, and I'll tell him how you're using the knife, and how you can kill rabbits with your bow and arrow."

"Thanks, I'll see you soon, Frase."

With bloody hands, and the smell of game on my skin, I was left to start my day. I needed another bath. Oh well, I'd have to clean up in the sea. I wished we'd had time for me to show Fraser my stallion, I thought. He won't believe his eyes when he sees the Thunder Child.

First I needed to rinse off the rabbit meat and the pelts in the Killy Willy, and get this sticky blood off my hands. As I plunged my hands into the river, a large cloud of blood joined the flowing waters down to the sea. For a few moments I stared at my hands and rubbed my fingers, feeling them getting clean.

What was interesting in those few moments was an awareness within my soul; I was beginning to understand what being clean on the inside meant. I had begun to talk to God about different things in my life off and on. It was better than thinking I was always talking to myself. If I was talking to someone then I knew I was not going crazy. I hadn't surrendered my heart to God; I still had too many questions that I needed answers to. But I knew very well that he was working in my life, and revealing himself to me one sign at a time, and I wondered how it was all connected.

As I picked up the rabbit meat and pelt, the seagulls squawked and circled overhead, hoping I'd throw them some meat. I was tempted to give up one of my rabbits. I felt lazy and did not want the bother of cooking them. I'd grown used to enjoying a variety of other foods lately. "No," I shouted back at the gulls. "I have to get used to eating wild food again, or I won't be able to stay living here on the cliffs."

My trips to Penmaen store to buy food and kindling were making a good-sized dent in my money supply. My only chance of income, as far as I could see, was to rob James' milk round again in the near future. I was too proud to ask my father for money. Oh well, I still had a bit of money left. I'd try and make it last as long as I could.

I finished washing the pelts in the ocean now, holding them in the waves. Then suddenly I heard the thunder of hooves in the distance. It was the Thunder Child, on his return gallop from Oxwich. Standing up, I braced myself, ready to be chased into the sea, for I was intruding into his time upon the Sands, but he galloped right past me, leaving me alone. "Thank you, Thunder Child," I shouted. "Wow, look at you go. You're as fast as the wind."

I climbed back up to the Tor and added my pelts to the others. It was time I tried my hand at sewing and started to

King of Gower!

make my blanket. Within a short time, I learned that it was a lot easier said than done, and oh, how I wished I'd thought of getting a thimble—as I jabbed my thumb several times trying to push the needle through the tough, inflexible skins. As long as I pushed the needle hard and straight, it pushed through, but it was hard work, and I had 50 to do. As I continued, my thumb and fingers ached. I tried to think of my finished blanket, and how great it would look, draped over my shoulders like a robe. Come on, Kings, you've got to get it done. Just think what Gay will say when she sees it.

I took several breaks to rest my hands, and I stopped for lunch. It was coming along now as the hours went by. As I ran out of one piece of twine, I cut off another from the roll, and I wove it through the skin side of the pelt and out through the fur. This way the skin would be smooth, and the joins hidden by the fur. I wanted it to be more of a fashion garment than for warmth, as I wasn't living in the Ice Age like my caveman predecessors were.

It was time for another break, so I laid it out flat on the ground. There were only six more pelts to sew, and my blanket was looking really good. From the fur side it looked like one large piece of fur, and you couldn't see the joins without pressing your fingers through the fur. I should do this with a sheep, I thought. Two sheep and a lot less sewing, and I'd have a sheepskin blanket for Gay.

Finally, in the late afternoon, I finished. I climbed to the top of the Tor and wore it like a robe over my shoulders. I felt excited and proud of my achievement, as I stood there as king of my castle. It was heavy and warm, and wrapped completely around my shoulders, and came down to my knees. "Wow, I'm the King of Gower!" I shouted across the lonely hills. They answered me back, saying, "You are indeed!"

After my celebration on top of the Tor, I decided to try out my father's camping lantern inside the cavern. It lit easily, and as Fraser had said, it was a great little room. As the light shone on the ancient walls, I wondered if this had been the first lantern lit in the cave, and the brightest light my cave had ever seen. Certainly that would have been true in caveman times, for they would have found out, like me, that the cave did not have the ventilation to have even a small fire in here. Maybe they were smarter than me and figured that out before smoking themselves out like I did.

I lay on my air mattress and put my robe over myself like a blanket. It was soft and warm with the fur against my skin, and the extra weight on my body helped me to feel secure. All of a sudden my blanket had increased in value. By day it would be my royal robe, and by night my warm blanket.

I didn't want to waste my lantern's oil by burning it in the day, so I placed candles in each corner and one big one in the centre of the floor close to my bed. What a cosy home I have, I thought, and I couldn't wait to show Gay tomorrow. One more sleep and I would see her.

The evening sky grew into a beautiful sunset, and I ate supper at the entrance to my cave. The sky was still half clear and there was no sign of rain clouds on the horizon. Tomorrow promised to be a dry day for me to show Gay my territory around the Tor. As I felt the cool wind on my face, I thought how nice it would be to have a fire tonight—and besides, I needed to cook the rabbits. They would only keep for a few days. I went inside and checked my kindling supply and driftwood. There was plenty for a fire tonight, and there would be enough left to have a fire with Gay tomorrow.

As I built my fire, I could see that some of the stars were already out, along with a crescent moon. The wind blew cool and clear, a westerly in from the Bristol Channel. Wrapping the rabbit meat in foil, I placed it on a stone in the middle of the fireplace, using the same design I'd used at Bacon Hole—a ring of stones around the outside, and a flat cooking stone in the middle. I did have my father's camping stove now, but it needed fuel. Oh well, I had to keep up my skills in cooking on an open fire. Soon I built up a good fire, and I could smell the meat cooking. I buttered a few pieces of bread to have with it, and continued to watch the night sky. There was always something to look out for when even a part of the sky was clear; satellites, the constellations, and even shooting stars.

My rabbit tasted good, much like chicken, only stronger. I couldn't go so far as saying my break from eating rabbit made me appreciate it. I think I was just really hungry. After finishing my food, I built up the fire again for warmth, and in the fire's light I wrote a poem about my home within the Tor.

THE GREAT TOR

Oh, Great Tor!
Great and mighty you stand.
Guardian of the sands from ages past!
From sunrise, and through endless setting suns,
Your majesty commands the changing seas.
Who am I to describe you ?

Cave Days

Not as other men is my plea.
Who have come and gone in your timeless presence,
Without "knowing" your majesty!
Your days began before the continents separated,
and the ice fields melted, and the great burgs raced along
the Labrador Sea.
You were here with the cavemen, and then watched the Vikings
Cross the sea, and now you are here with me.
I have made my home within you, my castle by the sea.
Here within your stone rooms, I am safe, and I am free.
Thank you. Your Majesty!
© *Kingsley Ross Hill*

Chapter Twelve

Sunset Colours of Love

I'd spent another night in the heart of the Tor, and Leathers Hole was surely my home now. I lay down at night in peace and woke up in the morning at peace. 'Fear' was no longer a part of my life, but was it the presence of God, or the absence of fear and companions that gave me peace?

I climbed to the top of the Tor, robed in my fur blanket. What a beautiful day. I had hoped for a nice day to spend with Gay, and I got one. There wasn't a cloud in the sky, just a light breeze, as the rising Sun sparkled its light upon the dancing waters, and I danced along the top of the Tor, like a King on his coronation day. In my heart, I wore a crown.

After breakfast, I put on my best jeans, jacket and boots, and headed off to meet Gay. When I arrived at the stables, she was already out in the field, practising some skills with Blaze. I watched her for several minutes from the fence. She looked so beautiful and graceful as she rode her horse. Suddenly she looked up and saw me, and then galloped across the field towards me.

"Kingsley!" she shouted excitedly, climbing down from her horse and kissing me. That answered my question immediately. She did still feel the same way as when she'd left, and it wasn't a dream.

"You're real," I said, and she laughed.

"I hope I am," she replied, "and you are still real too, Kingsley." We both laughed.

"Oh, it's so great to be real," I said, and I kissed her back and hugged her tightly. "It's great to see you Gay, I've missed you."

"I've missed you too, Kingsley, and I've been longing to see you."

Now I felt like I was on top of the world. A King with his Queen.

"I'll just finish my program with Blaze, and then we can go on our picnic, and we don't need to go to the store because I've got everything made."

Not only was she excited to see me, she'd already made us a picnic again.

After she had fed and watered Blaze, she said she had something to show me. "What is it?" I asked excitedly.

"Come and see," she replied, and I followed her into the barn. She handed me an old potato sack with something heavy inside it.

"What is it?" I asked.

"Look and see, Kingsley."

*

I pulled out a big trophy that had her name written on a plaque. It read: "Best Individual Skills Performance by Horse and Rider: Miss Gay Tripp."

"I won, Kingsley, I won. I wanted to win the skills competition more than any of the others, and I won it! It's also the first time a Welsh girl has ever won the competition, and the first time the trophy has ever left England. I get to keep it for a whole year, and I can try to retain it next year. My dad is getting a replica made for me so I can keep the trophy forever."

"Congratulations, Gay. That's such a wonderful achievement and I'm so proud of you."

"Thank you, Kingsley," she said, and kissed me.

Just then, Gay's mother pulled up in her car. "I'll take your riding gear home, Gay, and don't be back late. Hello Kingsley, I've heard so much about you."

"Hello, Mrs. Tripp, it's nice to meet you," I said, and I walked over to the car and shook her hand.

"Nice to meet you too, Kingsley. Have a nice picnic, you two, and remember, Gay, don't be late. I'll pick you up here at 7 o'clock."

"Okay, Mum, I'll see you tonight."

"So where are we going?" Gay asked, taking my hand.

"Have you ever heard of Leathers Hole?" I replied.

"Yes, I have. That's a cave up on the cliffs, isn't it? My mother and father went there once on a hike, but I've never been there."

"Well, I thought we could go and have a picnic on top of the Great Tor, and then I can show you the stallion. I named him Thunder Child." I went on to share with Gay why I had given him that name.

"He sounds wonderful, Kingsley, but is he really that wild? Will he really chase us into the sea?"

"Only if we walk on the beach during the time he likes to gallop from Pobbles to Oxwich," I explained. "Why don't we have our picnic first, on top of the Tor. It's so beautiful up there and you can see for miles, right across the Bristol Channel to Devonshire. Then after our picnic we can go and see the Thunder Child.

"I don't mind what we do, Kingsley, as long as I'm with you."

I cradled her face in my hands and looked deep into her beautiful eyes and kissed her. Trembling, I thought I was going to melt inside. We kissed gently, standing on the hilltop, for what seemed like hours, and the cool wind blew around us, making our kisses that much more warm and sacred. We could have kissed forever, we both confessed as we came up for air.

It was already the best day of my life, I thought, as I took Gay's hand and led her out towards the Tor. As we walked, her hand felt warm and soft in mine, and our souls spoke in silence, telling each other what words could not say.

It was Gay who broke the silence. "I love being with you, Kingsley. It's like we have known each other forever. Do you think our souls could have known each other before?"

"It's like my soul recognizes you, Gay. Like we have always been a part of each other."

"It's so beautiful, Kingsley. I've never felt like this before. Would we have felt like this, if we'd gone out together when we were in school?"

"I don't know, Gay, but I'm learning that there is a time for everything in life. When you were away in England, even though we had just spent that one day together, I felt that a part of me was missing, and now I feel I've found the missing part."

Gay's eyes filled with tears. "Kingsley, that's the most beautiful thing anyone has ever said to me."

We kissed again, and I felt her warm tears rolling down my cheeks. "I'm so glad we met, Gay."

"And I'm so glad too, Kingsley."

We stopped and kissed, and stopped and kissed, until we finally reached the Tor.

"I wouldn't care if we had never gotten here," I said, "I could have kissed you forever."

"Me too," she said, and we both laughed.

As we stood on top of the Tor, I knew it must be lunchtime, for the sun was high in the sky and it warmed our faces every time the wind paused to take another breath.

Gay had packed a lovely picnic. Salmon sandwiches, a garden salad, and cheese and crackers, and even chocolate biscuits and pop.

I sat with my back to a rock, and Gay leaned back against me. What more could I want, I thought, as I felt my arms around her, our hands and fingers touching and squeezing like we had been searching for each other for lifetimes and suddenly we had found each other.

"How can we feel like this, Kingsley?" she asked, turning and kissing me.

"I don't know," I said, "I'm just so happy we found each other."

As her head rested upon my chest, and the cool wind swept her long hair over my face, she smelled like sweet coconut, like the wild Gorse flower in the spring, and I thanked God I was alive.

After our picnic, I showed Gay my cave. "My gosh, Kingsley, you live in here? Oh my gosh, it's amazing. You actually live out here in the wild, in a cave? What's this? A fur blanket?"

"Yes, I made it from rabbit pelts."

"You caught enough of them to make a blanket?"

"It took me a while to catch them all, and then to make the blanket."

I lit the lantern, since the candles that had been burning since morning were starting to fade.

"Kingsley, this is amazing. It's like a room in here. Do you ever get scared at night?"

"I used to when I lived in another cave, but not in here. God watches over me and keeps me safe."

"How about your mum and dad, do they mind you being out here? Don't they worry?"

"No," I said, "they don't mind, and I go home about every two weeks to visit my brother, and my dad if he's home."

"That's right, you have a brother, don't you?"

"Yes, just one brother. Fraser is his name. He's a great brother. He was actually visiting me this morning."

After showing Gay my cave, I took her down to the beach to meet Thunder Child.

"Can we feed him?" she asked. "I have some carrots left from feeding Blaze. If he allows us to feed him, he will remember it the next time he sees us and associate us with giving him food. I found that out with the ponies on Cefn Bryn."

"I agree about the ponies associating people with food." I said. "But when you see the Thunder Child, you will realise that he is not like any other horse." I was sure that Gay thought I was exaggerating, but she would soon find out.

"If we are going to feed him, I think this would be the best time," I said, "while he's standing at his cave. But if we try to walk the beach while he's on his gallop, he will give chase, and even chase us into the sea."

"I've got to see this, Kingsley," exclaimed Gay. "I've never heard of a wild stallion roaming the beach. Usually they stay quite hidden, unless they are protecting the herd from danger."

"I'll show you. He's as wild as the west wind," I said.

༄

When we reached the Killy Willy, I took my shoes and socks off, and piggy backed Gay across. "Don't drop me, Kingsley!" she screamed, as I pretended to stumble a few times.

"Well, stop tickling me," I said jokingly, as I lowered her into the sand.

"Look," I said, pointing towards Pobbles." There he is standing in front of his cave. Let's go and meet him."

As we walked along the beach towards him, I felt a bit nervous. How would he react to the two of us? I felt like he was just getting used to me walking by him, but two people in his space…? Oh well, I need to trust, I thought, and I prayed a short prayer of protection under my breath.

"Are you praying?" Gay asked. "You don't have to whisper. I pray to God too, you know."

"God, protect us from this wild animal!" I prayed aloud.

"Is he that wild, Kingsley? Now you've got me nervous."

We soon reached Thunder Child, and Gay very calmly spoke his name, saying, "Hello, Thunder Child, my name is

Cave Days

Gay and I'm pleased to meet you. I have a horse named Blaze, and she wanted me to say hello to you. Can you smell her on me?"

He remained still, like a soldier on duty.

"My gosh, Kingsley, he's huge. He just towers over us. It's just like you said, he does look like he's guarding something inside the cave."

It was my turn to speak. "Hello, Thunder Child, you know me, don't you, old boy? This is Gay, and she's brought you some carrots."

Gay slowly reached into her pocket and pulled out some carrots. Moving her arm up slowly, she held the carrots up to his mouth. For a few minutes he just kept still.

"This is really strange, Kingsley. *All* horses like carrots. He reminds me of one of the Queen's guards at Buckingham Palace. Come on, Thunder Child, they're carrots."

Suddenly he lowered his head down to Gay's hand and munched on the carrots. I couldn't believe what was happening. My wild and fierce stallion was eating out of her hand. She reached into her pocket for another handful. This time she patted his neck with her other hand. "Kingsley," she said softly, "lift up your hand to his nose and let him get used to your smell."

His reddish brown coat gleamed in the sun, and he lifted his head up and down as if he was enjoying the fuss. Wow. Now my dream of riding him across the Sands one day seemed a little more realistic.

"You're right, Kingsley, he is the most amazing stallion, and we have to check out that cave."

"Maybe next time he goes on his gallop, we can have a look in there," I said.

Sunset Colours of Love

After our visit with Thunder Child, we carried on towards Pobbles. We held hands and followed the tide line high up on the beach. It felt so good to feel Gay's hand in mine and the warmth of the sun on our faces. Every once in a while we stopped and picked driftwood or shells.

"Look, here's a whelk shell, and it's the same colour as the sunset," I said.

"It's beautiful, Kingsley."

"I want you to have it," I said, putting it in her pocket and kissing her again.

"I could stay out here with you forever, Kingsley," she whispered in my ear. "Shall we watch the sunset tonight?"

"Yes," I replied, "and I'll make us a fire."

We walked down the beach to the waves to see what we could find. "I have a collection of glass fishing net floats that I found since coming to the cliffs to live," I said. "Would you like to see Bacon Hole? It's the first cave I lived in, and I'd like to bring my glass floats back to my new cave.

"I would love to see Bacon Hole, Kingsley. You're so brave to be living on the cliffs. I would be afraid, unless I was with you."

I shared more with Gay about Bacon Hole and its influence on my life. I talked about its darkness, and the light of my fires that I made as big as I could, trying to chase my fears away. I told her about my message in a bottle, and how my life was changing.

"That's amazing that you found a message in a bottle. I've never found something as special as that."

By the time we arrived at Bacon Hole, it was well into the late afternoon and we were getting hungry again. "We could always walk back along the cliff tops," I said, "and stop at Pennard stores for a snack."

I showed Gay my old throne. "This is where I started each new day," I said, "and got my weather report."

"Caveman weather station," she said, and we both laughed.

We climbed up upon the stone, and looked out across the Bristol Channel. I pointed out Devonshire in the distance. It was so clear that we could see the rolling hills of Ilfracombe in North Devon.

"This is so beautiful, Kingsley, and I feel so safe here with you, even though it's such a lonely place. I can feel the past all around us. It's like the walls of the cave are calling out."

"Yes, that's exactly what I feel when I'm here, Gay. It's great to have you with me and to share this with you. When I first came here, I imagined what it would have been like to live here in this lonely place, in the time of the cavemen." I shared with Gay so many of the daydreams I'd had when I first arrived at Bacon Hole. It was a wonderful conversation.

"What would it be like if it was just you and me, Kingsley?" Gay asked "…if we were the only human beings in the whole area, in caveman times?"

"Our love would be strong." I replied. "We would love and depend on each other in a way that modern man could never experience or understand. A love so pure and deep, without the distractions of modern living and other people. We would have to rely on and trust one another implicitly to survive. I would hunt and fish and keep you safe, my Princess."

"And I would cook and mend your clothes, my Prince."

Sunset Colours of Love

"Come with me," I said, lifting her down from my throne. "Come inside and see."

Gay stopped at the entrance, and stood there in the silence, just as I had done when I first arrived. "This is a very lonely place," she said, "and I can feel the past here in the still air."

"I know what you mean," I said, "and if you listen carefully, you can hear the voices of the cave family."

"Oh, let me hold on to you, Kingsley," she said, as I led her inside the cave.

"This would be our fireplace, Gay," I said, kneeling down at the circle of stones.

Suddenly our eyes met, and she said, "Here our children would play, and they would draw paintings of our family on the walls."

I cradled her face again in my hands and looked deep into her soul. In our kiss, it was as if the past, present and future were all together with us, and our hearts were one.

"Oh Kingsley, what if it were real? That we could live this life, and have a cave family together?"

"We would sing songs around the fire." I said. "Songs that told the story of our love and lives. The priceless, sacred love of a cave man and woman, and our children, all together as one."

Gay held my head and kissed me. "I wish it could be our lives, Kingsley. That we and our children were the only people on the whole of the Gower Peninsula."

"That would be so wonderful," I said, as I smelled her hair and kissed her again. "And this is what I will dream of always, from this time forth, Gay."

"I shall dream of it always too, Kingsley, my love, and let us be married under God's sky today! We must find something down on the beach and give it to each other when we arrive back at the Tor. It will be as a ring, and a covenant of our love."

It was time to head back to the Tor. Before we left Bacon Hole, I went back inside to get two of my glass fishing floats. One each would be enough to carry back this time. I picked out a green one and an amber coloured one from the pile. "You can play with the rest of them, Fear," I said aloud. "Be good now, you spooks, until I come and visit you again."

"Who were you talking to in there?" Gay asked.

"Oh, just Fear, and the other spooks that haunt the cave."

As we walked back along the cliff tops, Gay called out suddenly, "I found my covenant piece." as she bent down and picked something up from the path.

"What is it?" I asked. It had to be something small to fit inside the palm of her hand.

"You'll have to wait until we get back to your cave." she said.

"I will find something for you on the beach," I replied, and there it was, sparkling in the waves.

We kept our covenant pieces secret until we got back to the cave.

As we walked along the Sands, the sun sank lower in the sky, reminding our hearts that sometime soon our day would have to come to an end.

"I wish this day would last forever, Kingsley. Don't let it end, please!"

"This place and time will always be ours, Gay. No matter what happens, our love will always remain."

Sunset Colours of Love

She began to cry, and said, "Kingsley, I love you!"

"I love you too, Gay," and I held her in my arms and kissed her – with all of me that ever was or ever would be. I wanted her to feel all of my soul. I could not believe how strong this connection was so soon after meeting again. It was unexplainable.

"Oh God, how am I ever going to be able to go home and leave you here, Kingsley? Even for one day, it will be too hard. You're such a part of me already."

The evening Sun was almost setting as we arrived back at the cave, and the sky was full of oranges and reds, as if celebrating with us the colours of our love.

"Kingsley, look at the sunset, it's so beautiful, and just for us."

Having already prepared the fire, I told Gay to sit down while I went to the cave to get my fur blanket. Wrapping her in my blanket, I put a match to the fire. The dead Gorse burned instantly, and we soon had a nice fire blazing. We sat with our backs to a rock and held hands under the blanket. As she caressed my fingers with her hand, I knew she'd heard everything my soul had said to her in our kiss.

The sunset was indeed spectacular, a mirror of our wonderful day. We talked of the different shapes and colours representing the different parts and experiences of our day together.

"The red reminds me of our hearts, Kingsley, and the warmth of our love. The dark grey clouds around the red ones are like the people in the world around us, wanting and searching for what we have found. They stay grey and cold, until they find true love, and only then do their hearts burn red."

"The orange clouds remind me of our fire, and the passion within our hearts, Gay. All the grey and dark clouds will never be able to put out our flame."

Gay then gave me a heart shaped stone that she had found on the Cliff path. "This represents my heart, Kingsley, but I've given it to you."

"Thank you, it's the perfect shape of a heart, and I'll always carry it with me," I said, kissing her again.

I gave her a round rock, with a perfect white circle around the outside of it. I'd found it sparkling in the waves. "The circle represents our love that goes on and on forever, unbroken with no end. And because I found the stone in the waves of the sea, it symbolises travel, time and distance. It has taken time, travel, and distance for our souls to meet again, for we had met years ago on the school bus, and been at the same school, but only now is the perfect time for our souls to meet and connect as they have done. This is the season that our souls have found each other, and I am so happy, Gay."

And there under the sunset, we said our wedding vows!"

She kissed me then, with everything she ever was and ever would be, and my soul understood. We held each other so tight, until it was time for me to walk her back to the village to meet her mother.

As we walked along the Burrows, it was as if our souls had known each other before, long ago when God first made man and woman. I now knew what it meant when my grandparents had said it was not good for man to be alone.

"I'll meet you here again tomorrow, Kingsley," she said, pulling me behind a tree and kissing me, so her mother didn't see. I'll see you tomorrow at 10 o'clock."

Sunset Colours of Love

"Bye Gay, and sweet dreams."

"I'll meet you in the cave in my dreams, Kingsley."

…And with our eyes taking a longing look into each other's souls, it was goodbye until tomorrow.

I headed back to my cave. The night sky was clear and cool, and I built up the fire again and covered myself with my fur blanket. The fur was warm and cosy against my skin, but how could I close my eyes and let this day end? As I looked out into God's praising sky, I praised Him too, and thanked Him for the most wonderful day of my life! I sat at my fireplace for another hour or so, marvelling at God's handiwork in the night sky.

I wondered how man can deny God as Creator?—When his moon and stars shout out his praises, across the endless expanse of time and space, and the shooting stars dance.

As I closed my eyes to sleep, I heard Gay's voice calling me. "Kingsley," she said, "I am in my dream now. Come into the cave and meet me in your sleep. I am waiting for you, come now to me."

And I did.

Chapter Thirteen

Waltzing Through Spring

I woke from my dream, a wonderful dream. Oh, Angel of the morning, put me back to sleep, for I have been with Gay, and we have dreamed of a lifetime together, and I do not want to open my eyes.

Wake, Kingsley, whispers the morning wind, the dawn has broken to a brand new day, and at 10 o'clock you will be back with Gay! Wake up, wake up! Okay, I'm opening my eyes, and I'm ready to start the new day.

Robed in my fur blanket, I climbed to the top of the Tor and looked out across the Bristol Channel. The sea has on his emerald green today. That's what he likes to wear on these blue sky days. Sometimes he hides under the Celtic mist, only showing himself through little porthole windows, as he tries on different outfits of different colours. But by the time the wind asks to see what he's wearing, he seems to have always chosen a colour-coordinated wardrobe. My favourite is a navy shirt, with a turned over white collar, and with the azure trousers for evening wear. Some days it seems he doesn't care what he wears. Any old grey drab thing will do, and on those mornings, it takes longer for the birds to sing.

I had no idea what time it was. My night had been so fair. I closed my eyes and opened them again, hoping Gay would be there! By the look of the Sun, it was about 8 o'clock. His rays had not yet started to stare. Excitement filled my heart as I thought of meeting Gay.

After cereal for breakfast, I headed off to the village. How wonderful my life is, I thought, as I skipped across the Burrows with the warm Sun following me and smiling on my day. How would my Princess look this morning? – Her long flowing hair down to her waist, and a scent as sweet as the spring Heather. Oh, to take her hand again in mine, and hear our hearts talk in the silence of our listening souls.

Where could we go today? It would be nice to walk upon Cefn Bryn, or we could go and find Thunder Child, and have an adventure with him. Having reached the village, I went into the general store.

"Hello," said the lady behind the counter, "isn't it a lovely day."

"It certainly is," I replied, "a very beautiful day, and could I have some flowers please? Red roses would be perfect for today."

"Are they for that lovely young lady who rides the horse?"

"Yes, they are, how did you know?"

"Oh young man, your face gives it away."

"Is it that obvious?" I asked, smiling.

"Yes it is. You're absolutely beaming." We both laughed. "Look, how about I put three red roses mixed with these lovely green Ferns? They will tell the story of young love."

"That will be fine," I said, my face turning red.

"Oh, don't be shy," she said. "I was young once, and love is the most wondrous thing."

"It is, isn't it? I said, my shyness starting to leave me, "It is a very wonderful thing."

"Well, here you are, young man. These will make her heart sing…And what is your name?"

"Kingsley."

"Kingsley, what a lovely name. I think you're a very nice young man, and remember this, Kingsley, any nice young lady loves to have flowers given to her."

"Yes, thank you, I can't wait to give them to her."

"Bye for now, Kingsley. Call in again soon, and let me know how much she liked the flowers."

"I will," I said, and headed off to the stables.

This time Gay was waiting for me, having already finished her practice. Holding the roses behind my back, I walked towards her.

"Kingsley. It's so good to see you."

"It's so good to see you too, Gay. These are for you."

"Oh Kingsley, I love them! Red roses, thank you so much."

Tears filled her eyes, and she kissed me.

"You are so romantic Kingsley. I love that about you."

For a while we just stood there looking into each other's eyes and smiling, and our hearts did all the talking.

"I couldn't wait to see you today, Kingsley, and to go on another picnic."

"Where would you like to go today, my Princess?"

"I'd love to go up on Cefn Bryn again and have another picnic there. It's such a beautiful day. I've already packed our food. We do need to get something to drink in the store, though. I forgot to pack some drinks."

"We walked through the village hand-in-hand, and then went into the store.

"Hello, you two," said the lady. "I can see you like your roses," she said to Gay.

"Yes, they are beautiful," Gay replied.

I bought two bottles of orange juice, and then we started making our way up to Cefn Bryn. It felt so good to take Gays hand and to lead her up the path to the Bryn.

"You look beautiful Gay." I said, stopping to touch her face and run my fingers through her hair. Her perfume rode upon the gentle wind, and we kissed.

"You look so handsome, Kingsley. I love your curls and green eyes."

I smiled as I felt my soul basking in her words. "Thank you," I finally said, and her smile melted me again.

"Let's go up to King Arthur's stone," I said, "and have our picnic there."

"Yes, let's go up to Kingsley's Stone," Gay echoed, and I truly felt like a King!

I remembered the old man's words and I repeated them to Gay: "You can be a King up here, boy, and this can be your stone."

"He was right." I declared. "I am a King! You're my Queen, Gay, and you can share my throne with me!"

"I'd love to, Kingsley," she said, kissing me again.

Cave Days

Wow, I thought that yesterday had been the best day of my life, but today was turning out to be just as wonderful.

As we walked across the Bryn, like a king and queen, we noticed more flowers blooming around us. Spring was truly here. As we arrived at my stone, we were suddenly surrounded by a herd of ponies.

"Look at them all." Gay shouted in excitement, and we counted sixteen of them.

"This one is pregnant," she said, pointing to a white mare. "Look at her tummy. She will be due around May."

My thoughts went back to Thunder Child, and I wondered if he had a mare somewhere, with a foal growing in her tummy, or was he alone?

"I hope that Thunder Child has a mare of his own, Gay, and that he has the chance to have a family. I hate to see him chased away by the other horses. He is such a wonderful horse, and he deserves to be happy."

"You relate to him, don't you, Kingsley? You remind me of him, living out here, wild and free."

With her words, I felt my vulnerability. It seemed like she was looking into the secrets of my heart.

"Can I ask you something, Kingsley?"

"Yeah, okay, what is it that you want to ask?" But I already knew the words she would ask.

"Why did you come to the cliffs to live, instead of living at home with your family?"

"You're right, Gay. I am like the stallion as far as being wild and free is concerned. I believe that this is the way God created us to be. Free to live out our hopes and dreams. Not in fear and compromise, as I lived for so long. When I watch

Thunder Child trying to fit in with the other horses, it's like looking at a mirror of myself. I've never really felt like I fitted in with society. And it's not like I haven't tried. I have! I just haven't been able to make sense of what this life is all about …why I'm here on this earth. At home, trying to fit in, life seemed to have no real meaning and purpose to it.

"But out here in the wild, God is speaking to me, and revealing things to me through the quiet beauty. Ever since I was a child, I've known of his existence. Just look around us at the things he has made. The sea comes in for six hours—I timed it. Then it stays still for an hour, like its sleeping, waiting instructions. It doesn't come in or go out; it waits. Then all of a sudden it stirs, like a voice is calling it from above. Then it goes out again.

And then there's the moon, up in the heavens. It controls the tides. How fast they come in and how high they rise and fall. The sea only comes in so far; it never goes beyond its boundaries. Unlike people, who seem to have no order and direction in their lives. When I can't see the moon because of the heavy clouds, I still know it's there, just like God is there, even though we can't see him. When I can't see the moon, I can still tell how big it is, by the height of the tide and how fast the tide comes in and goes out. Everything has a design, an order, and a purpose."

Gay kissed me and said, "I love you just the way you are. You're not like anyone else I've ever met, Kingsley. You know and understand things that other people don't, and I love being with you."

"I love being with you too, Gay," I said, holding her in my arms and kissing her. "Your hair is honey and strawberry flavour today," I whispered.

"You mean I'm not coconut and wild Gorse today?"

Cave Days

"No, you're definitely honey and strawberry." We both laughed. As I looked deep into her violet eyes, her sweet love engulfed me, and then we sat on top of Kingsley's Stone and looked out across the emerald sea. We talked about our hopes and dreams, and we shared our heartaches and fears. It was a wonderful experience, to bare ourselves to one another, and to be completely accepted for who we were. Every fiber of my being reached out for Gay, and her soul reached out to me, and we danced.

We held each other for what seemed like months…and years…and eternities seemed to pass. It was like we had been searching for each other all our lives, and now we'd found each other.

As darkness fell, we started heading back to the village to meet Gay's mum. We walked down the path in the light of the moon, and we were late as we arrived in the village.

"Don't worry, my mum won't be upset at us for getting back a bit late," Gay assured me. And she wasn't.

"Hello Gay, and hello Kingsley," she said. "What a beautiful day it's been, and what beautiful roses you have, Gay.

"Kingsley got them for me."

"I was hoping they were for me." teased her mum.

"Oh mum, you have Dad to buy you roses."

"Did you have a nice picnic upon the Bryn?"

"Yes, Mrs. Tripp, we did, and I'm sorry we are a bit late."

"That's all right, Kingsley, I went for a nice walk through the village while I was waiting."

When Gay gave me a goodbye kiss, she whispered in my ear, "Let's meet in our dreams tonight, and I'll see you next weekend."

Waltzing Through Spring

I skipped back along the Burrows to my cave, and radiant with joy in my heart, I thanked God for being alive. As I sat at the entrance and watched the night sky, the air was crisp and clear, and the moon and stars shone brightly.

Well, it was Saturday night, and the new week would soon be upon me. The weekends were going by so quickly now, since Gay had come into my life. But the weekdays were going by slowly as I waited for Saturday to arrive. In some ways it was nice to have so much time to fish and explore this wonderful land of the Gower Peninsula. Surely there could be no other place as beautiful in all the world. With spring here now, and summer coming, it could only get better. I thought of how much fun it was going to be swimming in the sea again and body surfing in the waves. And now I had Gay to share it with. I would have to teach her how to body surf. It was going to be the best summer of my life.

There was also lots of time to think about what I was going to do with my life … I couldn't just live out here in the wild forever though. I dreamed of getting a job and saving for a motorcycle to tour around Great Britain. One day I would like to settle down and have a wife and family. Yes, I had a lot of dreams just waiting for me to live out.

Well, Kings, it's been a long wonderful day. I went into my cave, lit one of the candles, and retired for the night.

Sunday morning was another beautiful day. And the song and smell of spring filled the air. From the top of the Tor, I watched two ravens collecting twigs and animal hair to build and line their nests with. They flew back and forth from the heights of the Tor to one of the peaks of the three cliffs. Ravens are one of the first birds to start building their nests on Pennard Cliffs, and they often lay their eggs by the middle of February. It was the end of March now, so the ravens would have young in their nests. I watched one of them fly over me with what looked like a large shell in its beak. Suddenly he dropped it on a flat rock behind my lookout at the top of the Tor. Then he flew with what had been inside the shell back to his nest on top of the three cliffs. I went to the flat rocks to investigate and I found dozens of shells cracked open. There were mussels and clams and cockle shells, which confirmed that the gulls were part of this also, as the ravens only collected shellfish that were exposed by the outgoing tide. They much preferred carrion and small mammals that they hunted along the Cliffs. There was even the remains of quite a large fish, and the whole place stunk like rotten shellfish. I'm out of here. Yes, the ravens were feeding their young, all right. It was also time for my breakfast.

As I ate, the skylarks hovered above the Tor. They were in greater numbers now, not just the odd one or two as had been the case only a few weeks ago. In the springtime, the skylarks build their nests in the long grasses and Heather patches that grow along the cliff tops. They will often hover directly over their nests and sing the sweetest songs. As a boy, I would try and find the nests by keeping my eyes upon the patch of grass or Heather that I thought was directly below them. I did find a few nests using this method; but what I soon learned about skylarks was when I got too close to where their nests were, they would slowly hover across the sky, thus leading me away from their precious family below.

One day my father and I marked a nest with red tape so we knew exactly where it was. We observed the skylark right above, and as we slowly walked towards the nest, the bird led us away. On one occasion that I will never forget, my father and I stood over a nest admiring the eggs, and the skylark dropped from the sky to within six feet of us on the ground. It pretended that it had a broken wing, and it led us away from its nest. We followed it, and after we were a fair distance away from the nest, it tucked in its wing—the one that had previously been dragging on the ground as if it was broken—and then it flew off and hovered perfectly up in the sky again.

"Now that is one good parent bird," my father said, and I must agree. What an incredible bird.

Oh, I do so enjoy my daydreams, when they are memories so precious as these. My mother once told me that God watched over me closer than a skylark watched over its nest and protected its young.

Well, back to the present time. The wild Gorse blossoms cover all the bushes now, not just the sides that face south to the morning sun, and oh, their sweet, sweet smell.

I walked around the cliff top, smelling the bushes. Mmm, they smell so lovely, a combination of coconut and Hawaiian suntan oil blowing in the breeze, and Gay's perfume. I smelled till I was intoxicated with hopes and dreams of spring, summer, and Gay.

What was that sound? No it couldn't be.

"Why couldn't it be?" answered the skylarks overhead. "It is, it is," they sang. "It is the call of the 'cuckoo bird', announcing the official arrival of spring."

I listened again. "Cuckoo, cuckoo," he called, and I shouted with the skylark, and I danced with the spring. The cuckoo's call took me back to my childhood, where I was planting a flower garden with my mother. My brother Fraser was there too. Mum and Dad had made us a little rockery garden each.

"When is it spring, Mum?" I asked, as we pressed in the earth around the roots of a flower. I can't remember the name of the flower, but I remember its smell.

"Dig another little hole with your spade," she said, "and gently put the next flower into the hole. Be careful and push the soil around the roots, Kingsley." Then Fraser watered it with the watering can, and Mum said, "Now the plant will grow big and strong."

"Yes, Mum, but you didn't answer my question. When is it spring?"

"Yes, when is it spring, Mum?" Fraser echoed.

"It is when you hear the cuckoo call."

"Does the spring come without the cuckoo bird, Mum?"

"Well, it might come," she said, "but it's the cuckoo bird that tells everyone that spring is here."

That was the perfect answer, Mum. I can see that now, all these years later.

I decided to make this day something special. It was the day that the cuckoo came and announced the arrival of spring. I would go into the village and buy a special lunch to celebrate.

I bought a ready cooked chicken and heated it up over a fire, and I had a bag of potato crisps, and a large chocolate bar for dessert – Cadbury's Fruit and Nut, and I stuffed the whole thing in my mouth all at once. Well, I am celebrating, aren't I?

For the next few days I got back to my hunting and fishing. My money was running out, and I wanted to keep what was left for the weekends when I spent time with Gay. I also wanted to buy her a necklace to celebrate our love. I'd seen some beautiful Celtic crosses with birthstones in the middle when Gay and I had been in the general store on the weekend. She had picked one up and looked at it longingly.

I'll surprise her and buy one for her. Yes, she'll love it, and I'll give it to her next weekend. Now let me think, what was the price? They were expensive alright. I remember the lady in the store told Gay they were £17.

Gay was born in August like me, so the birthstone would be peridot. I pictured the cross on her slender neck and I couldn't wait to give it to her. I counted my money. There was only £22 left. Not enough to buy the necklace and another week's supply of food as well. What was I going to do? I couldn't go back to eating just rabbits and fish again. Not after our lovely picnics up on Cefn Bryn. I didn't mind eating fish a few times a week, but not rabbit any more. I was just trapping them for the skins now, and of course they were good target practice for my bow and arrow. I was getting to be a really good shot with my bow. Dad would be impressed when I told him how many rabbits I'd killed with my bow, and I'd show him my fur blanket.

Suddenly I had a wonderful idea. No, it was a bad idea, so my conscience whispered. It had been a long time since I had robbed James the milkman. He wouldn't be expecting anything now, and I was sure people would be leaving their milk money under the milk bottles again. Well, that was my plan then. On Friday I'd get up early and earn some money.

In the afternoon I went to the general store, and the same lady who had sold me the roses helped me pick out a beautiful cross necklace for Gay.

Cave Days

"You must care for her a lot, Kingsley. It is Kingsley, isn't it?"

"Yes," I replied, as the lady showed me the different designs. There was only one Celtic cross with Gay's birthstone. "I'll take this one," I said, "and how much is it?"

"It's £17, Kingsley, and it's my favourite one of them all. Peridot is a beautiful stone."

"Can I put a £10 deposit on it, and pick it up on Friday?" I asked.

She put it away in a little box, and as I left the store, I felt excited that I bought such a lovely gift for Gay. I knew she would love it, and I'd write her a poem and read it to her on Friday when I gave her the cross.

With the rest of my money, I bought food to last me for another week. Well, Kings, that's it, that's the last of your money. Let's hope you get a good take from James on Friday.

For the next few days the spring weather continued. The winds, however, were strong, and the sea was too rough to enjoy fishing off the rocks. Salmon bass fishing was often good when the sea was rough and the waves crashing. The big waves churned up the sand with shrimp and crabs for the bass to eat. I was looking forward to catching a really big one, but to fish off the rocks in the strong winds would be asking for trouble. So I spent my time during the day walking along the sands and re-exploring my favourite places.

The tides were quite low all week, which allowed me to walk all the way from the great Tor to Oxwich Bay, and then all the way back to Pobbles beach. I encountered the Thunder Child on several occasions when he wasn't standing guard at his cave, and I made sure I walked at the water's edge in case he charged me. He thundered towards me on three occasions, but veered away from me again before getting too close. Was he more accepting of me now, as I walked along the beach at the same time he was on his gallop across the Sands? I was getting braver, standing there and trusting that he wouldn't trample me, so it was probably a combination of both.

On Thursday morning I decided to walk along the cliff tops eastward to Bacon Hole, and pick up the rest of my glass fishing floats that I'd collected during the time I'd lived there. Glass fishing floats were getting rarer to find, and I'd had a feeling for a few days now, that if I didn't go and get them, someone else would come into the cave exploring and find them.

Along the cliff path, spring was in full bloom, and the Bluebells, my favourite of the wild flowers, were out in number. Their lovely blue and mauve shone like summer dresses, contrasting with the new green Ferns, whose shoots pushed up from the ground around them, like young men waiting for the next dance. What was that in the distance? A white Bluebell. I picked her gently and smelled her, and asked, "Could I have the next waltz?" What a chorus of praise surrounded me. Daffodils and Primrose lifted their heads, and then the field of wild Heather all in bloom. Oh, the beautiful fragrance filled the air as the wind whispered in gently from the sea. I had to stop and bask in the smell and colour, and I waltzed again with my white Bluebell, as we danced through the sea of purple Heather.

How far my soul has travelled from November grey to this wonderful sunshine day. As I arrived at the cave, I sat at the entrance and listened as always. Why was it that here, silence shouted so loudly?

"Fear, are you here?"

"Yes," came a voice from inside. "I'm still here, but I'm not here as often now."

"Why is that?" I asked "Did you miss me?"

"You could say that," he replied. "There's been no one here since you left."

"Oh well, keep your chin up, old man, it can't be that bad. Just like I said when I moved out, I'm sure in a few thousand years someone else will come and live here, and you can haunt them. Anyway, Fear, I can't stay. I've just come to get my fishing floats to take back to my new home."

I found the floats where I'd left them, against the wall in the heart of the cave. Fear was right. No one had been here since I had left. "Well, Fear, bye now. I must be on my way."

I made my way back along the beach with my bag of glass treasures over my shoulders. As I approached Pobbles, I saw Thunder Child standing outside his cave. He did nothing except stand on guard as I passed right in front of him. "Good day, old boy," I said gently. "I guess you have been on your morning gallop already. Well, old boy, I'm off back to Leathers Hole with my glass fishing floats that I found on the beach. Didn't want to leave them at Bacon Hole for someone to steal. See you soon, Old Thunder."

Chapter Fourteen

The Miracle

As I continued my way along the Sands, I crossed the Killy Willy, and then looked up at the great Tor. I then saw a sight that made my heart beat faster. There on top of the Tor Rock were a number of people. There were at least six of them, walking around like they were searching for something. The entrance to my cave, no doubt. Quickly I slung my backpack over my other shoulder and started to run. Hopefully I could get back and protect my dwelling before they found the entrance. My fur blanket was in there, along with my bow and arrow and knives.

"If I catch them in my cave, I will throw them to the ground." I said aloud, as I ran on through the sand. "I don't care how many there are of them, I'll take them all on. How dare they come near my home!"

Reaching the path up through the dunes, I scrambled across the Burrows to my cave, my glass floats banging together in my backpack. I hoped that they wouldn't break. As I arrived, I shouted at two men who were peering into the entrance.

"Get out of here. Get away from my house," I shouted.

"Your house?" said a voice from behind me. "It's a cave that belongs to the National Trust. We are a group of university students studying archaeology."

"Archaeology, my arse." I pushed the two of them out of the way. Running inside, I grabbed my spear and Bowie knife. "Get away from here!" I shouted again, with a weapon in each hand. The two men close to the cave looked at my spear and knife and turned tail like rabbits fleeing away across the Burrows. "And don't come back!" I shouted, throwing my spear. I didn't aim to hit them, but it landed close to their feet. I chased what appeared to be a teacher and four other students back down the dunes and on to the beach. They kept running and looking back until they saw I had stopped chasing them. "Don't come back!" I shouted again at the top of my voice. I picked up my spear and climbed back up to the entrance of my cave. I watched them until their bright jackets disappeared in the distance.

My feeling over the last few days about the possibility of having visitors had been correct, and with spring now here, and summer on its way, I could expect more intruders to my home. Opening a can of beans and buttering some bread, I ate my lunch around a small fire. A waste of wood, I thought, as I looked at my diminishing pile. But the smoke and the fire gave me a feeling of reclaiming my territory and cleansing the air of my foes.

Would my visitors come back, I wondered? Or tell other people that there was a mad man on the loose? Maybe they would report me to the police because of my knife and spear? They were quite right, of course; the cliffs, along with

The Miracle

the beaches and caves, belonged to the National Trust and the people of this wonderful Celtic land. But as the old man had said, I'm a Knight of Gower now, and nobody knows the secrets of the Gower like I do. Secrets revealed and discovered. That makes this place mine, doesn't it? I'm sure that Thunder Child agrees, and that's what counts around here, not what mere visitors think. I understand, Thunder Child, how you feel when someone is in your space. I don't feel so bad now, when I think about you chasing me into the sea. I just did the same thing, old boy, by chasing those people out of my territory.

I decided to be on the lookout for the next few days, in case they came back with more troops. I moved my bow and arrows, knives, and fur blanket to a small dry crevice that I'd found on the cliff face a few days before. That way, if I did get uninvited guests, there would only be my food and bedding to steal. I can't see them carrying my driftwood very far.... and oh yes, my glass balls...I must move them too.

Thoughts of Gay now entered my mind and heart, and I longed to see her. There was tonight and tomorrow night, and then I would see her on Saturday morning. I thought about my money situation and paying for Gay's necklace tomorrow. I needed seven more pounds for the necklace, and as much money as I could get, since this would be the last robbery of James' milk money. People wouldn't leave money out in milk bottles after tomorrow, I was sure of that, and James would be out looking for the thief.

For a few more hours I continued to stand guard in front of my cave. You're getting more like the stallion every day, boy! Yes Sir, I believe I am.

In the late afternoon, it got so warm that I decided to go and have a bath in the river. Gosh, the water was cold, but with my bar of soap and some heavy breathing, I had a good wash in the Killy Willy. Well Kings, you're a clean knight now. After my scrub in the river, it was time to put on some clean clothes. Not my best ones though. I would save them for Saturday and seeing Gay.

As the sun began to set, I decided to write my poem for Gay. As I wrote, I felt her in my heart, and the words just flowed from my soul. I could feel my whole being reaching for her. I wondered if she was feeling what I was feeling. Somehow I knew she was. "Can you hear me, Gay," I said softly. "Can you feel my heart? Will you meet me in our dreams tonight?"

Then on the breeze I could smell her fragrance, and she whispered, "Yes, my love, I will be waiting for you." I finished my poem and lay down my head. In our dreams we would continue our conversation.

☙

Friday came with the cry of the ravens and the mischievous chuckle of a magpie that was always nearby. Maybe the magpie was Jerry, here to keep me company on these long days. Well, James, here I come.

It was still dark as I climbed up the path to West Cliff, and on over to the road. People usually put their milk money out on Thursday night, as James delivered milk early Friday morning. Let's hope nothing has changed. I really needed to pick up Gay's necklace today and have enough money left over for food for at least a month. That was my goal anyway.

The Miracle

Remember, Kings, this is your last robbery, old boy. After this you're going to have to find another way of getting money—and getting it honestly, like finding a job. Suddenly my conscience spoke to me, and I heard my father's words. "Be honest, old son, for honesty and right living are their own reward. If you do wrong things, they will catch up with you and overtake you." Then it was my grandfather's words that spoke next: "God, who sees all things, is watching closely." And didn't I know it!

My conscience wasn't agreeing with my justification, but I went ahead anyway. I reached the first house. There were empty milk bottles, but no money.

What was that? A car passing on West Cliff road. I hid in close to the hedge until the beam of its lights had passed. Okay, Kings, on to the next house. Let's hope there's some money there. There was. A 10 pound note was stuck in the neck of a bottle. Good. That was more than enough for the balance on the necklace. Come on, Kings, keep moving. You've got to get enough to last you a month. At the next house was a five pound note and change. The next four houses also had money, and I was up to 50 pounds already.

It was getting lighter all the time now, and people were getting into their cars for work. Come on, Kings, just a few more houses. If you get 70 pounds, you will have achieved your goal. At the next two houses there was nothing, and I could hear a car in the driveway next door. Skip this one, Kings or you're crazy! The car was coming up the driveway to the gate. I glanced at the bottles, and then at the lights of the car. He wasn't quite up to the gate yet. There were notes in the bottles. It was now or never. Quickly I darted out from the hedge and grabbed the notes, and then jumped back into the hedge, just missing the beam of the headlights. The car stopped outside the gate and my heart nearly jumped out of my chest. "Come on, get back in the car," I murmured, What was wrong? Why hadn't he closed the gate? Had he seen me in his headlights? Was he checking the milk money?

I couldn't bear to just sit there. Should I make a run for it? No, he would see me then for sure. Please God, get me out of this mess! I promise I won't do it again! Help me get out of here without getting caught. Grandma's words came again: "Kingsley, your sin will find you out!" Just as I was about to get up and run for it, I heard the gate close, and then the car door being shut. My hands were clammy with sweat as I watched the car pull away. Breathing easier now, I opened my palm to find two 10-pound notes. That makes a total of 70 pounds, Kings. You met your goal exactly. Now let's get the heck out of here!

The dawn gave way to the morning as I walked back along the Cliff path. When I got to Pobbles, I peered over the cliff top to see if the Thunder Child was there. He was. I think he'd been there all night, as there were no fresh hoof marks on the sand nearby. It wasn't uncommon though for a stallion to stand outside a cave or overhanging rocks to shelter from the prevailing winds, but the fact that he hasn't moved made me think something had changed. Maybe today I would go and explore the cave while he was gone on his gallop to Oxwich.

Well, Kings, first things first. It's time to pick up Gay's necklace and then celebrate by having a wonderful breakfast. You have £70, enough to last you a month if you're careful. You can have breakfast at the cave – bacon and eggs. Then you can go and explore Thunder Child's cave. That should be a good full day.

As I walked to the village, my conscience began to bother me again. After all that God had done for me, in giving me Gay as my girlfriend, and helping me to live out here in the wild, and keeping me safe all this time ... and this is how I repay him, by robbing people of their milk money. "Stealing is stealing, Kingsley," Grandma's words echoed in my head again. "Wrong is wrong, and right is right." "Yes Grandma, you're right, and I'm sorry. I won't do it again. So can you leave me to get on with my day now?"

I arrived at the store. "Hello Kingsley, have you come to pick up your cross necklace? Just a minute and I'll go and get it...."

"I have this little pink box and ribbon left over from Christmas, and I thought you might like to put the necklace in here...."

"That would be great," I said. "Thank you very much," and I handed her a 10-pound note.

"You must have a nice job and be saving your pocket money to buy a nice gift like this."

"I catch fish and rabbits," I replied, my conscience bothering me again.

"Well, she is a very lucky girl to be getting such a beautiful necklace, and you say you catch fish. What type of fish do you catch?"

"Mainly bass, flounder and sole – and mackerel in the summer time. I can even catch skate in the river in the autumn."

"I'll tell you what, Kingsley, next time you catch a nice bass or some flounders, I will buy some from you. I love fresh fish, and usually I have to go all the way to Swansea market to get some."

"Okay," I said excitedly, "I'd like to catch you some fish."

"Okay, Kingsley, I'll see you soon then, and I hope your young lady enjoys the necklace."

"I'm sure she will," I said, "and thank you for the little box. Goodbye now."

"Goodbye, Kingsley."

As soon as I was out of the store, I undid the ribbon on the box and had another look at the cross and the little green stone in the middle. The stone is also known as "Evening Emerald," which was significant to Gay and I, given the evenings we had spent together. Our evenings up on Cefn Bryn were the most wonderful part of our days.

As the morning sun shone upon the little cross, illuminating the "Evening Emerald," it looked so beautiful, and I couldn't wait to give it to Gay tomorrow. "She will love it." I said aloud to the two sheep standing close to the store. "And now I have some orders for fish that I can sell too. It had been a good morning, apart from almost being caught stealing the milk money. Oh well, I had gotten away with it, and that would be the last time I would steal from James.

When I got back to the cave, I picked up my fishing gear and headed off to Pobbles to see where the Thunder Child was. He should be on his morning gallop by now. That would allow me to go and explore his cave, and then I'd do some fishing off the rocks at Three Cliffs Point. The tide was coming in, so it would be perfect for fishing. My goal was to catch a nice sized bass or some flounders, and sell them to Mrs. Davies in the store tomorrow when I went to meet Gay.

The Miracle

That would impress Gay too – to see me selling the fish I'd caught.

To my surprise, Thunder Child was still standing guard at his cave. That was three times this week he'd been standing at his cave instead of being on his usual gallop across the Sands. Maybe he was tired, or just bored from running? No, there must be more to it than that. I knew he enjoyed his gallops as much as I enjoyed my walks. One thing was for sure though, I wasn't going to risk going into his cave while he was standing guard. Not now that we had an understanding between us. After all, he now allows me to walk right under his nose when he's standing guard, and even when he's on his gallop, he doesn't chase me into the sea anymore. Yes, we have built a covenant of trust between us, and I'm not going to betray it.

I decided to go and greet him. "Hello, Thunder Child, it's good to see you, old boy." I gave him an apple, which he accepted, chewing loudly. "I noticed you haven't been on your gallops as much this week. Is everything all right, old boy?" He lowered his head and I patted his neck.

"We are becoming good friends, aren't we?" I continued in a gentle voice. "Do you know what happened yesterday? I had intruders at my cave. I chased them off, though, just like you do when someone comes into your territory. You taught me that, old boy, to stand and defend what's mine. Gay says you and I are alike. We both live out here in the wild, and we don't want to fit in with the crowd. The more I get to know you, the more I think she's right. I don't want to fit in with the crowd anymore. Do you, old boy? You and I are a breed of our own, aren't we." Thunder Child lifted his head up and down a few times and nudged me with his nose. "I'm glad you agree, old boy. Well, bye for now, I'm off to do some fishing."

As I reached Three Cliffs Point, it started to cloud over quickly and a cool mist was coming in from the sea. I hoped that it wouldn't rain, but I couldn't complain if it did. We had enjoyed two weeks of beautiful weather. If it just stayed dry for tomorrow, so Gay and I could go on our picnic, and I could give her the necklace and read her my poem while the weather was nice, I'd be very happy.

I stood right on the end of the rocks and opened my tackle box. As I didn't have any live bait, I decided to use a silver and green red gill lure. The red gill lure is a rubber imitation of a swimming fish or sand eel, and it looks like it's swimming because of the movement of its tail as it's pulled through the water. I've caught a lot of bass on red gills by retrieving the line on my fishing rod at different speeds. Sometimes the bass strike best with a slow-moving action, especially the larger fish. The smaller bass tend to like a faster movement.

Excited, I was all ready to make my first cast, when suddenly I slipped and fell. Desperately I tried to hold onto the rocks, but they were too slippery, and before I knew it I'd fallen into the sea. Trying to catch my breath with the shock of the cold, I tried to swim back to the rocks. I managed to touch them, but I couldn't get a grip; they were too wet and smooth. And the tide was too strong, slowly pulling me away, and then suddenly faster and faster, sweeping me right out to sea!

Somehow I managed to get my boots off and I slowly wriggled out of my heavy coat before it pulled me under. I swam furiously, trying to get back in, but the current was too strong. Panic gripped my soul, as I was getting further and

The Miracle

further out to sea, and my limbs were numb from the cold. I couldn't give up, and I continued to fight the current until I was exhausted.

Lying on my back, I cried out to God, pleading with him to not let me drown. Pictures of me stealing the milk money flashed through my mind, as if God was playing me a recording of my wrongdoing. "I'm sorry God! I'm sorry," I cried. "Please don't let me drown. I've got my whole life ahead of me yet. I'm not ready to die! Please help me get back to shore. I won't steal again."

Just as I finished praying, I felt the current ease, and I was able to swim. The tide had taken me a long way out, and I was at least half a mile down the Sands from where I'd fallen in at Three Cliffs, but strength seemed to come from nowhere, and somehow I was able to slowly make it back to the shore. As I crawled out of the sea, numb with the cold, I could hardly breathe. I had but one thought, and that was to get back to my cave and light a fire.

As I walked, my wet clothes clung to my skin and the wind was icy cold. Trembling, I struggled to inhale. My whole body seemed to be slowing down. Where was I? I couldn't think straight. It felt like I had been walking forever. Time meant nothing. Where was my cave? It had to be around here somewhere. As time went on, I became more confused. Was my cave at this end of the beach, or was it the other way? Looking up to the cliffs, I couldn't see the great Tor. The fog had come in thick and I couldn't see the cliff tops. I stood in a daze. Oh God, help me find my cave, I'm so cold!

Wait! There are the rocks where Thunder Child's cave is. It's this way.

Cave Days

I made it to the rocks, but I just stood there, having completely lost my sense of direction. It was getting harder to breathe, and I was shaking all over. Suddenly I stumbled into the cave and I managed to pull off my wet shirt. I tried to undo my pants, but my fingers were too numb and I didn't have the strength. Please help me! I need to get warm. I can't breathe!

Everything was a blur. I tried to make my way back to the entrance, feeling my way along the walls, but it was too dark to see anything. Which way was the entrance, and was I going deeper into the cave? Suddenly I tripped over something and fell, and I didn't have the strength to get up.

∽

When I woke up, the early morning light was making its way into the cave, and I found myself lying on something warm and furry—and it was moving. My gosh, where was I? …And what was I lying on?

I had come into the cave looking for shelter. That's right, now I remembered. It wasn't my cave. As I continued to lie there, I felt something move across my stomach. My gosh, what was that?! I'm lying on something alive! It's an animal…oh my gosh, it's a horse. I could smell it now, the strong smell of horse in the air. Something continued to move back and forth across my tummy! Half in shock, I slowly moved, sliding gently off the horse's belly and knelt beside what turned out to be a big mare, and she was pregnant. Putting my hand on her tummy, I felt the hoof of her unborn foal.

That's what I had felt when I woke up on her belly. I couldn't believe it. I had tripped and fallen on a horse and spent

The Miracle

the night sleeping on her belly. She had kept me warm through the night, probably saving my life. Surely without her warmth, I would have died of hypothermia. I continued to kneel at her side, and I rubbed her belly. The rays of the morning sun now moved across the cave, illuminating the walls, and then shining on us like a giant flashlight. I could see that she was a beautiful chestnut colour, and as I looked into her eyes, I could see that she wasn't afraid of me. She just lay there, gentle and peaceful like a wise mother. It was as if she knew how much I had needed her help. "Thank you, girl, for keeping me warm and saving my life."

Slowly I stood up and made my way to the entrance of the cave. Suddenly I stopped dead in my tracks. There towering over me was the Thunder Child! That was his mare and unborn foal inside. That's why he had been standing guard outside the cave all this time. Wow. Now if I could just get out of here alive and live to tell the tale.

As I walked out of the entrance in front of him, I half expected him to attack me at any moment, or at least chase me into the sea. Stallions are very protective of their mares, and especially when they are with foal. Should I run for the sea? Or pretend I'm not scared and just keep walking? I chose to believe in our friendship and I walked past him. Holding my head up high, I talked to him as I walked by.

"Hello, Thunder Child, you have a wonderful mare in there, and she saved my life. She's got your baby foal in her tummy. No wonder you stand so tall and proud. Congratulations, old boy. I think it's a baby stallion because he's got a strong kick like you."

As I walked by, he just stood there. It was as if he understood things too. This was working out better than I had anticipated. I thought I would be swimming to Ireland by now, but I continued to walk unchallenged. I talked to him all the way to the sea, and I shouted back; "Thank you, old boy, I didn't feel like swimming to Ireland. Not even for a guinness."

As I walked along the beach towards the Tor, I thought about the events that had happened to me. Having been swept out to sea and surviving was amazing enough. The currents of Three Cliffs Point are among the most dangerous in all of the Gower Peninsula. Many people have been drowned, having been swept out to sea like I was, and many have never been heard of again.

What was that in front of me? It was one of my boots, and there about 100 yards along the beach was my other one. It could easily have been my body that washed up, I thought, as I poured out the cruel sea from my boots. I remembered being too exhausted to swim any more, but somehow I still got back to the shore. It had to be God who saved me.

…And to think that I was numb with the cold and hypothermia, lost and confused, and I woke up on the belly of a pregnant horse. That was what I called a miracle!!!

IT'S SO GOOD TO BE ALIVE

As I walked along the tide line,
The sun's warm kiss fell upon my shoulders,
and I shivered no more!
Above the beach, the Daffodils
Were singing their last yellow songs upon
the cliff tops high.

The Miracle

Two skylarks, drunk with Spring song,
Hovered high above their quiet babies,
Who were snuggled in a secret nest
in the waving blankets of purple
Heather,
Which fragrance thrilled my soul,
And I danced with bumblebee and butterfly,
And sang with the cuckoos chorus and
the collar doves romantic song!
I sang "Thank you, God" for the springtime,
when life is mine,
I am so glad to be alive and part of
your song.
I shall sing and dance all my life long,
For it's so good to be alive.
© *Kingsley Ross Hill*

I continued on my way towards the Tor. In the distance, I saw someone coming towards me. As the figure got closer and closer, I could see it was a girl with long flowing hair. It had to be…?

"Gay!" I shouted, waving my arms. "Gay, it's me!"

"Kingsley!" She shouted back, "Is that you?"

She started running towards me, and she was crying and carrying something under her arm. I could see now that it was my coat.

"Oh Kingsley!" she cried, throwing her arms around me. "I thought you had drowned. I waited at the stables for an hour, and when you didn't come, I knew something must be wrong. So I went to your cave and you weren't there. I found your rods and tackle box on the rock, and then I found this coat. I thought you had drowned! I found it washed up on the beach with a pile of seaweed. Oh Kingsley, thank God you're safe! What happened to you?"

"Gay, all I can tell you is that it's a miracle that I'm still alive. I was swept out to sea, and I nearly drowned, and then Thunder Child's mare saved my life!"

"Thunder Child's mare saved your life? What do you mean?"

"Come and I'll show you." As we walked to the cave, I shared the whole story with Gay.

"Are you serious, Kingsley? The pregnant mare is in the cave?"

"Yes, I am. Just wait till you see her. She's beautiful."

When we arrived at the cave, Thunder Child stood tall and proud as he guarded the entrance.

"Here you are," Gay said, pulling an apple out of her pocket. Thunder Child lowered his head and took the apple from her hand.

"I'm just going to show Gay your mare, old boy," I said, and we went inside.

Oh, my gosh, Kingsley, she *is* beautiful." Gay said, feeling her tummy. "And she is close to giving birth. Put your hand here and you can feel the foal's hoof."

"I know. That's what I felt moving across me when I woke up."

"Kingsley, you are so connected to these horses. Something as wonderful as this doesn't happen to most people in a lifetime. I do believe God saved your life, and he used this mare to do it. My gosh, look at her, Kingsley." We sat quietly for a

The Miracle

few minutes pondering the miracle. "Do you know how many people have drowned off Three Cliffs?" Gay replied wiping the last of her tears away.

I was silent as the reality of God's role in saving my life sank in.

Gay held me tightly and began to tear up again. "I don't know what I would have done if I'd lost you. I love you so much, and I wouldn't want to live my life without you."

"I love you too, Gay. Don't cry. I'm safe now here in your arms."

"You know when you told me about the message in a bottle, Kingsley—well, I wanted to believe that God could be that personal, but for some reason I couldn't. But now I know that God is looking after you. He is watching and keeping you safe!"

"You know, Gay, when I was exhausted out at sea, I had no strength to swim in, and all of a sudden there was like a voice in my heart and a sense of peace, and somehow I was given the strength to swim to shore. Then when I woke up this morning on the mare's belly, I felt this feeling of belonging like I've never felt in my life. It was like I didn't completely belong to myself anymore. I know my life is worth more now," I said.

Just then, the mare lifted up her head and made a noise, as if she was trying to speak to us.

"I think she's agreeing with what you just said, Kingsley, but I'm worried about her. I don't understand why she came in here to give birth instead of being in the Valley with grass and water around her. Maybe she's sick, or maybe Thunder Child wanted her here for protection, knowing how hostile the other horses are to him."

Cave Days

"Yes, but there is plenty of grazing grass in the Valley, and Thunder Child and his family could stay on the other side of the river, away from the main herd," I said. "Anyway, I think we should find some food for the mare. She seems weak. Let's go to Pennard stores and get some carrots. Pennard stores are closer than going all the way back to Penmaen."

"Good idea," said Gay. "Let's get a bag of apples too."

As we left the cave, Thunder Child had started on his gallop to Oxwich. We could see him in the distance. As we walked along the beach, Gay took my hand. It felt so good to feel her hand in mine. I stopped and held her close and kissed her.

"Oh Kingsley, I was so worried."

"I was too." We kissed again, for what seemed like a whole springtime. Finally coming up for air, we continued on our way to Pennard stores.

We bought a five-pound bag of carrots and a bag of apples. I bought Gay one of my favourite Cornish pasties and a pop for lunch. We sat and ate our lunch overlooking Pobbles Beach, and in the distance we could see Thunder Child, thundering his way back across the Sands from Oxwich.

The warm Sun shone upon our faces, and Gay's hair pressed gently against my face in the spring wind. Her fragrance was sweeter than the wild Gorse flower, even more lovely than the dew-wet Roses in my grandmother's garden in the spring, where smell and memory do not separate, but hold hands and kiss forever. I am a King on high, sitting with my Princess. I thought of the necklace that I had bought for Gay, and I couldn't wait to give it to her, and look into her eyes, and read her my poem. I would do it tonight at my cave, before the sun went down.

The Miracle

We finished our lunch and got back to the cave. Thunder Child stood on guard again after his gallop. We fed him some carrots and another apple before going back into the cave. It was a great feeling to be bonding with my stallion, and I dared to believe what the old man had said. "He will choose you, boy, and you will be a true knight of Gower."

The mare crunched the carrots and apples like she hadn't eaten in weeks. Gay still thought there must be something wrong with her, as she was this hungry and hadn't left the cave for food. "We must keep a watch on her and feed her every day. She will need grass and water too," Gay said.

"I have a bucket at my cave," I replied, "and we can get water from the Killy Willy." Gay and I returned to my cave. We then carried a bucket of water from the river to the mare. She drank most of the water right away, obviously very thirsty.

Gay stayed with the mare while I filled up the bucket again. When I arrived back with the water, Gay said that we needed to help the mare stand up.

"She can't remain lying down, Gay said, otherwise her foal could die inside her. Come on Kings, help me to push on her side and get her to stand up." Gay and I pushed for what felt like a long time, and it seemed the mare was too weak to stand. "Come on Kings, keep pushing!" Gay said, "we have to get her up." Finally the mare made a grunting noise and climbed to her feet.

"She's standing," I said excitedly. "What do we do now?"

"Lets walk her slowly around the cave," Gay replied, "so that she can get some exercise. This will also help her with the birthing and strengthen her legs." We walked the mare around in a circle inside the cave for about ten minutes. Suddenly her legs began to shake and she stopped walking. "Lets help her back down to the ground," Gay said, "she's too tired to walk anymore." Slowly the mare layed back on the ground, and we both rubbed her tummy.

It was interesting, I thought, that the mare had saved my life, and now maybe I was helping to save hers. Gay was like a mother, fussing around the mare, rubbing her tummy and kissing her head.

"Kingsley, she is so beautiful. We will have to name her."

"How about Thunder Cloud? It goes with Thunder Child, and when her foal is born, we could name him or her Little Thunder."

"I like that. Little Thunder is the perfect name for the foal. Hmm how about Thunder Spring for the mare? Because she saved your life in the spring, and you introduced me to her in the spring."

"I like it," I said, "and it has more meaning than Thunder Cloud."

Gay laughed happily. "I feel like we have our own horse family," she said.

"We do," I said, and I kissed her.

"Oh, Kingsley, I could stay out here with you forever."

"Thank you for being my cavewoman," I said, and we both laughed.

As the afternoon grew into evening, we headed back to my cave. I made Gay close her eyes and sit at the entrance, while I went inside to get the necklace.

"Can I open my eyes?" She shouted.

The Miracle

"No, keep them shut." I shouted back as I snuck up behind her and put my hands over her eyes.

"What is it?" She giggled. "Come on, what are you doing?"

I sat right behind her, with my legs at her side. Gay lay back into my arms and rested her head on my chest, and I felt like such a rich man.

"Here you are." I said, putting the little box onto her lap.

"Can I open my eyes now?" She asked, leaning forward and looking back at me, her face blushing like the warm Sun.

"Yes, you can open them now," I said, putting my arms around her again and holding her tight.

She gently pulled on the ribbon and opened the box. Then she picked up the little chain and cross, and slowly laid it out in the palm of her hand.

"Oh, Kingsley! It's so beautiful. I love it. It's even got my birthstone on the cross. How did you know which one?"

"I'll never tell." I kissed the side of her neck.

"Oh Kingsley, thank you. I will treasure it forever."

"I'm happy you like it, and I have something else for you," I said, pulling the poem from my pocket. "I wrote this for you, I hope you like it."

"Oh my gosh," she said, her face blushing again, this time as red as the sunset. "Well, are you going to read it to me?"

"Yes I am."

Looking deep into Gay's eyes that were like a falling waterfall, I felt her love as I fell deeper and deeper into her abyss, and we danced.

Cave Days

THE GIRL WITH THE SUNSHINE IN HER HAIR

The spring wind blew cold, swirling through my hair, as I opened the post-office door.

I turned and looked because you were there, the girl with the sunshine in her hair.

I stood behind you, beholding a beautiful woman in riding boots, and horse tail hair.

I forgot what I came into the store for, and I tried not to stare! But there in front of me stood the girl with the sunshine in her hair.

Her voice is soft and gentle, and I tremble because I care. I haven't even seen your face yet, and I love you oh girl with the sunshine in your hair. When you turn around will you see me there? And will you care for this green eyed boy with the dark curly hair?

Suddenly you turn around, and you also stare! And your purple eyes sparkle, and seem to say, I care, I care! And still I try not to stare. And you say my name, "Kingsley...and your smile melts me there. And I want you, and I need you. Oh girl with the sunshine in her hair.

Oh, my soul, look! Look, she is there, my soul sings, and my heart skips, and I dance within, for I have met the girl with the sunshine in her hair.

Well, Kingsley, I must go now, she says. Wait, wait!

The Miracle

My heart cries. I want to come with you, and know what our souls can share! Don't go my love, with the sunshine in your hair, for I shall stand here again in the cold, if you are not there.

I will run and catch you. For what I feel for you is far greater than my fear! No, I will let you go my love, and believe that your soul has also heard.

And you will come back to me, as we walk through the years. For I know your soul also hears. Today I celebrate a love that is here, a love between a man and a woman so dear. I love you Gay! The girl with the sunshine in her hair.

© Kingsley Ross Hill

I looked into her eyes again as I read her my last line. She cried and smiled, and my heart melted as I felt my love for her pouring out of me. For moments – or was it months and years, or forever? – Our souls spoke and reached for one another.

"Kingsley, I love you so much. You are the love of my life!"

I held her face in my hands and kissed her, and whispered, "I love you too, oh love of my life!"

We kissed through eternity, and then I walked her back to the village to meet her mother. Gay said she would come and meet me each night after school, so we could care for Thunder Spring. After sharing with her mum what had happened, her mum agreed to her coming after school, as long as it wasn't too late.

"Bye Kingsley, I'll see you tomorrow."

"Bye Gay, bye Mrs. Tripp," I said with the thought of her kiss still lingering on my lips.

Chapter Fifteen

Welcome to the World

From my deep sleep, I stirred, and climbed out of my dreams of Gay, and horses, and swimming in the sea in the warm Sun. I climbed to the top of the Tor to have breakfast, and to look out across the golden Sands where the Prince and Princess kiss and hold hands.

Suddenly the Sun rose, making the sea orange, and the Rocks shone like gold, and I danced as the Sun continued to climb his ladder to the sky. As he passed the clouds, he shouted "Good morning on high," and I felt his smile upon my skin glow… And I shouted out, "Good morning, Sunshine, I'm in love, you know!" And he shouted back, "I know, I know, I'm happy for you, Kingsley. Bye for now, I must go." And he went across the sky, and he looked almost as happy as I.

Finishing my breakfast, I walked back down to my cave. I don't have to wait a whole week this time, I thought. Gay will be coming after school to check on Thunder Spring with me. For a few minutes I thought intensely about Thunder Spring, and sensed she was close to giving birth. Shall I check on her before going fishing? Collecting my fishing gear, I headed off to see her.

Welcome to the World

Thunder Child stood on guard as I gave him an apple before going inside. "Good morning, old boy," I said, rubbing the side of his head. "How are you? Did you have a good night? It looks like a beautiful day for your gallop across the Sands. One day I would love to come with you, and ride on your back, and thunder across the beach. That is, if you don't buck me off, old boy."

I went inside the cave to see the mare. She seemed to be lying in the same spot as where Gay and I had left her the previous evening. Kneeling down beside her, I rubbed her tummy and spoke to her. "Hello Thunder Spring, and good morning to you girl." She looked at me with her big brown eyes, and I continued to talk. "Thunder Child has been standing guard outside, my girl, and he sends his love. He's going for his gallop across the beach soon, and then he will be back to watch over you. Meanwhile I thought I would come and visit you, I didn't want you to feel lonely in here. I know what that feels like, and it's not nice is it?" She neighed quietly as if answering me."

Suddenly she seemed restless and lifted her head up and down with her eyes fixed on mine, as if beckoning my help. "What is it girl?" I said gently. "Do you need my help?" She nieghed loudly and then grunted, as if saying yes.

Then I saw it! There was part of the little foal's hoof sticking out of her. I turned on my flashlight and looked closer. My gosh, she was starting to give birth. What should I do? I wanted to run and get Gay, but she was far away at school. I got up and started to walk to the entrance. Thunder Spring lifted her head and made a noise that tugged at my heart, as if she didn't want me to leave. "It's all right, girl," I reassured her. "I will be right back." As I reached the entrance, I could see Thunder Child in the distance. He had started his gallop. "It's happening," I shouted, half expecting him to turn around and come back.

I walked out to the middle of the beach, in the hope that Gay had left school early and was on her way to the cave. There wasn't anyone around, only Thunder Child, who was now a speck in the distance. "Come back!" I shouted again.

"Oh well, I guess it's only me here," I said to myself, and I went back inside. Now there were two hooves and a whole head coming out, and a bag of skin and blood. I began to tremble with excitement. She was giving birth right now, and I was here to see it. Suddenly Thunder Spring lifted her head and made a deep grunting noise, and slowly and gently, out came the rest of the foal. The foal was half covered in the bag of skin and blood. Then Thunder Spring rolled over and climbed to her feet. What looked like an umbilical cord was still attached to her and the foal. She started licking and cleaning her newborn. The whole process had taken around 15 minutes from start to finish. After a few minutes, Little Thunder, as Gay and I had named him, scrambled to his feet and tried to stand. He stood and fell, and then stood up again and wobbled. This time he was up, and I shouted, "Well done, Thunder Spring, and well done, Little Thunder. Welcome to the world!"

I jumped and shouted in excitement, and I ran out from the entrance onto the beach to see if Thunder Child was back from his gallop. I could see him coming, but he was still a distance away, so I went back into the cave. Thunder Spring and Little Thunder were making their way to the entrance, and I stood against the wall of the cave as they passed and then followed behind them out onto the beach.

Welcome to the World

Just as Little Thunder was taking his first steps into this new, exciting world, Thunder Child arrived back. He shook his head up and down and neighed proudly as he slowed to a stop. He then smelled his son and nudged him with his nose, and said, "Welcome, my son, into the world!" I watched from the rocks, and my soul praised God for the miracle of birth. I thanked him for allowing me to be such a part of it.

Thunder Spring had given Thunder Child a wonderful son. "He's a baby stallion, Thunder Child," I shouted out. "Well done, old boy, and congratulations."

Thunder Spring stood still as Little Thunder drank his first milk from his mother. I stood and glowed in the joy of Little Thunder's birth for about an hour, and then I followed behind as Thunder Child led his new family across the Sands to the Three Cliffs Valley.

They stopped at the Killy Willy and drank before moving up the valley to graze. I followed closely, crossing the cool of the river and on up to the grazing area, for I was part of this new family too. After a short rest, Thunder Child led us to the Valley on the left side of the Killy Willy. He could see that the Three Cliffs herd was grazing on the other side of the river, including the other stallion who had often chased him away.

"Hey, you other stallion!" I shouted out, my voice echoing across the Valley. "You wouldn't dare to try to chase him away now, would you. There is only one true King in the Valley now, and that is Thunder Child." I shouted now at the top of my lungs, and Thunder Child's name echoed back across the valley three times, like clashes of thunder, and I said to myself, "I am sure he knows how proud of him I am."

Cave Days

For the next few hours, I stayed in the Valley and watched Little Thunder sleep, play and explore what it was like to be a horse and to be free. Thunder Spring grazed on the new shoots of grass, and Thunder Child often lifted his head, keeping a wary eye on the other stallion on the other side of the river.

It was time for me to eat too. So I headed back to my cave for lunch. It was now close to two o'clock in the afternoon, and the spring sun shone warm on the horses and me. On top of the Tor, the Ferns were growing taller as they reached for the sun. Most of the Daffodils were gone now, their life songs hidden away deep within their bulbs, as they waited for the next spring. But the Bluebells were in full bloom, and I walked over to a white one and said good afternoon. All his friends were blue, but he loved his colour; it made him feel like the bridegroom.

The yellow Gorse flower was beginning to lose its sweet spring fragrance, as summer's breath swept over the valley. Oh well, I would have to smell the sweet smell of my Gay all the more. There were still three hours before it was time to meet her, so I decided to go fishing, and to fill my fish order for Mrs. Davies in the general store.

I started fishing where the Killy Willy joined the sea. The tide was a long way out, but had just started to come in. Casting a soft crab into the river, and allowing the current to take it out to sea, I held my rod tight in anticipation.

In my experience, the larger bass only strike once or twice, and if you miss the strike and don't set the hook, you rarely get another chance at the same fish, although I once caught a larger bass with another hook in his mouth. I guess he wasn't once bitten and twice shy.

Welcome to the World

My line had been in the water for about 20 minutes, and I still hadn't gotten a strike. Some days you didn't get any strikes when it came to salmon bass; they just weren't in the area where you were fishing. But the mouth of the Killy Willy was generally quite productive, especially during the spring and summer months.

Catching flounders and sole was a lot easier, of course. There were often a lot of them feeding in the churned up sand at the river's mouth, but today I wanted to catch a nice bass to start off my fish orders. I could probably get paid five pounds for a good one.

After winding in and casting out several times, I wondered if I would have to resort to catching flounders. If there were bass around, they weren't biting. As the last of the afternoon sun warmed my face, I dreamed of the summer months and the arrival of the mackerel. In early July, sometimes even earlier, the mackerel arrive off the Gower coast. They travel around in huge shoals. Hundreds come in close to the rocks, and I would cast my feathers or spinners into the bubbling mass of fish. I have many wonderful memories of catching them with my brother Fraser. Once we caught over 100, and we went door to door in Pennard village selling them. In those happy fishing days, it was those of us who caught the first mackerel of the season that made most of the money. After a few weeks of the season, you couldn't give them away.

Suddenly I felt a strong tug on my rod tip. Quickly I lifted the head of my rod up to feel the bite. Yes, he was on alright, and starting to run. Keeping the tension on my line, I let the fish run. As soon as he stopped running, I wound in, keeping the tension on. The dorsal fin broke the surface, and I could see it was a beautiful bass. I held my rod up, holding the weight of the fish, and I brought the landing net up underneath with my left hand. Then he was safely in the net.

"Yes!" I shouted to a black-backed gull who was sitting nearby, hoping to get a piece of the action. I took the bass to the river's edge and gutted it. I left the head and tail on it, so Mrs. Davies could see how big it was, and when Gay saw the size of it, I'd be a hero.

Time was getting on, so I dropped my gear off at the cave and carried my proud catch to the village. I wanted to show my bass to Gay and Mrs Tripp before I took it into the store to sell.

Gay and her mum finally arrived. "Well, what a beauty!" exclaimed Mrs. Tripp. "Yes, what a nice catch." Gay echoed.

"I caught it about an hour ago, I said. "I had promised Mrs. Davies in the store that I'd catch her one."

Gay's mom said goodbye and we were on our way to the store.

"I'm really proud of you, Kingsley," Gay said, taking my hand.

"Thanks," I said, landing a kiss on her lips.

We opened the door and went into the store.

"Oh my word, Kingsley, how big is it?"

"About eight pounds, Mrs. Davies."

"Now, how much do I owe you?"

"Well, I would like to get some more orders from you, Mrs. Davies, so I'll give you a good price on the bass."

"How about five pounds, Kingsley, and I'll put in another order for next week."

Welcome to the World

"That's fair, thank you very much," and she handed me a crisp five-pound note from the till.

"And how do you like your Celtic Cross necklace?" she asked Gay. "I happen to know this young man thinks the world of you."

"Oh I love it." Gay replied, blushing.

As Gay looked at me and smiled, I felt like the wealthiest man in the world, and it was such a good feeling to have sold the fish and earned some honest money. I left the store with my Princess in one hand, and a five-pound note in the other. "I've got the money, honey, if you've got the time."

"I've got the time, baby. Let's go."

Five steps down the road, Gay turned to me and said, "Now tell me about Thunder Spring. How is she doing?"

"Oh my goodness, I forgot to tell you. Are you ready for this?"

"No, no, don't tell me Kingsley. She didn't!"

"She did. She had her foal today."

"Oh no, I missed it. I dreamt she had her foal last night. Kingsley, I'm so disappointed that I missed the birth. Is it a baby stallion or a mare?"

"It's a..."

"No, no. Don't tell me," she said, covering my mouth. "I want this part to be a surprise!"

"Okay, I won't tell you."

"Are they still in the cave?"

"No, Thunder Child took his family to the valley. Come on, I'll show you."

We climbed down the dunes and on to the beach. When we arrived at the valley, Thunder Child seemed wary and uneasy as we approached, but once he recognized us, he lowered his head to graze again.

"Oh my gosh, Kingsley, it's a baby stallion. Thunder Child has a son. Somehow I knew it was going to be a boy, and look at Thunder Spring. She doesn't look like she's lacking any strength now."

We sat at a distance and watched for a while, before Gay called out, "Here you are, Thunder Child," and she pulled an apple out of her pocket.

To my surprise, Thunder Child lifted his head at the call of his name and came over and took the apple from Gay's hand. Thunder Spring and Little Thunder soon followed, and Gay gave the last apple to the proud mother. Little Thunder came and suckled milk from his mother, as Gay and I stood just a few yards away.

"He's just beautiful, Kingsley, look at him." No sooner had Gay finished speaking, when Little Thunder came right up to us and sniffed us with his brand new nose, and we both patted his shining new fur. "Oh, my gosh, Kingsley, oh my gosh, look at him."

I'd never seen Gay so excited. "I didn't think Thunder Child would let us come this close," I said.

"He obviously trusts us. As you said, we are part of his family now, and he knows it."

All of a sudden we heard the call of the other stallion across the river. Thunder Child's ears perked up instantly, and raising his head, he shouted out his own claim in horse language that Gay and I could both understand.

"That was his reply to the challenge of the other stallion," we both said at the same time.

Welcome to the World

...And Thunder Child said, "Just you try and cross the river, and I'll come after you." Thunder Child stood tall and proud as he fixed his gaze on the other stallion.

"Yes, I think he looks bigger, and definitely more proud, since he's become a father," Gay said.

"I agree, he does look bigger, and one day soon he's going to challenge the other stallion for the leadership of the Three Cliffs herd."

"Have you ever seen two stallions fight?" Gay asked.

"Yes, once when I was a boy. My father took me out to watch them, and I thought they were going to kill each other!"

"How about you?"

"No, I've never seen a fight, but I've heard they can fight to the death, unless one of them backs off."

"Well, one thing I know, our Thunder Child isn't going to back off, or run away from him again. Not only will he fight, but he will win."

"I think you're right. I just hope he doesn't get badly wounded in the fight. He's got a family to look after now."

We stayed with our horse family until dusk, and I walked back with Gay to the village. When Mrs. Tripp arrived, Gay told her of our adventures.

"That's wonderful, Kingsley."

"Yes, Mrs. Tripp, it was amazing, and it was a baby stallion too. Gay and I named him Little Thunder."

"Oh, and before I forget, Kingsley. Could you catch us a fish? I'd be happy to pay you for it. My husband and I love fresh fish.

"Yes, Mrs. Tripp, I'd be happy to catch one for you."

"Thank you, Kingsley, and you can call me Helen."

"Okay, Mrs. Tripp, thank you. I mean Helen." Gay and I both laughed.

The car pulled away, and I was a hero. What an incredible day. I'd made money, and I also had two more orders, although I wouldn't charge Gay's mum for the fish. That is, unless she insisted on it.

It was a night to celebrate. My life was getting brighter and brighter, just like the days of spring. Since I had met Gay, my whole outlook had changed.

I celebrated by having a fire outside my cave. How different it was, to have a fire of celebration, rather than a fire to chase away my fears and gloom at Bacon Hole. Thank you, God, for shining your light into my life, and taking away my darkness.

The night air was cool and clear, and the moon reflected its light on a circle of sparkling sea, out on the bay. It looked like an enchanted pool, with silver dancing ripples, where mermaids swim and watch the night skies. The Knights of the Round Table bathe and soothe their wounds, their strength regained in the silver light, as they ready for the next battle protecting the Gower.

"Tis true, boy! The Gower, she has many secrets."

"Yes Sir, she does!"

"You ride the stallion, boy, and you will see much more."

As I threw another log on the fire, I couldn't remember a time when I had felt so happy as I did now.

Slowly, the night clouds came and tucked away the day in their blankets, and this special day fell asleep and dreamed with me, under my fur blanket.

Those dreams have never really ended. They are tucked away in my memory chest, to be brought out again and again, along life's path. Sometimes they come out all on their own, just to say good morning, or to take away November's grey. Yes, days like this last forever, and in our souls they come to stay, and we only take out one at a time, one per rainy day.

For the next few days, Gay came to spend time with me after school. We stayed in the valley, watching our horse family learn and grow. On Wednesday evening, the other stallion dared to come halfway across the river. Thunder Child stared for a moment, and then thundered into the river after him, chasing him away.

Gay and I both shouted, "Thunder Child, hooray."

For the next few hours, both stallions stood at each side of the river watching each other.

"Thunder Child is getting ready to challenge the other stallion for the herd," said Gay.

"I think you're right, Gay. In fact, I'm sure of it. Did you see how quickly he went into the river chasing him away?"

"Yes, and it's going to be a terrible battle when they fight. I'm afraid for Thunder Child. He's big and strong, but so is the other stallion. What if he gets badly hurt?"

"He'll know when he's ready," I said.

On Thursday evening, Gay stayed home with her family. She had told me the day before that her mother and father had something important to talk to her and her sister about. I decided to go and visit Fraser at the house, and do my laundry and have a nice bath. As usual I watched the house for a while from the back field, to see if my father was home. Though I was free to come and go as I liked, I was always aware of my father's wishes. Knowing that, in his heart, he wanted me to go and live with Grandma and Grandpa, or at least get a job, made me feel awkward around him.

From the field, I couldn't see anyone in the house. I climbed over the hedge and went around to the front door. My Dad's car wasn't there, just Fraser's motorcycle. I opened the door and went inside.

"Fraser," I called out.

"Kings!" I heard him call back from upstairs. "I'll be right down. How are you doing, Kings?" he asked, as he ran down the stairs.

"Great, Fraser, and how are you?"

"Oh, I'm doing good. Work is going well, and I've almost paid off my motorcycle loan."

"Well done." I said, feeling a bit envious.

"And I'm going to buy a car next, Kings, as soon as the bike's paid off."

Instantly I went into a daydream and imagined driving Gay around the countryside in my own car. Suddenly my father's words echoed in my heart. "If you apply yourself, Kings, you can get a job and buy yourself a motorcycle or a car. If you work hard for six months, I'll loan you the money for a down payment."

My father's words were appealing to me in a way they hadn't been for a long time. Since I'd met Gay, I found I desired to do more in my life, and achieve what my brother and peers were doing in their lives. I heard my best friend Mitch's mother's words again: "Our Mitch has finished school, and is going to be starting university, Kings!" What a contrast to me, leaving school. On the last day of school, my headmaster offered me a £10 note if I promised never to come back to Gowerton School again.

"You're the worst behaved pupil since 1968, and we don't want you back." There wasn't much humour left now in being a high school kick-out.

Welcome to the World

My brother spoke and woke me from my daydream. "How's your girlfriend doing, Kings? All the boys in the village are jealous because you're going out with Gay Tripp."

My heart started smiling again at the mention of her name. "Oh, she's great Fraser. She's more wonderful and beautiful than I could ever tell you."

"Her sister was in the village the other day, Kings, and she told Mitch that Gay is madly in love with you, and you're all she ever talks about." Now I was beaming. "I don't know how you do it. You live on the cliffs like a wild man. You have no job or income, and yet the most beautiful girl on the Gower Peninsula is in love with you. Only you could do it, Kings, only my brother."

"Thanks Fraser, I'll take the compliment, mate."

"Oh, and another thing, Kings, Gay's sister said you gave Gay a silver necklace, and she hasn't taken it off since. How could you afford that if you're not working?"

"I am working," I said. "I'm selling fish now. I've got two more orders for bass this week."

"You're a great fisherman and hunter, there's no disputing that. No one could do what you're doing, living out there in the wild."

"Thanks, Fraser, you don't know what that means to me, to hear you say that. I love you, man."

"I love you too, Kings."

"Listen, there is one more thing, Kings. James came round and talked to Dad. He said you've been stealing the milk money, only he can't prove it. The police are involved now too. They're looking out for whoever's doing it."

"What did Dad say when James came over?"

"He told him to get off the property and not come back."

"Dad said that?"

"Yes, he did. He really is there for you, you know. He hasn't forgotten about your magpie. He told James if anything, he should be paying you damages."

"He really said that?"

"Yeah, he did, Kings. I was standing right next to him when James was at the door."

"I feel 1 million pounds richer, Fraser, after hearing that. Thanks for telling me. Dad really went to bat for me, didn't he? I'm feeling so good right now. I wish I'd brought some beer, and we could celebrate."

"There's cider in the fridge. We can have that. I'll get us some."

Fraser handed me the cold bottle. "Here, try this, it's Woodpecker. Your favourite, remember?"

"I remember alright," I said, taking a nice long gulp. "I don't often get a treat like this. It's mainly just the basics out on the cliffs. But Gay makes some wonderful picnics! Then I eat really well."

"Let's sit on the couch, and we can have a few more ciders while you're doing your laundry."

"That's great, Fraser, I appreciate being able to get my clothes washed."

"Well, one does have to keep up appearances, even when you're a cave man, if you're dating Gay Tripp," Fraser quipped.

"Yes, especially when you're courting Gay Tripp," I echoed back, and we both laughed.

"Now tell me about James. I don't care if you robbed him. So did you do it?"

"Of course I did it. I robbed him twice."

"Good for you, Kings, and I hope you got a decent amount. No money can compensate for what he did to Jerry. All the kids in the neighbourhood loved him, and you were heartbroken. You were home from school for two weeks, remember, Kings?"

"Yes, I remember alright. I'll never forget. I can't rob James any more, though, or I'll get caught. I almost got caught the second time. I had to jump into the bushes and hide to escape."

"It's good that you know when to quit. You've given him something to think about, and made a bit of money too. Well done, Kings, here's another cider."

"Thanks, Fraser. I think the wash is done."

"Just chuck them in the dryer and they should be done in about 40 minutes."

"How's Dad?" I asked, as I threw the clothes in the dryer.

"Oh, he's fine. He left for Devonshire this morning to visit Grandma and Grandpa. He said he'd be back on Sunday. Why don't you stay the night, Kings, and I can give you a ride to Penmaen again in the morning."

"That would be great, Fraser. Thanks."

Chapter Sixteen

Orange and Indigo

Fraser dropped me off at Penmaen in the morning as planned, and I carried my bag of clothes to my cave. It had really been great to spend time with Fraser, and now I could put on some nice clean clothes for Gay. She would be coming to meet me after school. I wondered what her mother and father had wanted to talk to her about. Hopefully not me, after all, I didn't have the greatest reputation in the community. Not only was I 'The Wild boy', but now a suspected milk money robber. Oh well, I have other qualities, and titles too, like 'Knight of the Gower'.

I decided to rest in my cave for the morning and then go fishing in the afternoon. It would be great to catch a bass for Gay's mother, and give it to her when I went to meet Gay at the village. She'd be impressed that I filled her order so soon.

The tide was about halfway in when I started to fish. I fished in the same area as I had on Wednesday, right where the Killy Willy joins the sea at Three Cliffs. I used a soft crab for bait this time, and a float so I could see the line moving out in the current.

Orange and Indigo

The current of the river soon took my line out to where I wanted it, about 50 yards out to sea above the river bed. Tightening the drag on my reel, I sat down and watched my float bobbing in the tide. A few times it went down beneath the waves and came up again slowly—probably just the drag of the tide, or a piece of weed on the line. Then suddenly it went down fast and there was a bend in my rod. I pulled gently so as not to pull the hook out of the fish's mouth, while also keeping the tension on the line so the fish wouldn't throw the hook. It was a bass alright, and a good-sized one. He started to make a run, and keeping the tension on the line, I let him run. He continued to run and I was running out of line on my reel. Adjusting the spool on the reel, I increased the drag on the line. After that, the fish tired, and I began to wind him in. I brought him in closer and closer as I watched for his dorsal fin to break the surface.

"There it is, and it's a big one." I shouted out loud. Continuing to pull in gently, I brought the bass into shore. Then dropping my rod, I pounced on the bass amidst the waves. This was worth getting wet for. I had him and he was about 10 pounds.

I gutted the bass in the river, and then headed off to the village to meet Gay.

There were a few people walking out on the Burrows as I strode past with my proud catch. "That's one nice fish," people commented, and I was getting more excited to give the bass to Gay's mum. It's wonderful what catching a nice bass can do for your self-esteem.

I waited in the village for them to arrive.

Cave Days

"Oh, what a lovely fish." Gay's mum said. "Look at the size of it."

"I just caught it, Helen," I said.

"Well, thank you Kingsley, and here's five pounds."

"You don't need to pay me for it, Mrs. Tripp. I'm happy to catch you one."

"Come on Kingsley, take the money, it would cost me three times that amount to buy it, and a trip into town."

"Well thank you, Mrs. Tripp, I mean Helen!"

Gay was unusually quiet, and I wondered what was wrong.

"Bye, Kingsley, and remember you two, don't be late."

As Gay and I walked towards the valley, she continued to be quiet, and I could feel that her spirit was heavy.

"What is it, Gay? I can feel you're troubled."

She tried to get some words out and then began to cry. "Kingsley," she sobbed, "I'm going to have to move away."

"What do you mean, move away?" I choked back, feeling instant pain in my heart.

Gay cried uncontrollably. "My dad's taken a job up in England, and we're moving in September."

I felt numb inside as she continued. "They have the house up for sale already."

"What do you mean, moving away?" I said again, holding back the tears, and continuing to feel pain in my heart.

"I have to move away to England. I can't believe it. Do you remember when I was up at the horse show? Well, my mum and dad saw this house and fell in love with it. And my dad applied for a transfer to work out there, and he got accepted. They even offered him a promotion if he moved to the area. I'm not going. I'm going to run away. They didn't even consider me or my sister. They just sat us down on Thursday night and read us our rights with no discussion.'We are moving to England, girls'. I'm not going! I'm going to stay here with you. They can't do this to me. My life is here on Gower."

What could I say back? I felt stunned at the thought of losing Gay. If she moved to England, I'd never see her.

We walked on in heavy silence. It was like a death. Wake me up from this nightmare, please. I'd been the happiest I'd ever been in my life, and now this.

Gay spoke up again. "I love you Kingsley. My life is here with you, and I'm not going"

"I love you too, Gay, and everything is going to be all right. It's only May, and we have the whole summer together yet. We've got plenty of time to come up with a plan."

"I'm not going Kingsley. I'm not leaving you."

"I know, and somehow it's all going to work out. I'm going to think about this. We love each other, and no one is going to take that away from us."

"Kingsley, promise me you won't let them take me away from yo.!"

"I promise." I took her in my arms and kissed her like I'd never kissed her before.

"I love you so much, Kingsley. You're my life, and Thunder Child and Thunder Spring, and Little Thunder are my family. See, I'm as wild as you now, my prince."

"I don't know about that," I said, "I'm crazy too," and we both laughed. "So no more tears."

"No more tears," she echoed back, and she kissed me.

The heavy cloud that had hung over us was gone, at least for now, and we carried on with our day. It still seemed strange not to see Thunder Child on his daily gallops, thundering across the Sands to Oxwich.

I noticed people were coming down to the beach more often, now that it was lighter in the mornings. People were walking their dogs before going to work, and even coming down with picnics and staying for the day. I could understand Thunder Child not wanting to come down to the beach, with all these people going by. He would get tired of chasing them into the sea. I could always give him a hand though. Go back to my cave and get my Bowie knife and spear.

"And get arrested at the same time," Gay added.

"Yes, but for a good cause, don't you think?" We both laughed.

"Yes, I suppose I must learn to share this paradise." I said.

"Thunder Child is a family man now. He's got better things to do than stand outside his cave and chase people."

"Yes, you're right, he sure does, and I have you to take care of now."

"Oh really, wild man? This girl can take care of herself out here now."

"Oh can you now, Princess," I said, landing a kiss on her lips.

"No, Kings, I can't. I need you to take care of me, and kiss me like this forever, and as long as I can run free with you and the horses, I'm a happy girl."

We spent the rest of the day as we always did, walking hand-in-hand, running and laughing, only now we walked barefoot on the warm sand, and danced in the waves. For "blazing June" was upon us, and we sang the songs of May.

Orange and Indigo

LOVE AND COLOURS

Kingsley and Gay, and May

Blazing June and the glorious May came out one
day to play.
They played with King and danced with Gay
on the most beautiful summer's day.
We held hands, and ran, and sang, and fell,
and loved, and rode the sea on wild horses that
took us to lands far and near.
There we swam and kissed in mermaid pools!
And climbed rainbows to clouds above,
where we lay in heathered meadows and
shared the secrets of young love.
A place where time stands still, where there is only now
and tomorrow's shadow never falls.
It is where the four winds blow, and only two may go.
Past to present, and present to past,
all together in one big "know!"
One is orange, and the other Indigo.
They are the colours of our love, you know!
Yes my love, I know.
I know you are orange, and I am Indigo,
And together we make the most wonderful rainbow.
Yes my love, I know,
I know I am orange, and you are Indigo.
I love you Indigo.
© Kingsley Ross Hill

After watching the sunset, which had become a tradition for us, we walked back to the village to meet Gay's mother.

"Oh Kingsley, I want to be able to see you next weekend, but I have exams the following week at school, and my parents are making me stay home the whole weekend to study."

"But I will see you the following weekend, right?" I asked, feeling insecure. I'd had enough bad news for the day.

"Yes, of course," she answered, and then kissed me. For a few minutes I felt better again.

"Bye Gay, bye Helen."

"Bye Kingsley, see you in two weeks."

As I headed back across the Burrows, Gay's words "see you in two weeks" echoed back and forth from my heart, where I felt pain, to my head, where I tried to reason why Gay hadn't said she would try and see me some evenings this coming week. Could she go two weeks without us seeing each other and feel okay with that? Or could she really not get away because of her studies? Well, her mother and father were certainly serious when it came to her applying herself to her school work, that was for sure, unlike me who was a high school kick-out. My folks were doing well if I even showed up for school, yet alone passed any exams.

Gay had often shared with me about how she had to pass exams, otherwise she would lose her riding privileges. I guess I was just feeling sorry for myself, and the thought of losing her at the end of the summer was really starting to hit me again. I had done so well being strong for us throughout our day, trying to focus on our present time together, but now the future seemed such a haunted place to go, for this teenager in love. I tried to cheer myself up by thinking of the summer holidays. They were only a month away now, and then we could see each other every day, not just on weekends.

For the next several days, I went up to the stables and practised riding Blaze. It made me feel closer to Gay. Mrs. Griffith would often see me riding as she looked down from the farmhouse window, and she came out and gave me tips on how to ride better. Gay had taught me a fair bit about riding, but there was a lot more for me to learn.

"Now you be careful, Kingsley, and don't push Blaze to go any faster than that."

Little did Mrs. Griffith know that I was practising so I could try and ride Thunder Child. One day when I thought Mrs Griffith wasn't looking from the window, I made Blaze gallop across the field. I did okay for the first few minutes. "Faster, faster Blaze," I shouted excitedly. We neared the end of the field and Blaze turned sharply to avoid the fence. I tried to hang on the best I could, but off I came, landing on my stomach on the hard ground.

Oh, the pain. I could hardly breathe.

"You silly man," I heard a voice say from behind me. "I told you not to go faster than a trot."

"I know, Mrs. Griffith, and I'm sorry. That was a stupid thing to do."

Well, Kingsley, you have learned the hard way. Come on lad, try to get up."

I stood up, still winded, and Mrs. Griffith made me walk around the field for about 10 minutes before letting me go on my way.

"I think you're all right now, Kingsley! You may have a few bruises in the morning. I hope you have learned your lesson."

"Bye, Mrs. Griffith, and I have learned that lesson."

In the afternoons and evenings, I spent my time watching the horses in the Valley. I crossed the Killy Willy and studied the other stallion and the Three Cliffs Herd on the other side of the river. Wherever I went, thoughts and memories of Gay followed me around. Was I in some way saying goodbye to her already? It sure felt like it. I'd remember a time or place, and something we had done together, and I'd feel this great sadness come over me. Then my heart would feel such longing for her, her smile, her touch, and the smell of her hair. My soul breathed her in like the sweet spring air. I could hear her happy laughter in the wind, and feel her warm tender kisses on my neck!

"Oh how could I ever live without her?" I asked the Sun. It felt like my first heartbeat had started on that first day I saw her in the Penmaen store. I would never forget her beautiful flowing hair as I stood behind her at the till, and her shapely woman's body, in her riding gear. I remembered that my heart began to beat faster and faster as I anticipated her turning around and me finally seeing her face.

I have known her for only months, I said to myself, yet I have touched her beautiful face, kissed her lips, fallen deep into her eyes, and caressed her soul, and my heart does not want to beat without hers. I have dreams of sharing a lifetime with her, and our last heartbeats being spent together.

As I continued to spend time with my horse family in the Valley, Little Thunder continued to grow each day. Strong

Orange and Indigo

and steady on his feet now, he ran around playing with some of the other foals that had been born shortly after him. Gosh, he was fast, taking after his father more and more. Thunder Child spent less time grazing with his family now. He stood most often on the top of the hill and watched over them from up there.

A few times, I watched the other stallion and some of the other horses try to cross the river and come and graze with Thunder Spring and Little Thunder. Down the hill the Thunder Child charged. Chasing them back to their own side of the river. I learned a lot more about how territorial stallions are in the wild. I'm taking good notes, I thought, for sometime soon I would be getting more visitors to my cave, for sure. This time I won't throw my spear near them, or flash the blade of my Bowie knife. I'll just chase them, shouting and charging like Thunder Child. I guess it was true what Gay said. Thunder Child and I are becoming more alike.

༄

The two weeks had finally gone by, and Gay was coming to see me this evening, after finishing her studying. I felt nervous as I walked across the Burrows to the village. Would she really be there? Or had her parents already whisked her away to England, leaving me only memories? Come on Kings, it's only been two weeks—though it seemed like a lifetime. My mum once said to me, when I was a young boy and laughing at two teenagers kissing, that it was love that made the world go round. Today, Mum, I know what you meant. It is love that makes the world go round, and without it, it would surely stop.

Cave Days

When I arrived at the village, Gay and her mum were already there. Gay and I ran into each other's arms, and I swung her around me.

"Oh Kingsley, I've missed you so much. It's so good to see you. I couldn't wait another day."

"I missed you so much too, Gay, and I couldn't wait another minute." I continued to hold her oh so tightly.

"You two behave," her mother said, "and I'll see you back here tonight, Gay. No later than nine. Don't be late. Bye, Kingsley."

"Bye, Helen."

"So how is our horse family?" Gay asked, after we had hugged and kissed again.

"Oh, they are doing great. Little Thunder is getting bigger every day, and Thunder Child spends most of his time watching over them from the hilltop. He chased the other stallion a few times when he tried to cross the river."

"Sounds like he's being a good husband and father."

"Yes, he is."

"Well, let's go and see our horse family, and make plans from there."

As we climbed down from the Burrows to the beach, we were surprised to see Thunder Child galloping past us on his way to Oxwich. "My gosh, he is resuming his runs." I said. "What about Thunder Spring and Little Thunder, and the other stallion?"

"I wouldn't worry about them," Gay said. "You should see a mare when she thinks her foal is being threatened. She will even fight a stallion off."

"That, I haven't seen yet."

Orange and Indigo

"It's true, us girls aren't just a pretty face, you know."

"You're not?" I argued jokingly.

"No, we are not," and she thumped me on the shoulders.

When we reached the Killy Willy at Three Cliffs, Thunder Child went flying past us on his return gallop.

"He's stopping at his cave. I felt sure he'd head up to the Valley to be with his family."

"Let's go and see him," Gay said. "I brought some apples and carrots."

Thunder Child stood again at his cave, and we fed him. "He's becoming tamer all the time," I said, "but to watch him gallop across the Sands, he's as wild as the West wind."

After Gay and I had eaten our lunch, I had an idea.

"A wild and crazy idea." she said.

"But it could be done."

"If you try to climb on his back and ride him, he will buck you off, as sure as the sun is in the sky. He's a wild stallion, Kingsley, and he can't be tamed"

"The only way to ride a horse like him is on his terms," I said.

"Then he's not like any other horse I've ever known," said Gay.

"He's the Thunder Child."

"You do have a special connection with him, Kingsley! I've been around horses since I was a little girl. And horses can feel and sense a person, and even know their emotions—whether they are lonely or sad, or happy or afraid. I know it may sound crazy, but a horse can mirror what's going on inside us, and act on it!"

Cave Days

"No, it doesn't sound crazy at all, Gay. I believe it's true. I know that I have a special connection with Thunder Child. He knows me and feels me inside, just like I have a special understanding of him."

"Thunder Child knew that he needed us to help his family in the cave." I continued. "Just like I needed Thunder Spring to keep me warm and stay alive. I'll never forget walking out of the cave and seeing him towering over me. At first I thought it was all over, that he would trample me, or at least chase me into the sea, but he just stood there peacefully, with a knowing look in his eyes. I really want to ride him, Gay. Can you imagine if I could ride the Thunder Child? I'd be the King of Gower!"

"You are already the King of Gower," she said, and kissed me. "If you want to try and ride him," said Gay, "we can go up to the stables and get a saddle. I have my old one there. It's really heavy, though, and it would take a lot of effort to carry it this far, and then carry it all the way back again.... I'll tell you what, next Saturday after my practice, why don't we bring my old saddle and tack, and see if we can *persuade* Thunder Child.

"That sounds great. Do you think I could practice during the week on Blaze? I did practise a bit last week while you had your studies."

Gay seemed really excited that I'd been riding Blaze. I didn't tell her that I'd fallen off trying to gallop, or that Mrs. Griffith had seen me fall.

"That would be great if you could ride him, Kingsley. He doesn't get ridden enough. And I know Mrs. Griffith who owns the stables will always agree to let you ride him."

We walked up to the farm, and talked to Mrs. Griffith.

"I thought you might have had enough after your time last week, Kingsley," she said with a twinkle in her eye; but she didn't tell Gay that I'd fallen off.

"Thank you," I said under my breath, happy to retain my pride, and she agreed to me coming over and riding Blaze again.

"You can drop by any Wednesday or Friday morning, Kingsley. If I'm around, I can give you some pointers, and you know where the gear is."

"Thank you, Mrs. Griffith, thank you," I said excitedly. The excitement wasn't so much about riding the horse as much as it was about her letting me do it for free. I guess Blaze really did need the exercise.

Before meeting Gay's mum, we had time to go down to the Three Cliffs Valley and visit Thunder Spring and Little Thunder. Gay was so excited to see them. I had seen them most days, but it had been two weeks for her.

"Gosh, Kingsley. Little Thunder has grown so much, and you're right. He is much like his father—so strong and fast. He will soon be eating grass shoots and other plants in a few months. I think that must be one of the most exciting times for a young horse – trying out the different tastes of all the plants. Rather like you in the sweet shop."

"You've got that right," I said laughing.

We visited our horse family until it was time to meet up with Gay's mum, and as always it had been a wonderful day.

"See you next week. Bye, Kingsley."

"Bye, see you next weekend."

The next weekend came, and I sure wasn't ready to ride Thunder Child. I'd wait until late in the summer and try then.

Cave Days

That way I would have time to practice riding Blaze on Wednesdays and Fridays, and by late summer I should be ready. Gay thought it was a wise decision, but I wondered if it was partly cowardice. Would I really be able to ride Thunder Child?

∽

Along came the summer holidays, and blazing June gave way to July, and the sea was now warm enough to swim in. I'd start my day with my usual walk across the Sands to Pobbles, and then say "Good morning" to Thunder Child, who continued to stand in front of his cave most mornings.

By mid-morning he would head up to his hill, and watch over the Valley. As he headed off to his hill, I would head back to the Tor for breakfast. I would then go for a swim in the sea, which soon became a big highlight of my day. On the high tides, the waves got big, and I loved to body surf, letting the waves sweep me right into the beach. Then I would run back, jumping over the waves, and wading out to catch the big breakers. I would choose one big wave to carry me back in.

Oh, the water felt so great on my skin, and the warm Sun and wind began to tan my body. My favourite thing to do, when the breakers weren't too big, was to stand beyond the waves with the warm sun on my back and watch the waves form from behind the swells as they journeyed their way onto the beach. Then, as the crashing waves receded, I could feel the undertow pulling at my heels, as my feet sank into the soft sand.

As I looked towards the shore, the song and rhythm of summer sang all around me. Cefn Bryn, the mighty Hill, was now arrayed like a King in his summer glory. His crown was the illuminating Sun on his summit, with the wild purple Heather gleaming like jewels. This contrasted with the belt of deep green Ferns that he wore around his waist like a gown. And there at his feet, the wild Gorse, still in yellow flower. Above was the blue sky, with kestrels and buzzards on the wing, and as I stood in the sea, I started to sing.

Gay would meet me in the sea, and I would swim with the most beautiful girl on the beach. We danced and laughed, and kissed, and held onto each other tight as we were swept up the beach with the singing sea. We walked the tide lines and found treasures, sang songs and whispered things that became love letters. We made two big hearts as big as houses and wrote in the sand: Kingsley and Gay forever and a day.

When we got cold, we ran up the beach to the sand dunes, and there we lay and kissed in our warm bed of sand. The warm breeze whistled softly in the long grasses, and the smell and songs of summer filled the air. Hand-in-hand we didn't have a care. Each night when Gay went home after the sunset, only to return on the morrow, I thought a lot about my life, and what my mother had once told me. She said that when you are in love, you look at the whole world differently. The little things that seemed so ordinary before are no longer ordinary anymore. They are so much more valuable when you have someone to share them with. "Mum, you were so right."

Throughout the course of the summer holidays, Gay and I scoured most of the Gower Peninsula, and at the end of each day, we watched the sunset together. Each sunset told a different story about the wonderful heavens and the earth. My favourite time of the day was in the evening, because that's when He brings out his paintbrush and tells me stories in the sky.

Cave Days

We walked the seashore in the cool of the evening, and we shared our hearts, and our dreams that had been born in the springtime. We fell asleep in the afternoon Sun, and woke up tangled in each other's arms. Sometimes, when Gay could stay late, we lay down in the Heather and watched the stars in the night sky. I wrote her poems and read them to her. I grew confident and strong, and so very happy.

Sometimes we watched the sunset up on Thunder Child's Hill, and gave thanks for what we had been given. From up there, you could look out over such wonderful things. Maybe that's why Thunder Child loved it up there so much. Some evenings he would stand with us and look out across the Valley. We could see the other horses, and the Killy Willy winding its way to the sea, which shone like silver under the moon.

I also liked to come up here alone and talk to God. This hill had become my sanctuary ever since I found out that Gay would have to move away. It was the place where I poured my heart out to Him. Each time we talked He seemed to know exactly what I needed. He gave me assurance, a knowing, and that peace in my heart that told me that everything was going to be all right—even when the day came that I would have to say goodbye to Gay.

I was already living out part of the plan He had for my life, out here on the cliffs wild and free, and one day when I had to leave the Gower Peninsula, I would not be alone.

Slowly, summer began to grow old, but Gay and my love remained so young. Gay and I, in our own ways, came to terms with the fact that one day soon, we would have to say goodbye...

Orange and Indigo

SUMMER, YOU'RE GROWING OLD

Now you summer, must grow old,
for autumns winds are blowing cold.
How many secrets do you hold,
now your leaves have turned to gold?
Tell me...
I'm listening, summer old.
Soon these winds will break your mould!
And you will vanish into the season's fold.
Oh summer, your growing old!
Many stories will be told,
about your warming centrefold.
Oh summer, don't grow
Old. For we have found your pot of gold,
which in your fragrance you do hold.
Oh summer, don't grow old.
We can feel your hands, they are so cold.
Oh summer, you're growing old.
But to your hands we will hold, until every leaf is story told.
And the autumn
Winds will blow us cold. Oh summer, don't grow old.
We will always remember our days of gold,
which in our souls can never die
or grow old. Oh, our summer, always, always, gold!
I love you Orange! I love you too Indigo!

Poem by Kingsley Ross Hill and Gay Nightingale Tripp
And summer of 1976

Cave Days

It was now the last week of August, and I waited at the stables for Gay to arrive. Blaze had already been sold, and I too felt his loss as I looked around the empty field. He'd given me my first experience of riding a horse, and now that he was gone, I wished I'd ridden him more.

Isn't that true of so many things in life? You don't really know what you have until it's gone, or going away. Gay said that she couldn't take Blaze with her because there were no stables close to where she would be living. "And even if there was, I couldn't have a horse," she said, "because I'm starting university in September."

As Gay's mother's car pulled up, my stomach tightened and I wondered what I'd be doing at the end of the month. My qualifications were "high school kick-out" and "worse behaved pupil." I'd be going to the University of Pobbles Beach in September. Boy, cheer up. It's the finest school of its kind. They can't teach you anywhere else what you're learning here, boy. No Sir, they can't, but my confidence wavered as I heard Helen's last words: "Don't forget, Gay, you must be home early tonight. We still have a lot of packing to do."

"Wait a minute, Mum. Wait!" Gay called out to her mother as she started to drive away.

"Oh yes, the saddle. I almost forgot." her mother said as she pulled up in the car again. "Kingsley, we have something for you. Can you help Gay lift it out of the back of the car?"

"Yes, Mrs. Tripp," I said, opening the trunk.

"Gay asked if she could give you her saddle, and my husband and I agreed that we'd like you to have it, for being such a wonderful friend to Gay."

Orange and Indigo

"Thank you, Mrs. Tripp, thank you very much. I would love to have it!"

I thought for a moment what it would be like if she was giving me Gay instead. That wasn't going to happen though, was it? But it was a nice thought.

Back to the saddle for a moment. "Thank you, Helen, and I wish you and your family every happiness in England." Guess that's what you call lying through your teeth. I don't want you to go to England and take away my Gay. No, I'm not lying through my teeth. I do wish you a nice life in England, just leave Gay here with me. We will even come and visit you, especially when the rains come.

I felt myself crying inside. Come on Kings, save that for later. I carried the saddle over my shoulders and we headed off over the Burrows to my cave. The saddle was heavy, all right, just like Gay had said it was, and I was glad to put it down.

Gay took my hand and said, "I want you to ride Thunder Child with this saddle. I know that eventually he will let you ride him, and this is the best saddle to do it with. It's the best saddle I've ever had. This is my most treasured possession that I can give you, Kingsley, and I want it to remind you every day of my love."

As she spoke, my eyes filled with tears and she began to cry too.

"I love you Kingsley, I love you so much, and what you have given to me, I will carry with me all my life. Our love will always be in my heart."

When we sat down at my cave, Gay read me a poem that she had written for me.

Cave Days

THE SONGBIRDS SONG

The songbird sings a song,
so sweet that God in his heaven smiles.
Only one song he sings,
and many lonely hearts hear it.
But for only two,
the song is the same.
Listen my heart to the chorus,
he sings our song.
The song of our own hearts.
We sing and dance as our souls take flight,
having been woken from our winters sleep,
by the songbirds song of love!
As we sit here together,
you are in me and surround me at the same time.
Your voice sweet and gentle,
blows as the sea breeze over the fragrant hill.
I breathe you in, and my soul rejoices,
as I touch and taste the purity of your heart,
In this song I've never sung before,
yet my soul knows every word.
A love song, as innocent as children,
who discover that they speak the same tongue,
and somehow know they are one!
Touch me again my love!
That I may tremble, and fall into your green
Mysterious eyes, where I see you,
and you see me,

Orange and Indigo

our souls melting
Together, deep, deep, I travel within your soul,
where no one else has ever been.
Suddenly, I see myself and your soul melting together.
I am breathing with your breath, and beating with your heart.
Oh breathe for me my love!
And beat for me my heart!
For I have fallen so deep, because I followed my heart.
I am here inside you my love, and you are here with me.
I sing to you, Kingsley, my love, with the songbirds song.
One song. It is our song of love!
© *Gay Nightingale Tripp*

Not being able to hold the floodgates back any more, I began to cry. I held Gay tightly in my arms as our warm tears rolled down our cheeks and mingled on each other's faces.

"I love you, Gay, and that's the most beautiful poem that anyone could ever write for me! Thank you so much. I will keep it always."

"And I will always have your love—right, my Prince? Otherwise I can't handle this. I can't go to England unless your love goes with me."

Kissing her tears away, I said "You will always have my love, Gay, and there will always be a place in my heart that can only belong to you." I felt my heart tear.

She kissed my tears away and smiled at me, and I felt God's strength and peace. Slowly, our sadness turned to joy, and we shared and celebrated what had been the greatest year of our lives and we carved our names on a tree. "Kingsley and Gay, Forever Love!"

Cave Days

We made a last fire, and she had me read the poem I'd written for her three times, and God blessed us in seeing the most beautiful sunset we'd ever seen together.

"It's the most beautiful of all his sunsets, Kingsley, and he painted it just for us as a celebration of our love."

"Yes, and every colour and shape represents something wonderful we have discovered and shared together. Well, are you ready for me to escort you across the Burrows to your waiting limousine?"

"Yes, my Prince! I'm ready. You may take my hand."

As we walked toward the village, I could see, in the distance, Gay's mother's car. So many feelings and emotions rolled like waves upon my soul, and like a piece of driftwood on top of the breaking surf, my heart came crashing onto the beach. I am so glad that God is a collector of broken hearts, and that he picked mine up and held it tight in his palms.

"Goodbye, Gay, I love you."

"Goodbye, Kingsley, I love you."

"Bye, Helen, and have a safe trip to England."

"Goodbye, Kingsley, and thank you for being such a wonderful friend to Gay, and I hope you enjoy the saddle."

I stood and watched the car until it disappeared in the distance, and Mrs. Davies came out of the general store.

"You look like someone has just taken your heart away, Kingsley."

"They have, Mrs. Davies, they have."

"How would you like to come over to the cottage for a cup of tea?" she asked. "We can talk."

"I'd like that, Mrs. Davies," I said, trying to hold back my tears.

"I'll just lock up the store, Kingsley, and we'll go have a nice cup of tea."

Mrs. Davies lived just a short distance away from her store, and we were soon there.

"Now you sit down and I'll put a pot on," she said. "So your sweetheart has gone away to England to live."

"How did you know?" I asked.

"Well, apart from the look on your face, Gay's mother came into the store last week and mentioned it. She said she was afraid that the two of you were going to run away together and elope somewhere."

"I almost wish we had." I said.

"Well, I'm proud of you, Kingsley, that you didn't. Running away would have been the easy thing for you to do, and that would never have worked out for either of you. You have shown 'good character,' and earned the respect of Gay's family. As time goes by, you will both see that you did the right thing, and you'll have a lot of respect for one another."

"Yes, but it hurts so much, Mrs. Davies," I said, bursting into tears. "I really love her."

"I know you do, Kingsley," she said, putting her arms around me. "Life has many wonderful things to teach us, and in some of Life's lessons, it also takes away from us—often the things that we hold most precious."

"You're right about that, Mrs. Davies!"

"Yes, but all these experiences will make you a stronger person, Kingsley. Life's lessons are sent to equip us, not to break us. God allows heartbreaks as well as joy, so that we can help and relate to others. I know that this doesn't sound very inviting to you now, because your heart is broken, but you will be able to use this experience later in your life, and if you're willing to trust him, God will work everything out for the very best in your life."

I knew she was right and began to feel encouraged again. As we talked I decided to share my story of the message in a bottle with her, and how, through 'Thunder Spring', God had saved my life.

"Kingsley, that is a wonderful testimony. It's so exciting to hear how God is working in your life. There is no doubt he has great plans for you. I have been learning to trust him for over 45 years. I was about your age when I first asked him into my life, and I can tell you this, He has always been faithful to me all these years. It hasn't all been easy, mind you. Sometimes it's been very difficult to trust, but I know He wants the best for me."

"Thank you, Mrs. Davies, for sharing with me, and for the nice tea and biscuits."

"That's quite all right, Kingsley, and you may call me Maggie, now that we know each other more. Now you remember this: everything will work out. You just have to keep trusting."

"Yes Maggie, I will, and thank you again."

"Bye, and do stop by again soon. I'm ready for another fish when you can catch one."

"Okay Maggie, see you soon."

Chapter Seventeen

Life Goes On

I arrived back at my cave and I lay down in my sleeping bag at the entrance. As I watched the night sky, my heart went out to Gay. I pictured her lying on top of her bed thinking about me, and missing me, as I was missing her. Could she feel my heart going out to her in longing? After playing our last day together over in my mind, it was time to get some sleep, and as I drifted off, I thought about what Mrs. Davies had said.

Over the next few weeks, I slowly came to terms with carrying on my life without Gay. I missed her more than I could have imagined, but life goes on, and I tried to keep myself occupied, mostly because there was no choice, otherwise the loneliness would cry too loud.

The summer weather continued, and so did my walks along the beach. I followed the same route as Thunder Child, travelling from Pobbles to Oxwich and back. After breakfast, my swims at Pobbles continued to be the highlight of my day. My walking and swimming was keeping me in excellent shape, and I had a tan to match my muscles.

Cave Days

I rarely felt lonely as I swam in the sea. There were lots of people swimming at Pobbles now that we were at the height of the summer season. I did, however, feel lonely when I saw couples together holding hands. As I looked around, there were lots of beautiful girls. Some I recognized from school, others were obviously on holiday with their families, but none were my Gay. As the weeks went by, I still felt her love in my heart, and I often asked God to send her my love.

Some things that we say to other people can speak for a lifetime. So often I recalled Gay's words to me, and mine to her. Powerful words, still loving and affirming me, long after they were spoken. I remember her saying, "Kingsley, if your love doesn't come with me, then I can't go. I can't carry on without your love." My love for Gay had certainly gone with her, and it still went out to her. I could feel it every day, and her love came to me too! Love is truly a wonderful thing, and when it is real, it transcends time and distance.

MR BLACKBIRD

Oh, Mr Blackbird, sing me a song,
Even though my heart is broken, and only my memories linger on.
Do not sing me a sad song, but a "happy one."
For I have lived many lifetimes, even though I am very young.
My soul is enlarged. I am old and I am young,
And I have been given knowledge of the Holy One!
Sing, Mr Blackbird, sing me a song. Sing me a "happy song."
For I have loved and been loved back,
And I have tasted love's first kiss.

Life Goes On

Tender and innocent, heaven sent bliss.
Sing me a song, Mr. Blackbird, as you cannot send me a kiss.
Sing me a "love song," one that I will remember,
Like the love in my heart, that will last all my life long.
Sing, Mr Blackbird, sing me a song!
© *Kingsley Ross Hill*

After my swim, I often returned to the old oak tree where Gay and I had carved our names. I liked to write poems there as I looked out over the waves crashing onto Pobbles Beach and listened to the sounds of summer.

In the evenings I prayed and talked to God a lot, and the more I prayed and opened my heart to Him, the more conscious I became of his presence. Quite often during the day, He would bring to my mind and heart a remembrance of something I had talked to him about. At times when I missed Gay so much, I would walk to Penmaen village and talk to Mrs. Davies. She was always there for me with wisdom and encouragement. God spoke to me through her every time I needed Him to. It wasn't only through Mrs. Davies that God was speaking to me.

One day I shared with God what was the most difficult part of my day. It was in the evenings when the teenagers at Pobbles Beach would be walking as couples, hand-in-hand. I watched them swim in the sea and then run up the beach to the warm sand dunes to hug and kiss. I was reminded of what I'd found, and what I'd lost. Left with my memories of Gay and a hole in my heart, I would tell God exactly how I felt, seeing those other couples when I had lost Gay.

When you walk the beach at sunset, people seem to stare at you when you're alone, as if to say: "Why don't you

Cave Days

have someone in your life? Why are you out here alone? What's wrong with you?"

The very night I shared this with God, I went for a walk along the beach, and a girl came up to me and asked if she could walk with me. Surprised, I said yes, I don't mind at all. I'd never seen her before. She was a beautiful girl, and it turned out that she was here on holiday from England. As we talked, she shared with me that two months before she had had to leave a relationship with her boyfriend, because her family had moved to another county a long way away.

We walked and talked for hours that night, and I was able to encourage and comfort her in a way that I could never have done if I hadn't gone through my own loss with Gay. As I talked and shared my experience with my new friend Autumn, I realised just what Mrs. Davies had meant when she said that my soul had been enlarged by my life experience. What a wonderful gift it was for me to relate to and understand what Autumn was going through. As I comforted her, she also comforted me in return. It helped me to know that someone else was going through exactly what I had gone through, and in many ways was still going through.

God heard and answered my prayers by sending me a friend. Autumn was on holiday for two weeks, and we swam in the sea together, and I showed her my horse family in the Valley. I also got to share my faith in God with her, by telling her the story of my message in a bottle, and the miracle of Thunder Spring saving my life. Some days I took her younger brother fishing, and in the evenings we watched the sunset together.

Mrs. Davies was always keen to hear about my adventures, especially about my experiences with God. "You're

Life Goes On

getting to know Him personally, Kingsley. This is very exciting."

One day when I was teaching Autumn's brother to fish, I caught a really large bass. It was all of 12 pounds, maybe bigger, and I couldn't wait to give it to Mrs. Davies, who was waiting for me to fill her order.

"Goodness gracious, Kingsley, look at the size of it! You're getting to be a really good fisherman. Mr. Tucker in the village has been fishing for years, and he rarely catches fish as nice as this. I'm going to give you £10 for this one! There's enough meat on it to last me about three weeks."

"Oh thank you, Mrs. Davies, I mean Maggie. Thank you so much."

"You're welcome Kingsley, and remember: He will supply all our needs."

How different my life was now. I was able to bring in regular money from my fishing and not steal any more. I think he was working on my conscience.

The two weeks that Autumn and her family were here on holiday went by so fast, and I was soon saying goodbye to her. How nice to have spent time with her and make my days less lonely.

It wasn't until days after Autumn had gone back to England that I realised just how much my relationship with God had grown. I was slowly learning to trust Him. I talked to him about everything, my hopes and dreams, my doubts and fears, things that I'd never felt comfortable telling anyone else. You could only tell so much to a horse.

Summer finally grew too old to shine, and autumn's face stared at me again. Children were back at school and the golden sands became hushed again, and it seemed just overnight that the families and teenagers, along with their music, smells and toys were gone. Only the odd person walking their dog, and the bird watchers, and bad boys who didn't go to school came down to the beach. And that's just the way Thunder Child and I liked it. Well, most of the time, that is. I miss the girls, but he likes it this way *all* the time. I guess that's one way we are different, old boy.

As I walked along the high tide line, the waves were washing away the footprints of my summer stories. There was only one story left. It was Gay's and my footprints that we'd made high up the beach, on that first day we'd held hands and walked across the beach together. Suddenly the last wave reached it, but it left footprints there. Picking the wildflowers from the dunes, I put one where her foot had been and the other on mine. One was orange, and the other indigo. They are the colours of our love, you know. Yes, my love, I know!

I think of you being like the rising of the sun that warms and kisses me, and delivers me from the cold dark night. I miss you, my love, and I need you. Come to me and comfort me now. I need to feel your touch and smell your long flowing hair.

I headed back to my cave for the night, and dreamed of my summer stories, and each one ended with Gay and me together again: "Good morning, my love."

After having breakfast on top of the Tor, I went for my morning walk across the beach. Carrying my sandals, I walked along the water's edge. The cool waves crashed over my feet, and I took some deep breaths of fresh air. Looking to the hills, I said good morning to Cefn Bryn. He answered back this morning through different colours.

Life Goes On

Above the Bryn, the sky was a clear blue. His purple robe of Heather was still there, but it wasn't its royal purple any more, but a lighter hue of mauve. The Ferns around his waist had turned brown, and only patches of green Ferns remained, like sparkling buckles in a belt. The yellow Gorse at his feet had lost their flowers, and the brown bracken contrasted with the grey rock of his crown.

"That is a nice autumn outfit, Mr. Bryn," my soul called out.

"Thank you, young man. I prefer my summer wardrobe though, don't you?"

"Don't remind me, Mr. Bryn. Winter is coming, but autumn is lovely, isn't it?"

"Yes, it is young man."

After my morning walk I followed the Killy Willy from its mouth at the bay, up towards the valley. I thought I would visit Thunder Child and his family, as it had been a few days since I'd seen them. As I walked upon the soft sand of the river bed, the water ran clear before me. This told me that the horses weren't drinking from the river up ahead. If they were, there would be clouds of murky water running down with the clear water. The river was at its lowest this time of year, which allowed me to walk through its deeper pools, including one at a bend in the river that turns into a mysterious whirlpool once the rains have begun. As I walked on, I kept a lookout for skate, as they would soon be returning to the Killy Willy at the end of the autumn season.

Flounders and sole darted away from my intruding feet, but there was no sign of any skate yet. I was looking forward to catching one for Maggie. She always gave me great praise when I caught a nice fish.

The Skylarks were flying overhead in greater numbers now, with their young having left their nests and learned to fly. Oh, how sweet their song. Obviously they were singing songs of their spring and summer stories, and I whistled and sang mine too.

I crossed the stepping stones to the other side of the river, where I'd last seen my horse family grazing. As I turned the corner, I could see that the valley was empty. There were no horses at all. Thunder Child and family were gone. For a few minutes I just stood there, as a sense of loss came over me. First it was Gay and now my horse family had gone. It wasn't a loss like losing Gay, though. The horses had just moved on to another area on the Gower, and if I searched hard enough, I'd be able to find them. It was rather like the loss of a season, that I had been such a part of. I'd always imagined myself moving on with them, starting the next chapter of my life with my horse family at my side.

As I examined the grass on each side of the river, it had been eaten down to the roots. The horses had gone to find new grazing, that was for sure, but I'd expected at least a visit to say they were moving on. I am at least half horse, you know. In the evening I went to visit Maggie for a tea and a talk. "The horses could be in any number of places, Kingsley," she said. There are at least ten different herds on the Gower Peninsula, and they roam around, as you know, looking for fresh pasture."

Maggie knew more about horses than I'd thought. She said that during the autumn, and especially in the winter months when there was little or no growth of grass, that they roamed in smaller herds, some just in small families, so that an area of grass could sustain them longer, and that mares with young foals would also stay together. "I've watched the horses for years, Kingsley. Long enough to know that you and your stallion have a unique relationship."

"They call you 'the wild boy' in Pennard, but I know you better than that, don't I. You have many wonderful gifts. One of them is understanding and appreciating God's creation in a unique way, and your poetry is wonderful. You must keep writing. They can't teach you the way you write. It's a special gift from God which he will use in your life in the future."

"Thank you Maggie. You have always encouraged me so much."

"It's true, or I wouldn't say it. God is going to do something special with your life."

There it is again. God speaking to me through Maggie. They were just the words that my heart needed to hear. I left Maggie's house encouraged as always.

"Oh, and one more thing," Maggie shouted from the porch. "This letter came for you at the post office yesterday."

I ran back to Maggie to get the letter. Suddenly my heart was beating faster. Could it be a letter from Gay? I hurried back across the Burrows to my cave to read it. I held it, and smelled it, and the address stamp was from somewhere in England. What else could it be, other than a letter from Gay? Well, here goes.

It turned out to be a letter from Autumn. First of all, I felt disappointed. I'd only known Autumn for two weeks, and she'd taken the time to write to me. Why couldn't Gay write? But in my heart I knew the answer. It would be just too hard.

'Dear Kingsley. It was so nice to meet you and share some special days with you. My brother Brian is still talking about the big bass you caught. You gave him such a gift in teaching him how to fish. As for me, my life has changed so much because of meeting you. Thank you for sharing with me your experiences in your relationship with Gay. I know you loved her very much. You have no idea how much it helped me in dealing with the loss of my relationship with my boyfriend Chris. Thanks again and whoever you meet in the future will be one lucky lady. I will never forget you, Autumn.'

I went from feeling sorry for myself, to feeling joyful for what she shared in the letter. I'd come to the cliffs, rebellious and lost, and with a big hole in my heart, and now my life was being filled with meaning and purpose. Maggie's words echoed again in my heart. "God has a wonderful plan for your life, Kingsley."

I ended the day by climbing up Thunder Child's hill and watching the sunset. The whole valley lit up in orange light, and the Killy Willy flowed silver, praising its creator all the way to the sea.

The following day I woke up to heavy rain. For an hour or so, I was glad of it. It had been almost two months since we'd had rain – a rare drought for grey-skied south Wales. The wind was still warm, and I stood at the entrance of my cave in my shorts. The cool rain felt refreshing on my skin. When my shorts were soaked through, I went back into the cave to change. Maybe I should've washed with soap in the rain, I thought. That would have saved me washing in the river, which would cool quickly now with the rain falling.

The rain remained heavy for the next three hours, and the novelty of its refreshment wore off. All of a sudden I was back to staying inside my cave again. Memories of Bacon Hole pressed against the pages of my mind.

Life Goes On

"My life is different now!" I shouted out to loneliness and fear, who were standing at the entrance to my cave and wanting to come in. "No matter how grey and wet it gets, I don't have to feel gloomy or sad anymore, so I suggest you spooks get out of here and go back to Bacon Hole."

Putting on my warmest clothes and raincoat, I climbed to the top of the Tor for my weather report. The sky was grey as far as the eye could see, and the rippled sea reflected the same grey below. Far out in the bay, some white horses rode gently on a stirring wind.

I thought of Gay. She would be well into her studies now at university, and I wondered how different her life would be living in England? For a few minutes I actually thought about a boyfriend she might have met. "She is the most beautiful woman on the whole university campus," I said to myself. "So there will be many young men interested in her. I think I feel jealous. Yes I do."

I pictured myself riding Thunder Child across the university grounds with a sword in my hand and chasing away any man who came near her. "How's that for being passionate, Thunder Child? I'm getting more like you every day, old boy! I must say, that was a nice daydream. I enjoyed that. Especially chasing people away with a sword."

"Tell them to leave my Princess alone," I shouted out to a raven flying overhead.

Well, what was next for me? Gay was gone, having started a new and exciting chapter in her life. My best friend Mitch was starting university too, and Thunder Child had left the Valley with his family. My school teacher's words spoke to me again: "If you don't concentrate on your school work, Kingsley, you're going to be left behind."

Cave Days

It's amazing what a grey and rainy day can do to one's psyche. Left behind! "I'm not left behind." I shouted. "There is a wonderful plan for my life," and I read my message in a bottle verse again.

"Did you hear that, Fear? God has a wonderful plan for my life, and he's taught me things that they could never teach me in university.'

"Yes, I heard you the first time."

"Well shut up then and leave me alone. God loves me and I'm a Knight of Gower. I have a friend who is a stallion, nd I'm going to ride him across this land like a King surveying his kingdom."

"Well done, boy. You know who you are."

"Yes, Sir, I do."

"And they can't teach that at school either, can they?"

"No, Sir, they can't."

"Well, boy, when are you going to ride Thunder Child?"

"Soon, Sir, as soon as I can find him. He's left the Valley and I don't know where he is."

"He'll be back, boy! Now don't you bother going looking for him. Remember what I told you. He will find you."

"When, Sir?"

"At the end of the autumn, after the Harvest Moon. Then his mare and foal will be ready to be on their own."

"Thank you, Sir, and where are you going?"

"Where the wind blows free, boy, where the wind blows free!"

"That's on Gower, Sir!"

"That's right, boy, on Gower. You wait for the stallion, boy, then you can leave."

Life Goes On

"Wait, Sir! What do you mean, wait for the stallion and then I can leave?"

"You're a Knight now, boy, and you can go anywhere you want, and be anything you want in this world. Now wait for the stallion."

"Yes, Sir, I'll wait."

Days, and then weeks went by, and still Thunder Child did not return. Even though I had money to buy food, I hunted and fished again to pass the time. The grey skies and rain remained, and my hopes of an Indian summer were dwindling fast. Oh well, at least it wasn't torrential rain like it had been last autumn when I'd lived in Bacon Hole. But it was cold at night in my cave, and with the cave's poor ventilation, all my fires had to remain at the entrance. It had been fine in the summer, but not now with the cool autumn air blowing around and about. I never thought I'd say this, but I actually missed my rip-roaring fires in the heart of Bacon Hole – even though I had had Fear and other undesirable companions as my cave mates.

Had I grown brave and fearless, even to the point of missing creatures from that dark abode? Or was my present isolation making me crazy? Gay's words suddenly answered my question, and affirmed me—as always. "Kingsley, you're very brave living out here in the wild."

"Thank you, I am brave," I spoke aloud. "And if God is for me, who can be against me?" My soul answered: "no one!"

∽

My spring and summer stories seemed to fade away into the grey of yesteryears, though only months had gone by since I'd lived their golden adventures! Each Friday evening, I went and had supper with Maggie and this soon became the highlight of my week. It was good to have something to look forward to, and to have some routine in my life, apart from putting on my fur robe every morning and evening, and climbing up to the top of the Tor to look for Thunder Child returning, like the father waiting for the prodigal son.

Maggie continued to encourage me, sharing more with me about God. She became both my counsellor and friend. There was nothing I couldn't share with her. Surely God had put her in my life for this reason. Last week she told me that God lives outside of time and can see the past, present, and future altogether at the same time. Wow, to be able to see the past, present, and future all at once. I wonder if he could find Thunder Child for me?

I shared with Maggie about Autumn's letter, and how I had been able to help her.

"That's wonderful news, Kingsley! You can see how God is already using you in his plan to reach out to other people's lives. I am very proud of you for having learned so much."

Before I left to go back to my cave, Maggie gave me a Bible and signed it. With my Bible in one hand, and a freshly made loaf of bread in the other, I made my way back across the Burrows to my cave, and I felt excited about God and the wonderful things he was doing in my life.

Chapter Eighteen

Around the World In Five Days

It was the first Friday in November, and I went over to Maggie's for supper, as usual. After our meal and conversation time, Maggie asked me if I'd look after the cottage for her and feed her animals while she was away. She was going to Bristol to visit her sister for two weeks. I felt honoured that she would ask me to look after her place, and I eagerly accepted. "I shall be leaving next Saturday morning," she said, "so why don't you come over on Friday as usual and I can show you what needs to be done with the animals."

As I headed back to my cave, the autumn wind blew cool on my face, and I looked forward to having the comfort of the cottage. The cold wind reminded me that I had a whole week to wait yet, and that I needed to keep myself warm and occupied.

I sure missed my swimming in the ocean, and those warm summer evenings. Alas, it was time to say hello again to "November grey."

"Tell me, Fear, how long is November grey?"

"Oh not long, don't you remember? It's forever and a day!"

Each morning and evening I climbed to the top of the Tor to look out for the return of Thunder Child, but he stayed away. Would he wait for the harvest moon before he returned? Or had he vanished forever behind the sunset? Nay, he will return. He knows I am waiting for him.

The days were becoming all the same again now; grey, grey, and grey. I couldn't wait to see the blue sky again. Oh, how was I going to make it to Friday?

On Monday morning, I felt so lonely that I decided to go and look for my horse family. In my dreams I pictured Thunder Child and Thunder Spring with Little Thunder grazing in a secluded meadow, somewhere on South Gower. So with my backpack and Bowie knife, and a few days supply of food, I set off to see the world of the Gower Peninsula, and hopefully find my family.

It would be a different journey than the warm and romantic adventures that Gay and I had enjoyed during the summer holidays, but it would still be a wonderful journey. As the old man said, the Gower has many secrets. Well, I'd be gone until Friday, and then I'd head over to Maggie's. That would give me five full days to find them. I would start my journey in the direction of Oxwich Bay and continue westwards taking the cliff paths.

The wind blew strong as I crossed the Sands, with gusts that took my breath away. Oh, how I wished Gay was with me, or even my friend Samantha. They were far away in different lives, but always as close as my imagination could bring them. Today I would walk with Gay and feel her warm hand in mine, and try not to think of her having met someone else, as my dreams often told me. I would go back to the time when she was mine, "all mine," in those happy lifetimes of June, July and August, when our love was all there was, and it would never end. As the frigid wind blew, it reminded me that nothing lasts forever.

Having climbed up the path to Oxwich Point, I looked back across the golden sands to the great Tor and the Bell rock. In the distance, the peaks of the Three Cliffs looked spectacular as they watched like guardian angels over my beloved Pobbles Beach. The Bell rock reminded me of an adventure that I'd hoped to have had with Gay. I wanted to take her mackerel fishing off the rock when it became an island at three-quarter tide. How romantic that would have been, together on an island underneath the moon and stars. I became jealous again, of whom I imagined her being with at university. Come on, Kings, pull yourself together, man. Life goes on, you know. Yes I know, but she hasn't even written to me once yet; she's probably having a wonderful time and not even thinking about us…? Well, life has to go on, Kings; you just have to be thankful for the time you shared together. Yes I know. But can you just let me live in my yesterdays just for today; you know what I mean. Yes, I know what you mean.

I continued on the path at Oxwich Point and headed towards Port Eynon. Port Eynon Bay is the second largest indentation on the Gower coast with its fine sandy bay, backed by its adventure-seeking dunes, and ending at Port Eynon Point. Such wonderful memories greeted me as I beheld Port Eynon Bay. My mother and father had kept their caravan at Port Eynon when my brother and I were young boys. It was my first experience of caravanning and family holidays. We would build boats out of the fine sand, using our buckets and spades, newly bought each summer from the old Post Office and general store. I liked the shiny red bucket with white stripes, while my brother liked the all-blue bucket.

Dad would announce that it was low tide, and time to start building a boat. Dad would start by drawing out the shape of the boat with one of our spades, and Mum would help Fraser and I to fill our buckets with wet sand, freshly dug in front of the singing waves. We could shape the sand while it was wet and make wonderful designs on our seagoing vessel. For a while, we would follow the receding tide until our trips back and forth to fill our buckets got quite a distance from our boat, which looked more wonderful with every fresh load of wet golden sand. But soon the tide would turn, and Mum would say, "Come on boys, we need to make the walls thick and high, so the waves won't come in and sink the ship."

Sometimes the walls of our boat would be up to my waist, and we would all sit inside until the waves crashed around us, and we were off to sail the seven seas. Here and there the walls would crumble, or a wayward splash would come over the top, and we would all shout: "Quick! We need some more sand," and we'd try to build up the wall again fast. Eventually the conquering waves with their Viking ships broke through one of the walls, and for a few minutes our boat turned into a swimming pool. Then Dad would shout, "Pirates ahoy, abandon ship," and we would swim in the sea until we got cold or found a jellyfish to inspect on the Sands.

Port Eynon village lies on the western end of the bay, with its sister village Horton on the eastern side. The two of them are separated by the sand dunes of the Burrows. Horton tumbles down steeply to the sea, like a little boy running faster than his legs can carry him. I have little memory of Horton, other than it was the other place that could never be as nice as Port Eynon. As a boy, I was happy to stay in a place that I found and soon loved. So why would I want to go anywhere else in the world than the Gower Peninsula?

But as we grow from boys to men and girls to women, many of us like to explore those new places that we hope to find, but that often live only in our dreams. Yet somehow we know they are real, and we set off to find them somewhere in this wide, wide world! Maybe twice or thrice I remember going for a walk to Horton, riding "high on my father's shoulders," from where I once thought I could see the whole world, or at least everything I wanted to see. "Hey Dad, what's that? Let's go over there."

"Okay Kings, hold on tight," and he would run holding my legs as I bounced on his shoulders. Now that I am older, I know that all I needed to see, I could see from high upon my father's strong shoulders.

Doesn't every little boy see the world from his father's shoulders? Sadly, no. My father was "my gateway to the world," and for that I am so very thankful. I am too big to ride on my father's shoulders now, but you know what? I can ride on God's shoulders now. I am never too big to ride on his shoulders, and you can too if you'd like to.

My memory of Port Eynon village is vivid, even today. It had, and maybe still has, the most wonderful post office and general store. Far more wonderful than even Maggie's Penmaen store. I would go and investigate it today, as I was in need of a rest and some lunch. As I climbed down the path to Horton, I could feel the muscles pulling in the back of my legs, and I was glad to be on the flat sand again. I noticed how fine and white the sand was, compared to the larger, yellower grains of Oxwich beach. There were more shells up on the tide lines here too. Hungry now, I made my way across the Sands of Port Eynon Bay and on to the village. Port Eynon takes its name from a Welsh prince of the 11th century, who was supposed to have built a castle on this spot. The little village is clustered around the church like so many of the settlements around the Gower, and they all owe their existence to the Norman conquest.

It was my conquest now, and I wondered, would the little village and store be the same? Alas, things had changed from those early family days. There were four new stores in the village now and also a larger shop that sold everything a family could need for the beach—even fish and chips, and ice cream to go. Where was the old Post Office? As I followed the single lane road deep into the village, the old houses welcomed me, as if understanding the need of my soul to go back in time! Their roofs were thatched with grass, and their stone fronts painted with white and pastel pinks, and even yellows that reminded me of summer's colour, in the midst of winter's grey. Old whitewashed walls marked out the boundaries of people's friendly gardens, where gnomes stood around and fished, and wished at the wishing wells, and flowerpots sat blooming out the village news on wooden window sills. They sang a song that my heart loved to sing, called "Yesterday Once More."

Around the next corner was the Post Office. It seemed smaller now than when I was a boy, just like so many other things in life when I looked back and my memories were big. I opened the door and went in. "Hello," an elderly voice called out. I turned to see a rather stooped-over old lady stocking the shelves.

"Mrs. Hodgkins!" I exclaimed.

"Why yes, young man. How did you know my name? You're not from the village, are you? Do I know you?"

"No, I don't think so," I said. "When I was a boy, my mother and father had a caravan at the caravan site, and my brother and I would come in here and buy packets of football cards with bubblegum inside. We also bought marbles and sweets here."

"Yes, those were the good old days," she said, her voice perking up at my words. "They don't make the football cards any more, but I still have lots of sweets. I don't sell much more than the basics now. The locals still come and buy their milk and newspapers, but the new store right at the beach sells the buckets and spades, and the rubber rings for swimming. Of course I still sell the stamps because we are still the Post Office.

As she continued to speak, an old red and white striped pail with a little red spade in the corner caught my eye. It was just like the ones my mother and father had bought for Fraser and I. "I remember these old metal buckets and spades," I said in a deep daydream.

"Yes, and that's the last one I have!" She replied. "They're all made of cheap plastic now, made in China, and they never last."

"How much is it?" I asked. "It would be perfect to put my shells and precious stones in."

Cave Days

"I'll tell you what, young man. I have two bags of coal in the backyard, and I need them carried into the store for the winter. You carry the bags in for me, and you can have the bucket and spade."

"Thank you," I said gladly. "My name is Kingsley."

"Kingsley. What a lovely name. My name is Mrs. Hodgkins," she repeated. I hurried out to carry in the coal.

"Could you tell me where in the village I could get a Cornish pasty and some pop, Mrs. Hodgkins?"

"Just a minute," she said, disappearing into the back of the store. Then she returned with a box of Cornish pasties and a can of Pepsi. "The locals still come and ask for pasties," she said, "and these are made right here at the farm near the village."

"I'll take two, and I'll have a bottle of dandelion and burdock, which I see there on the shelf."

"That will be 1 pound and 50 pence, please, and thank you for carrying in my coal. It is far too heavy for an old lady to carry."

"I'm glad I could help," I said, picking up my bucket and spade, and I put my pop and pasties into the bucket.

"Have a nice day, Kingsley, and drop in any time."

"You too, Mrs. Hodgkins, and goodbye for now."

I went back to the seafront to eat my pasties. The tide looked like it was a long way out now, and the rocks were exposed in front of the point. As I swigged down my pop, I remembered a time when my father had taken my brother and me out to the point at low water. There was a cave out there, but you could only get to it when the tide was at its lowest. My father had shown Fraser and I a fossilised dinosaur bone on the wall of the cave. I thought I would try and find the cave. When Gay and I had come here, the tide was too far in for us to go and explore the cave, but today would be perfect.

Once I'd walked out to the point, it was easy to find. The cave's entrance is large, and the rocks are green and slippery in front of it. Not far into the cave, I found a fossilised bone on the wall. It was much as I remembered it when I had been here with my father. In this cave were found the remains of mammoth, woolly rhinoceros and red deer, among other animals.

After re-exploring the cave, I climbed up the path to the headland. From here, one can look out over a mysterious part of the coastline. Stretching out from what is called "the Salthouse" is a little spit of low land called "Sedgers Bank" And further out toward the sea's edge lies a group of lichen-covered rocks called "Skysea." Both Sedgers Bank and Skysea remain uncovered at high tide, although the white froth—or white stallions of the sea, as I call them—bury Skysea when there is a gale.

When it is low tide, the whole shore changes its character. A great wilderness of rock pools is exposed, with mysterious deep hollows and mermaid hair seaweed that sways softly in the current of the clear magic waters. 'Have you ever seen a mermaid, boy?' No sir, but I believe there is such a thing. My father once saw a woman with a fishtail on Port Eynon beach. 'No doubt that's true, boy. I've seen one myself.' Yes sir, I hope I will see a mermaid one day. 'You will boy, if you walk Port Eynon beach after dark. She is searching for her love who is buried in the old church yard. Mermaids live forever, and humans don't, at least not down here. So don't marry a mermaid, boy, or you will break her heart.' No, sir. I won't.

Cave Days

Well, it's time for me to get back to my journey of finding my horse family. I'd seen no signs of any of the herds so far. Maybe they were more inland seeking shelter from the sea winds? From Port Eynon head, I now walked what is known as 'the Magnificent 5 Miles." This breathtaking walk, which is unquestionably the finest Cliff walk on the whole Gower coast, starts at Port Eynon head and continues westward to the Worms Head at Rhossili beach. I have decided not to share with the reader all that I have seen along these "Magnificent 5 Miles" for fear that my book would become a tourist guide, rather than the autobiography which is my goal. So I will leave much for the reader to come and discover for themselves, and in particular, why this five-mile walk is called magnificent.

After travelling about 40 minutes along the Cliff path, I headed inland for a while to shelter from the strong sea wind. I came to a little hamlet called Overton. Here I found a few little farms with sheep and cattle, typical of the main livestock here on Gower. Overton also has a little village green and a duck pond. There, nibbling on the grass green, I found part of my horse family. I'd had visions of searching most of the Gower Peninsula before I found them. But there was Thunder Spring and Little Thunder, and I was so happy to see them. How Little Thunder had grown. They both recognized me right away and came over to greet me. Hello, old girl, I'm sorry I have no carrots or an apple to give you. I've missed you all so much. So much so that I came looking for you. It's too lonely in the Valley without my horse family, you know.

I picked some long stems of grass from the hedgerow and fed them to Thunder Spring, as Little Thunder danced around us and then suckled on his mother's milk. There was no sign of Thunder Child here. He was far too wild to be on a village green. I sensed he was a long way away, somewhere roaming the moors of Cefn Bryn, or running free on the North Hill of Rhossili Downs. I would rest here for the remainder of the day, reunited with Thunder Spring and Little Thunder. I thanked God for helping me find them, and for keeping them safe. Had I not come inland to shelter from the sea wind, I would have continued along the coastal path and missed them.

    I felt excited again about there being plans for my life, and being led to find the path of which I should go. Now please go before me, and help me find Thunder Child also. As I watched Thunder Spring and Little Thunder together, I thought of all the life lessons they had taught me. Thunder Child was the protector of his family, keeping them safe from other horses and people who would come too close and do them harm. Just like in human relationships, 'trust' must be earned and discerned before he trusts another to come close to his family. He would protect his family with his life, if necessary, by fighting off other stallions. The mare was also a protector, as well as being the main nurturer, just like a human mother.

    I watched Thunder Spring chase away some children who came too close to Little Thunder here on Overton Green. What lesson was I learning through this? I didn't have to try and win God's love to be accepted. I just had to put my 'trust' in him, and come to him just the way I am, with all my faults and weaknesses, and he didn't chase me away like the other stallions and the herd of horses that wouldn't accept Thunder Child when he tried so hard to 'belong'.

    As I continued to read my Bible, the verses that I read came alive to me, and brought light and understanding to my life situations. I'd never read a book that was 'alive' before, and that spoke to me in regard to my exact life experiences. It's far too wonderful to explain really, but I was learning that God actually inhabits the Bible, and this is "utterly fantastic" to have God himself speak to you personally through the scriptures, and you recognize yourself within the stories and characters that you're reading about. What an amazing thing.

    As the curtains of the day drew closed upon the western sky, it was time for me to find shelter for the night. My legs felt too tired to walk all the way back to the Tor, and besides, it would soon be too dark to see along the cliff tops. There were no caves that I knew of around here where I could sleep, so I decided to curl up in my sleeping bag on the green, and use my backpack as a pillow. I felt safe having my horse family so near. Thunder Spring and Little Thunder seemed content to nibble on the grass, and eventually they lay down for the night. This was my cue to close my eyes and get some sleep. My body felt warm in the sleeping bag as the cool autumn air breathed on my face, and the gentle wind caressed my head.

    My dreams, as always, went in search of Gay. Tonight I held her tightly in my arms, and we talked of our adventures finding Thunder Child together. We found him on the North Hill of Rhossili Downs, overlooking the beach and the Worms Head. The next thing I remember, it was morning in Overton village. Thunder Spring and Little Thunder were walking around grazing, and the dawn chorus was in full song. A robin was singing the most joyous song above me in a tree, and a thrush and two blackbirds were busy hunting worms on the green. I quickly rolled up my sleeping bag and stuffed it in my backpack, as I heard voices and a dog barking on the other side of the stone wall that separated the village green from the road.

"Good morning," said a man coming onto the green with his dog. Thunder Spring's ears pricked up immediately and she stood on guard at the sight of the dog. The man seeing the horses called out and put his dog back on his leash. A good idea, I thought. Two horses running through the village would cause quite a stir. I smiled as I remembered a time when I stampeded a herd of horses through the housing estate where I lived in Pennard village as a boy. That event is still talked about on old Brown's Drive, Fraser tells me. It was quite the day alright. There were horses running through wooden fences, flower gardens ruined, and manicured lawns looked like the Blitz of World War II! Oh yes, I mustn't forget Mrs. Boisey's greenhouse. I'd never seen so many broken panes of glass, but that's another chapter in the adventures of Kingsley Hill's childhood.

After saying good morning to Thunder Spring and Little Thunder, I walked into the village in search of food. There seemed to be nothing open. It was still early, however, just after eight according to the clock tower on the church. It struck me that Overton is the sort of little hamlet where the stores open only when people actually feel like getting up. Maybe they don't open at all in the winter time. I waited outside a little store for it to open. The sign in the window said 'Open 8:30 AM to 4:00 PM.' It was now 8:45, and there was no sign of movement as I peered in through the dirty window. Suddenly I heard the rather loud noise of a deadbolt being unlocked behind the old wooden door. Slowly it creaked open, and there bent over was an old lady. How can people get so old? She didn't look unlike Mrs. Hodgkins at Port Eynon, only more stooped over.

Cave Days

"Good morning. Are you open?" I said, startling her.

"You frightened me," she said. "I thought you were a robber."

I was quite tempted to say, "I don't do that anymore, Madam. I've found other things to do now," but I thought better of it and bit my tongue.

"Just a minute and I'll open the blinds and you can come in," she said grumpily.

"Well, young man, I open up when I'm good and ready to open up these days. I must have my cup of tea in the morning, and my toast and marmalade. Then I'm ready to start the day. Now what can I do for you, young Sir? I'm sure you don't want a stamp. You young people don't know how to write letters, do you, or at least you don't like to. My grandchildren never write to me, and they are quite old enough to read and write. What are you carrying that bucket and spade for? You're a little too old to be making sandcastles, aren't you?"

"No ma'am, never too old for that. I put my treasures and special stones in here."

"What are you doing in the village anyway? There aren't any school holidays yet, are there? What is your name anyway?"

"Oh, I'm Kingsley, and I'm exploring the Gower."

"Oh you are, are you. Well I'm glad that you haven't come to rob me. So what can I do for you? You won't find any treasures in here to put in your bucket. You will have to go back to the beach for that."

"I was hoping to buy something to eat, like some Cornish pasties."

"Well, there are no more Cornish pasties, but I have some pork pies and two scotch eggs. They were fresh in yesterday."

"I'll take them all, please, and a bottle of pop. I'm going to need plenty of food today, because I'm going to walk along the cliff tops to Rhossili."

"You be careful on those cliffs at Rhossili. A lot of people have fallen to their deaths from those cliffs."

"I'll be careful, and thank you for the warning."

As soon as I left the store, I ate one of the scotch eggs for breakfast. I'd save the rest for later in the day. Yum. Scotch eggs are like a meal in themselves. I'd forgotten how filling they were. On the outside they have a skin of breaded batter, which covers a ham-like meat, and the cooked egg is in the middle. Nice as they are, in my view, you just can't beat a good Cornish pasty.

So off I went climbing up the path to the clifftop. It was a rather dark and dismal day, but it wasn't cold and I didn't feel rain in the air. I had learned to feel the rain in the air since coming to the cliffs to live.

I'd been walking only a short distance when I heard the sound of horses. Excitedly, I hurried to where they were. There were three mares and some large foals. I counted four before one of the mares gave chase. I ran into a thicket of Gorse bushes that had a bit of a path in the middle. Fortunately, when I was a distance of about 60 feet away from the herd, the mare stopped her chase. There were no stallions to be seen, but with a charging mare, maybe they didn't need one. The old man said, when you have a charging mare and no stallion, you will have interrupted a women's lib meeting, and you better get the heck out of there, boy. Yes Sir, I'm out of here.

Cave Days

Another lesson learned from the horses is that both parents guard and protect their young. They work as a team, each providing a unique parenting skill specific to being a male or female. They can also parent individually at certain times during the care and nurturing that a foal needs to grow into a healthy happy horse.

When Thunder Child is present with his family, he is the protector of both the mare and the foal, and when he is absent, the mare takes over the protecting role. When he returns, the mare readily gives him back his role as protector and provider for the family. Gay and I thought it was very romantic how the horses knew and understood their roles in family life. I marvelled how God had built this instinct and understanding into a horse's makeup. As I viewed my horse family, I thought that these roles brought peace and contentment to their lives. They didn't have to try and be anything other than what God had designed and equipped them to be.

How often roles are misunderstood or distorted in human families, and, sadly, in my own. But God was teaching me a lot out here, even through herds of horses I was learning about how family life should be. I looked forward to being a good husband and father one day, and having my own family, just like Thunder Child. He's a great model for me to follow.

I walked along Overton Cliffs, westwards to Rhossili. Here the coastline maintains a splendour that is both thrilling and mysterious and with each new viewpoint, God's handiwork becomes more and more breathtaking. There are exciting rock formations like the curious triangular rock that is known as "The Knave," and the impressive overhanging of nature's art near "Deborah's Hole." This is yet another bone cave. Here fossils of prehistoric fauna, and also some cave dwellers splints for hunting, were discovered.

As I continued walking, I passed the narrow gullies of Foxhole and Butterslade and the impressive limestone prow of Thurba Head. This is in my view the most precipitous of the Gower Headlands. It drops 200 feet into the sea. As I stood there on the mighty cliff, I felt Gay in my heart. For it was here that we had stood holding each other tightly as we peered over the edge on this same walk during the summer holidays. As we beheld this mighty rock with its feet immersed in the sea, while here on its top the clouds were so low, we stood like young gods looking down from heaven! How great God himself must be, to have made such a place of majesty. Oh Gay, I miss you so much, I wish you were here with me.

The Knave rock guards the Eastern side of Mewslade Bay, and Mewslade runs down from the hamlet of Pitton, which is on the main Rhossili Road. After sitting down and eating a pork pie and my remaining scotch egg, I rested for a while and dreamed of Gay. All this walking was tiring work, and I felt I could sit here for a whole day just thinking. As I thought of my summer journey with Gay around the Gower, it became evident that my memories were becoming more precious with the passing of time. I was supposed to be getting over her and not thinking about her so much, wasn't I? Then why do "the gentle winds of memory stir" and why does my heart continue to experience this longing. Time does not take away. Surely, then, love is forever.

After resting on the Knave for an hour, I took the path inland to the hamlet of Pitton. I had found Thunder Spring and Little Thunder on Overton Green. Surely there would be some sign of Thunder Child soon. He wouldn't be that far away from his family, would he? Could he be watching me from a secret hideout somewhere? "He will find you." The old man's words echoed again.

When I arrived at Pitton, it was indeed a small hamlet. There was a farm and a few old houses, and a shop, and that was it. It wasn't that I was expecting more from a little village or hamlet, for it is a charming little place, like the village of Port Eynon, where time stands still.

But where was my stallion? And why all of a sudden did I feel this need to find him? Was he in trouble and needing my help? Or did I just need to connect with this missing part of my family? It was as if in my soul I knew that finding him again was going to play a big part in my future here on the cliffs, and in some way our experience together would bring to a conclusion my time here in the wild. Riding him was something I knew I needed to do, but what else was in store for us? Suddenly I remembered my long ago dream that I would find him on the north Hill of Rhossili. I would soon find out if my dream was true.

From Pitton cross, I headed down the path to Mewslade Bay. This was Gay's and my absolute favourite place that we had found together in all of Gower. The path runs down a slade alongside a high limestone wall and crags that guard it on either side. Then suddenly you come to the Bay, one of the most dramatic in all of Gower. When Gay and I stopped in our tracks to behold the Bay, we both exclaimed that we had found our most sacred place, and I was both happy and sad to see it again.

Thurba Head rises sheer from the Sands as if pointing to heaven. Westward are the equally impressive rocks of Jacky's

Around the World In Five Days

Tor. Jacky must have been some woman to have those rocks named after her. It had been low tide when Gay and I discovered Mewslade Bay. We swam and kissed in the sea, and body surfed as the crystal clear waves washed us up on the beautiful yellow beach. As you rise from the waves, Thurba Head towers over you.

At low tide, Gay and I had walked from Mewslade past Jacky's Tor, then on under the towering crag and razor-edged ridge of Devils Truck and the imposing rock tower of Lewes Castle into Fall Bay. Today, the tide was too far in for me to walk across the Sands of "Gay and Kingsley's Bay", so I climbed back up the path to the clifftop, and headed towards Tears Point, appropriately named today, I thought, as I felt so much like crying.

∽

Tears Point guards Fall Bay to the west and its shape seems gentle and kind, like a lonely longing lover, compared to the succession of limestone pinnacles and sheer rock that lift up so boldly and confidently like a knight raising his sword from the Sands of Mewslade and Fall Bay. My art and history teacher Mr. Richards told me that this was the rock climbers favourite place in all of the Gower Peninsula.

When the tide comes in, the Sands at Mewslade and Fall Bay disappear under the waves. You can't swim for at least two hours around high tide. It's a good time to cuddle up and tell stories with your girl, I found out. If you are alone, you can listen to the mermaids calling out from the waves, and learn stories about the Bay. I am told that if you come here in winter during a strong south westerly, winds drive the Atlantic rollers, and Mewslade fills with flying spray, and the thunder of the waves shout with the voices of lost sailors.

Around the corner from Tears Point is, in my view, one of the most spectacular sights on all of the Magnificent 5-mile walk, and that is the land's end of Gower, "The Worms Head." Yes, dear reader, I couldn't keep it a secret after all. The truth is, once you have walked the Magnificent 5-mile walk, you just have to tell someone, for it is so wonderful. The "Worm," as it's called in Gower, is one of the most amazing headlands in all of Britain.

The Worms Head really does live up to its name. It looks like a huge serpent or dragon, coiling its way out to sea, with its huge head rearing above the waves as if hissing to everyone who sees it: "Go west, go west, young man!" For its head plunges into the sea westward, as if it is leading the way. The Worm speaks with other voices too. When the wind drives in from the west, making the spray leap up from the blowhole on the outer head, it sounds out a strange, vibrating, booming sound that can be heard in the village of Rhossili itself.

When we were boys, my mother and father would take Fraser and me out for a Sunday drive. If we were well behaved, we would get an ice cream in the village, and my father would drive out to the car park on Rhossili Cliffs that look out to the Worms Head. When I looked out at it, I felt it was calling to me deep in my soul, and I had this desire to walk out to its very furthest point. At high tide the Worm becomes an island. But about 2.5 to 3 hours after high tide, the ebbing waters begin to leave what is known as the ship way — the channel between the Worm and the mainland.

Around the World In Five Days

My father once said, if you do walk out to the Worm at low tide, you must remember that you only have about three hours on the Worm before you get cut off by the tide. And if you don't get back in time, you will be marooned on the headland until the tide comes all the way in and goes out again. Growing up on the Gower, I heard frightening stories of people who drowned after getting cut off by the tides and trying to swim back to the mainland. It seemed each summer one or more unsuspecting tourists drowned, either trying to swim after being cut off, or falling to their death from the high rocks of the head. This, along with my father's warnings, was enough to stop Fraser and I from fishing alone on the Worm. We went with a fishing club, or with experienced locals who could read the weather and the tides.

Gay and I had hoped to cross out to the Worm and explore it when we were on our journey, but time and tide would not allow. Today, as I looked out to it from Tears Point, it called out to me in a silent voice, saying 'come and explore my secrets'. So I decided that before I returned to Maggie's on Friday, I would try and make the time to explore the Worms Head. First things first, though, I needed to find Thunder Child. It was late in the afternoon now, and the evening shadows were beginning their dark dance out over the waters. I had passed my refuge at Deborah's Hole, a long way back along the Cliff walk, but the dancing shadows told me that I had just enough time to get back there before dark. The sky looked heavy now with rain, and I could feel it in the air coming in from the Worms Head! My legs were heavy as I walked back along the path and itched where the wild Gorse had pricked through my jeans. At least I'd have shelter and be dry in Deborah's Hole.

Cave Days

    Tomorrow I would look for Thunder Child on North Hill, and if there was enough time and the conditions were right, go out on the Worm. The night clouds joined the wind and crossed the Bay quickly, and it was almost too dark to see when I arrived back at the cave. It was a good job that Gay and I had already explored the area, otherwise I'd have lost my way. Thank you, my love, for leading us back. Exhausted, I lay in my sleeping bag at the entrance and went right off to sleep.

Chapter Nineteen

Good Morning Deborah!

Wednesday morning at Deborah's Hole was as grey as November could be. With the light but steady drizzle and a thick cold mist hanging over the cliffs, I couldn't even see the sea. Well, good morning to you too, Deborah. I was expecting at least a kiss, not the cold shoulder like this. Oh well, all you girls can't all be as warm as my Gay, I guess.

Once in a while through the thinner pockets of mist, I could see the seabirds on the wing. I had a feeling of being closed in, and I wished the wind would get up from his sleep and blow open the windows of my day, but he remained a snoozer, and my feeling of being hemmed in grew to loneliness. What was I doing on this adventure? I asked my soul. Why am I looking for Thunder Child, I answered, trying to bring some meaning to what I was doing here this morning. The Cliffs are a lonely place in the mists. Familiar paths become mysterious and even frightening when you have lost your way. "I am not lost," I spoke aloud, as I left the cave to climb up the rocks to see if there was a break in the mist. There was nothing I could see, only thick mist, or was it fog? I could only see about 15 feet in front of me. It seemed too dangerous to walk any further away from the cave when I couldn't see. So I made my way back to Deborah and waited for the fog to clear. Suddenly, adding to my isolation, came the haunting sound of the Port Eynon foghorn. Then another horn from one of the light ships far out at sea echoed back in solemn conversation. I felt like a ship lost in the waves. How desperate are sailors lost at sea, I thought. I pictured a ship having run aground on the sandbar far out from the Bay, with the waves crashing over their ship and the drowning sailors shouts carried on the wind, as my father had told me stories about.

Many sailors drowned on the sand banks off Port Eynon, he said, before they put the Helwick light ships to warn the sailors away from the banks. When the wind becomes a northeaster, you can still hear the cries of their lost souls in the sea winds.

The foghorns sounded again, and I gripped the fog damp grass with my hands, making sure I wasn't lost at sea, for the spirits of the drowned sailors of the Helwick Sands were calling out to me.

"Fear, is that you?"

"Yes it's me, and I've caught up with you!"

"So what's wrong, Fear? Did you get lonely at Bacon Hole? Don't you remember me telling you to keep your chin up, old man, because I'm sure in a few thousand years someone else will come and live in the cave for you to haunt. Now clear off! Leave me alone and go back to your lonely cave. I have God in my heart, you see, and He will fight for me, you must flee."

When there is no fog and you can look out on the sea, even on the calmest days you can detect the sinister presence of the Helwick Sands by a line of darker blue. When the wind

Good Morning Deborah!

blows the waves break white with foam. They run due west from Port Eynon Point for five miles, and the East Helwick buoy off Port Eynon shows how narrow the channel is between the Shoal and the shore. The western end is marked by the Helwick Lightship, which you can pick out on a clear day low on the horizon. The presence of the Sands indicates that, for all its summer beauty that Gay and I enjoyed so much, this is a cruel coast for ships.

It was around midday when I saw the Sun behind the fog. Soon after, pockets of blue sky appeared, and the fog lifted like a man taking off layers of clothes before the warming sun. I too took my jacket off and basked in the warmth. The Port Eynon foghorn stopped its conversation with the Helwick Lightship, and shouted out instead, "you can carry on with your day now." So I did.

Within half an hour I had reached Tears Point again, and almost the whole sky was blue before me. As I turned the corner, I could see the spectacular view of the rock at the end of the world, the Worms Head. No matter how many times one sees the Worm, it provokes deep feelings as it calls out, either in the loud silence of its splendour, or in the mysterious language of the Blow Hole that booms across the sea to where you are in Rhossili. Even when you're walking with a group of people, it always seems that the Worm is talking to you personally. He talked quite plainly to my friends and I when we were boys. Some of us he frightened, and others, like me, he bid to come and visit with him. I never had to listen very hard to hear what he was saying. The Worm tells it the way it is.

The tide this afternoon was high, and the Worm had changed to an island. There would be no going out to visit with him today, not when he's wearing this wardrobe. Maybe tomorrow? Today I would walk up to the beacon of Rhossili Downs, following my dream of finding Thunder Child up there. Not having had breakfast yet, I headed into Rhossili village first. The Worms Head pub was open, but I didn't have enough money for a pub meal, and the general store was closed, so I walked back to the end of the village to the cafe that looked out towards Rhossili Downs.

The cafe was warm and dry and had a nice waitress who said, "Would you like a tea or coffee? We have freshly made scones this morning too."

"I'll have a cup of tea and one of your warm scones, please, and with butter and jam." As I sat at the table near the window, I scanned the hills for any signs of horses, though I doubted that Thunder Child would be with a herd. More likely he would be roaming alone somewhere, enjoying his own company.

After finishing my tea and scones (Yes, I had another one. They were so good with thick warm butter and enough strawberry jam to sink a ship), I walked up the hill path. It was well trodden by local village residents walking their dogs and collecting their thoughts with walking sticks and wives, or just with sticks having escaped their wives for an hour or three—depending on how loud the woman shouted, that is. Out here a man can be free, the old man had said. Like a teapot brought to the boil, when he got back from his walk, all was calm again. The man and his wife went off for another walk together, and she was no longer the crazy woman, but his sweetheart again.

In the summer when Gay and I had climbed the path, there were several tourists exploring the Downs, but today the

Good Morning Deborah!

path through the Gorse was less colourful and it was lonely. I only saw one man walking his dog, or was the dog walking him? They looked alike.... as men and their dogs often do. The only difference between them was the four legged one stopped to pee, and the two legged one didn't. I said good morning to both of them. Halfway up the hill, I rested and watched two ravens doing some acrobatic flying over the hills. They were quite something to see, diving and dancing on the winds from the sea.

Even from halfway up, the view looking back down to the village is wonderful. You look down over the farm fields with their grey stone walls. As one inspects them from below, you can see that each wall is made up of individual stones, sitting one upon the other and fitted to perfect shape and size. What skills those farmers had to have to build those stone walls so well. Some have stood for over 100 years or more, and generations of the farming families have kept them up. You can find fossils on the walls that tell stories of even the most ancient days.

It was time to continue up the Hill to the summit of the Downs. The cliffs on which Rhossili stands are 200 feet high and are a fine viewpoint, yet the view from the top of the Downs is even finer. The beacon is the highest point in Gower at 632 feet. Suddenly I became excited as I saw a herd of horses coming down the hill. There was no stallion with them, just mares with their foals. It gave me encouragement to see them, though, and I greeted them like long lost friends.

"You have made some friends," said a woman with her dog coming down the hill behind them. "If you want to see a wild one, there's a big stallion on the other side of the hill. It chased me and my dog." She protested.

Cave Days

I tried not to smile at her serious face, but I knew it had to be him. My heart raced with excitement as I hurried up the remainder of the hill, and there he was, thundering across the Downs with two other horses. "Thunder Child," I shouted. "I've found you, old boy. I've been searching for you everywhere."

I watched him run with the other horses until he was almost out of sight on the far side of the Downs, then he came thundering back towards me. He slowed to a trot and came right over to greet me. He allowed me to lift my hand and rub his head. "It's good to see you old boy, I've missed you. Thunder Spring and Little Thunder send their love to you."

Wow. I felt like a King up there on top of the hill, reunited with my stallion. His reddish brown coat was shiny and silky in the afternoon sun. He was obviously in good health.

"Where have you been, old boy? Roaming the Downs and chasing the mares? I hear you have been naughty, scaring a woman and her dog." He lifted his head up and down in agreement, and he had a mischievous gleam in his eye.

"It's good to see you too, old boy, and how do you like your new territory?"

"It's good," he said, "I like it a lot. It's beautiful up here, isn't it? And there's lots of space to chase the girls."

Suddenly he was off again, chasing the other two horses. I'd seen when they'd stopped galloping that they were both mares, and I shouted out, "Well done, Thunder Child. You have found yourself two new girlfriends, and I don't even have one."

As I watched the three of them disappear again in the distance, I felt as wild and free as they did. "King of the Castle", or at least joint heir with Thunder Child as we shared the Kingship of the Gower Peninsula.

Good Morning Deborah!

I didn't mind sharing it with him. As you stand on the beacon, the highest point on the Gower, it's not just the height that thrills one's soul, it's the uniqueness of what is below. From up there, you don't need to be a Red Kite or a Hawk, and you are certainly no ordinary man. You are changed, your soul enlarged. You're not the same coming down as you were when you came up. If you are, you are a blind man indeed, having missed the sights and sounds of some of God's greatest creation, a creation that praises him so loudly.

Behold, my soul, for here before me is the most wonderful place on Earth. Thunder Child and I are in agreement on this. And it is said that God himself walks here in the cool of the evening, just like he did in Eden.

"Who says so?" Says you.

"I do," says I, "and so does my stallion, as we look over the wonderful things He has made."

I spent the rest of the day up on the Downs with Thunder Child and the mares. They ran for hours until dusk, and then rested on the hill. I sat nearby and looked out with them across Rhossili Bay, until the curtains of the day were drawn.

I awoke Thursday morning, warm in my sleeping bag, as a gentle wind stirred and the smell of the sea caressed my senses. Thunder Child and the mares had already left the hill to start their day.

Rolling up my sleeping bag, I found 1 pound and 50p that must have been in the back pocket of my jeans. What a pleasant surprise to start my day, I thought, as I added it to my remaining change. At least now I could have a cup of tea and a scone in the village. Sometimes small blessings are really big ones.

Cave Days

When I arrived at the cafe, the same waitress as the day before was there, and she said I could have bacon, eggs and toast for three pounds. I just had enough to buy my breakfast. As I sipped my tea, I thought I would have to catch some more fish when I got back, and sell them in the village. Well, I'd found my horse family. I had achieved the goal I set out to achieve, and I had also found so much more. This journey in many ways had helped me to say goodbye to Gay, and hello to what was ahead for me.

I was becoming more aware that God was working in my life, but there was still so much that was a mystery in both my awareness and experience of his presence. I had also learned to take more notice of my dreams, for through them I had been guided to find my horse family. Was this God speaking through my dreams or was it connected at all? I believe they were because my dreams had told me right. Thunder Child was roaming the hills on top of Rhossili Downs, and I had found Thunder Spring and Little Thunder on the way. Surely this was no coincidence.

Well, should I go back to the great Tor and catch some fish and sell them in the village before I go to Maggie's tomorrow? No, I'd come this far. I couldn't go back until I had walked Rhossili beach and been for an adventure out on the Worms Head. It's a nice day too, with lots of blue sky.

After finishing my bacon and eggs, I walked out onto Rhossili Cliffs to see what the tide was doing. It was quite high but looked like it was going out. There was wet sand already a good distance in front of the breakers. Indeed it was going out. This would give me time to walk Rhossili beach first while the tide was continuing its way out, and then climb out to the

Worm this afternoon at low water. With spring in my step, and excitement in my heart, I climbed down the steep path from the village to the beach.

Walking westwards with the Worms Head behind me, I headed towards Burry Holmes, which also becomes an island on the high tides. The distance from the Worms Head to Burry Holmes is about three miles, so it was going to be a long walk. I walked high up on the beach as the tide was still about three quarters of the way in. One reward in walking high up on the beach is the pink and red stones. They are all pushed up in a pile by the strong Atlantic breakers. I spent quite a bit of time along my walk picking up stones of various shapes and colours. The rocks are of old red sandstone, which is the backbone of Rhossili Downs and Cefn Bryn.

My favourite stones to find are the flat square or rounded ones, which are a deep pink colour when dry and a darker red when dipped in the water. By the time I had walked for half an hour, I had quite a collection of them, and my backpack was heavy. What was that at the foot of the dunes? It looked like a heart-shaped stone. It was a perfect heart shape with a marble line going right around it. It made all my other rocks look ordinary in comparison. It was just as well, because my backpack was too heavy to carry now. So I dumped the rest in a pile up on one of the sand dunes. They were too precious to leave on the seashore. At least up here in the dunes they wouldn't get washed away and buried again by the tide. I hoped one day to return and collect them, so I put a marker of driftwood on the dunes to show me where I had left them. The beautiful pink rocks accumulate almost the whole length of the beach in front of the dunes.

On the sand dunes the long grasses grow, as tall as bull rushes or reeds. These grasses make some of the dunes secluded unto themselves like little rooms. I thought of bringing a beautiful girl here. Maybe Autumn, if she ever came back to the Gower for another holiday. We could collect some of the most precious stones and decorate our own secret room.

For once I didn't think of bringing Gay somewhere. It was one of the places we had never explored together. As I placed my last marker of driftwood over the buried treasure of my stones, I remembered I had a notebook and pen in the pocket of my backpack. I decided to write a poem within my secret sand dune room. The grass grew tall around my room in the shape of a horse shoe – just leaving a small entrance as a doorway. On one side of my room grew a wild Daisy bush and it was still in flower, as if it lived outside of the winter season, and it reminded me of the long sunny days of summer. So I decided to write about the daisies in my sand dune room.

WHEN THE TALL DAISIES BLOW

The wind rides in with the laughing sea,
and the sun-drenched Daisies stir.
A gentle waltz and then a lively dance,
But their eyes are always upon their lover, the sun.
They twist and turn, to high tides burn,
their secrets only told in the wind.
Upon the high beach where the driftwood roams
in the waves,
And dream of becoming islands in the dunes.

Good Morning Deborah!

The tall Daisies lift their heads up high
And follow the sun until the wind's song grows silent,
and they no longer stir.
Slowly they turn their heads again,
and follow their white and yellow dreams
To somewhere behind the purple fading sunset.
And the wild oak whispers,
it's the end of the day,
And the tall Daisies bow down good night and
dream of another yellow May.
© *Kingsley Ross Hill*

After walking for another half an hour, I came to a stream that flowed out between the dunes. Long before you reach it, you can see the trail of wet sand that runs right to the sea. I found out later that this stream is called Diles Lake, which seems a rather strange name for a stream. I also found out that the stream originates beyond the high beacon of the Downs above, and is also known by Gower locals as the divide between South and North Gower.

As I crossed the shallow stream I now stood in North Gower. It became significant to me that Gay and I had never crossed this boundary together. We had turned around last summer before crossing the stream. So here on this day, standing in North Gower would signify my officially letting go of Gay and moving on in my life. I recalled my prayers to God, asking his help and strength to face the day, and the time after, when Gay and I would go our separate ways. And now he had more than answered my prayers, beyond what I could have hoped and dreamed. Finding God for me was like finding a hidden treasure in the sand. It's like finding gold coins from a sunken ship. You find one and enjoy spending it as part of your discovery of who God is. And then it's as if he hides more coins in the sand, so we can find them and experience the excitement of discovering more and more of who he is. For when we walk with Him, we never walk alone.

When I was a boy I became a Liverpool football club fan, and they have a song that they sing at Anfield, their home ground. The song is called "You'll Never Walk Alone," and when you sing the words along with thousands of other people, you can't help feeling emotional, and you have the feeling that, no matter what happens in your life, you will never really walk alone again. The Liverpool fans are so friendly, and they treat you like family, especially when they find out that you have travelled hundreds of miles from South Wales to come and support the team.

YOU'LL NEVER WALK ALONE

When you walk through the storm
Hold your head up high
And don't be afraid of the dark
At the end of the storm
There's a golden sky
And the sweet silver song of the dark
Walk on, through the wind
Walk on, through the rain
Though your dreams be tossed and blown
Walk on, walk on,

Good Morning Deborah!

with hope in your heart
And you'll never walk alone
You'll never walk alone

Walk on, walk on, with hope in your heart
And you'll never walk alone
You'll never walk alone
© *Gerry and the Pacemakers*

I was always touched by the words of the song, even when the team didn't do well, but as the challenges and hardships of life carry on, as they always do, one does often feel like they are walking alone. They don't have hope in their heart. It's hard to walk on in the wind and walk on in the rain without hope in something that will last. People need something that will always be there to help them pick up the pieces of their broken dreams, and to show them a golden dawn.

I continued to make my way across the Sands to Burry Holmes. The word Holm comes from the old Scandinavian word "Holmr," meaning a small rounded island. Burry Holmes forms the northern tip of Rhossili Bay. It is a small limestone tidal island, only accessible for approximately 2.5 hours, each side of low water. I have only been out onto the island a handful of times, and that was with my father on exploring expeditions when I was 10 or 11 years old. We never did see a Viking, much as I wanted to fight one with my father's sword. I do, however, remember my father pointing out the mediaeval ruins of a small chapel, and I could feel the strange and desolate atmosphere, like I was back in a remote past. Very much like the feeling I had when I first stood outside the entrance of Bacon Hole.

Cave Days

My father had this wonderful gift of being able to make our expeditions that much more exciting. Like talking about what it would be like to time travel, to visit ancient civilizations and epic events in history. That's why I wanted to fight the Vikings, and at 10 years old I wanted to polish my father's swords and have them ready for when the Vikings came back. I also wanted to fight with Lord Nelson, against the French, and put a sword through the belly of Napoleon. Unfortunately that stuff all happened long before my time. Dad cheered me up by saying that Lord Nelson won anyway, without our help, and Dad did say that Lord Nelson would be pleased that I was polishing the swords in case the French ever tried to invade our island.

At the highest point of Burry Holmes, my father let me push his sword into the ground just like King Arthur, and at the age of 10, Burry Holmes became my island. No Viking has dared to come ashore ever since. From the highest point, or "sword point" as my father and I renamed it, you can look out over white horses breaking over the dangerous sand bank of the Burry Estuary. White horses with fallen riders, my father called the waves. I stood at the Cliff with his sword to see if any Viking rider would ever climb back on his horse again. Alas, not one ever did. We had conquered them.

As I approached my island today, the tide was still too far in for me to go out and explore it again, so I climbed up the sand dunes and then on up to Rhossili Downs. From there I could see the rolling hills of Carmarthenshire in mid-Wales. I rested there on the Downs for about an hour, and then climbed back down to the beach. I didn't want to miss the tide falling just low enough for me to climb out to the Worms Head.

Good Morning Deborah!

By the time I reached the south end of the beach again, it was well into the afternoon, and the sun was already lowering. What was that up ahead where the waves were just letting go of their claim? It was the wreck of a ship. Quickly I took off my shoes and socks, rolled up my jeans and walked into the water and over to the structure. The sea was chilling and the waves strong as they crashed around my knees. So much for keeping dry. Suddenly I remembered I'd seen this wreck before. I recognised its ribs sticking up out of the sand, and where it was in relation to a landmark on the cliffs above. It was the wreck of the Helvitia, and I hadn't seen it since I was a boy playing on the beach with my mother and father. Now I stood amidst its ancient frame and the crashing waves as a young man, and I felt a quiet gentle voice speaking within my heart.

This ship has been buried all these years, hidden amidst the crashing waves and the shifting sands, and I had found it again.

Above the sound of the waves, I now heard the voice become louder, saying, "Kingsley. This is the wreck of the Helvetia, which ran aground on the beach in 1887, just as your father told you. Only one man survived. The other members of the crew perished in the waves. For the man who survived and lived in the village of Rhossili for a while, it was a new beginning in his life, and yet for the others it was the end of their lives. You see, Kingsley, a shipwreck is either an end or a beginning. A reminder of the watery grave of lives lost, or a launch pad to a new life ahead for the survivors. Mankind has taken my hands off the helm of their lives and tried to steer the ship of life without me. A sunken ship and a lost crew is the result."

Cave Days

As I continued to stand between the broken ribs of the Helvitia, I felt sad because I was seeing a picture of my own brokenness. Then I heard the voice say, "cheer up, do not be sad, for this wreck doesn't signify the end for you, Kingsley, but a wonderful new beginning. I am the saviour of broken ships. This is why I have come to stand with you in the waves today. You came to live in your cave's and on the beach to try and make sense of your life which was falling apart, and you have found me. I want to steer and navigate the helm of your life, Kingsley, and show you *wonderful things that you do not know, and take you to places you have never been. For I have kept your dreams in my heart and I love you.*"

"Yes, I answered, but I am broken inside. I feel so unworthy of having a happy and successful life, because I feel it's my fault that my family has fallen apart."

"Kingsley, Listen to my words. It is not your fault. Again I tell you what your heart needs to hear. It is not your fault." Still standing in the waves I lifted up my head and looked out to sea, and in the distance I could see a sailboat with its coloured sails hoisted proudly. Then the voice spoke again.

"The ship that you see sailing with its sails up in the wind, colourful and free, are like the lives of those people whom my hand is steering. As I steer and navigate your life upon the open waters, do not be afraid of the wind and the waves. Remember, it is I who am with you at the helm of your life. I, who the wind and the waves obey."

"Yes, God," I cried out, as I continued to watch the sailboat sailing by with its colourful sails, high and happy in the wind. "I thank you God, for saving me from a shipwrecked life. I want you to take the helm, and navigate my life."

Good Morning Deborah!

As I continued my way along the beach towards the Worms Head, my heart glowed with the words and revelations. I danced my way along the beach, for when God meets with us, we are changed, and made new from the inside out. "How I want to follow you, upon the seas of this life, knowing it is you who steers me to what is ahead."

As I reached the south end of the beach, I had to climb the steep path again to get back up to the village, and then walk out on the cliffs to take the path to the Worm. Once you climb down from the cliff paths, you come to what is known as the Shipway. The Shipway is the low-lying rocky causeway that leads out to the Worms Head itself. It is on this stretch of rock where one can easily get cut off by the incoming tide if you're not very careful. It was late in the day, so I wouldn't have much time to cross the Shipway and explore the Worm, and get back before dark, and tomorrow was Friday. I needed to get back to Maggie's to take care of her cottage. She would be expecting me quite early in the evening.

I stood at the beginning of the Shipway and pondered. If it got too dark, I would have to stay out on the Worm all night. The thought of being marooned on the "Rock at the End of the World" was a frightening prospect, but the adventure was also calling loudly, and I did have my sleeping bag and jacket. Oh, what should I do?

Chapter Twenty

The Rock at the End of the World

The call of the Worm, along with my spirit of adventure, won over my hesitation, and I found myself crossing the Shipway. Many of the rocks are sharp and jagged and it was difficult to keep a straight line while I jumped from rock to rock. There is also a spur of low-lying rocks out beyond the Shipway called the "crabert," a great crabbing area where one can catch edible crabs and even lobsters in the holes and crevices. Once in a while I stopped to explore a rock pool or gully, but there would be no time for any crabbing today. That fun and adventure would have to wait for another day.

  I continued on, scraping and grazing my knees here and there as I pounced from rock to rock like an escaping tiger. When one has walked a fair way out along the Shipway, there is a definite sense of aloneness, and a feeling of being exposed to the mysterious and potentially dangerous surroundings as you glance toward the safety of the mainland. Then as you look ahead to the Worm which now looks much bigger and intimidating than it did from the Cliff paths, there is a feeling of being cut off already, and thoughts of what it would be like to be marooned were already in my mind.

Carefully looking at the tide, it seemed to have reached its low, for it was still like a sleeping serpent. It would stay out for an hour and then start making its way in. There wasn't a lot of time so I needed to make the most of it.

Once across the Shipway, along with my cuts and bruises, I climbed up to the first and biggest of the three humps upon the Worm. One could call it a camel as well as a worm, especially when the blowhole hissed, but the rock at the end of the world is long, and its shape is more like a worm. This first hump is called the inner head, and is flat and grassy on top, and I had a feeling of safety up here as I looked back upon the treacherous rocks below.

As I continued, a group of hikers passed me on their way back to the shipway. "Don't get cut off," the leader of the group said to me. "You only have about three hours and then you won't be able to get off."

"Thank you," I said. "I'm just going to make a quick trip out to the end and back."

"Good luck."

"Yes, thank you. Bye now." He was quite right. I needed to get a move on. Making my way now from the inner head to what is called the middle head, I passed over a section of rough rock. It wasn't difficult, just stony and hard compared to the soft springy grass on top of the inner head.

I came now to one of the most spectacular and mysterious parts of the Worm, "The Devil's Bridge." The Devil's Bridge is a huge natural limestone arch which you cross from the middle head to the outer head. My mind flashed back to how my father had had to coax me to cross over it when I was a boy, as I looked enviously at him already having crossed to the other side. Even today I walked quickly across, not stopping to enjoy the incredible view which the bridge has to offer, for the Devil's Bridge is a spectacular balcony, where one can see out over Rhossili Bay, with the sea birds screaming and nesting below. The only time I ever felt comfortable standing in the middle of the Devil's Bridge was with my father's strong arms around me. We could look at the danger below, and I would feel so safe. How different the world seems when fear shows his face and whispers his lies.

As I crossed the bridge and stood on the outer head, it is difficult to describe the strange and wonderful feeling within my soul that I experienced there, but I shall do my best to do so.

First of all, I believe it to be one of the most powerful revelations of God's greatness and majesty. Here, He is reverently feared, praised, and worshipped by wind, land and sea. Secondly, the outer head is a place apart. It is a haunting rare place on the Earth's surface, full of wild air where the four winds converse with the crying gulls and the thunder of the sea. The strange, tormented hissing and booming sound from the blowhole is always in your ears like screams of drowned sailors calling out from the waves of Rhossili Bay.

I now reached the end of the Worm, and I tried to see what I could without getting too close to the edge. I could see how the Cliff plunged over 100 feet into the sea. As I peered over, the sea at the end of the Worm looked restless, like it was on an endless search for peace. The waves thrashed and swelled and crashed into the rocks, for they could find no peace.

The Rock at the End of the World

I thought the waves mirrored my soul before I found the safe harbour of God's grace and love.

It was time for me to leave this rock at the end of the world and get back to the mainland before I was marooned. Turning from the cruel sea, I started my way back to the middle head, and the Devil's Bridge, which I decided to rename "the Balcony of God." As I walked along the view was fantastic, and I soon reached the Middle head. I was making good time, as I could see plenty of the shipway left for me to get back on. Suddenly my foot went into a pothole and twisted.

The pain! I jumped three steps on my other foot and fell onto the soft grass, but the pain in my foot was throbbing. Undoing my laces, I took my shoe and sock off and inspected my ankle. It was swelling and it hurt to touch. That's just great. I shouted, "I twisted my ankle." Putting my shoe on again, I took a few steps. Oh, the pain. I couldn't even walk, let alone cross the rugged rocks of the shipway. I tried putting all the weight on the heel of my foot, but I was off balance and in too much pain to go further.

Well, that was it. I was going to be stuck out here on the Worm. I hobbled to the edge of the Cliff top and looked out across the shipway. The tide was coming in and quickly now, and the light was slowly fading. I watched enviously some people at the far end of the shipway who had almost made it back to the mainland. Oh well, I would just have to make the best of it, and I heard my grandmother's words saying, "We have to thank the Lord for the small mercies, King."

What small mercies? I thought. Then I thought of one. It could have happened on the outer head, and I'd have that much further to hobble, and then I thought of another mercy.

Cave Days

What if I had twisted my ankle out on the shipway? I could easily have been drowned in the strong currents as the tide swept me off into the open sea. At least I was safe here now, and I did have my sleeping bag and jacket, so I could keep warm. I didn't feel very thankful for the blessing of being safe and warm, but I did pray and thank God that I wasn't stuck out on the shipway.

It was going to be a long night, so I found a soft area of grass and pulled out my sleeping bag. At least I had a room with a view. I looked out across Rhossili Bay. "This might even be the penthouse suite." I said to Mr. Seagull resting nearby. He didn't answer. I guess he knew better.

"Hey you know what, Mr. Gull? When you're stuck out on the rock at the end of the world, you have to lower your standards a bit. What was that you said, Mr. Gull? Something about room service? Yeah, the room service is pretty poor around here. In fact, they didn't even offer to take my jacket when I came into the hotel. Don't you squalk at me, Mr. Gull. Oh, *you* are the room service. Well, if you're expecting a tip, you can forget it."

The night clouds soon rolled in thick and heavy, and the Sun closed his eyes behind the horizon, and I heard an old familiar voice whisper in my ear. "Kingsley. It's going to be dark soon, and you're marooned all alone out here on the Worms Head."

"Why, it's Fear. I was wondering when you were going to show up. I can't say it's nice to see you though, but please carry on. I'm trying not to listen."

Fear continued his conversation. "And don't forget that nobody knows you're here, and what if there's a storm during the night? You will be blown over the cliff to your death in the waves below."

"Oh, Fear, you're such a pessimist. In all my years I've known you, I've never heard you say one positive thing. This is such a bad relationship, you know. Things really aren't working out between us. I want a divorce."

"Only God can divorce me from you, Kingsley."

"You're right. You're right, Fear, that's the one true thing I've ever heard you say. Actually you didn't say it. In my battles with you, God is revealing to me that he is the only one who can help me have victory over you. Fear is a faith battle."

"Oh Kingsley, shut up and listen. God isn't going to help you. The only help he gave you was twisting your ankle, but I've come to visit you, all alone on the Worms Head. Doubt and Confusion send their regards to you. They couldn't come with me now because of a prior engagement, but they did say they would be coming later on in the middle of the night. You'll know, Kingsley, when you hear the drowned sailors screams and the Devil himself goes for his walk across the Worms Head. They don't call it The Devil's Bridge for nothing, you know.

Oh, that's right Kingsley, you haven't been here all night before, have you? Well, what happens about 2 a.m. in the morning is, the Devil starts his walk, and he walks every inch of the Worms Head, and searches for anyone marooned on the island by the tide. And when he finds them—and he always does—he picks them up and carries them on his shoulders all the way out to the blowhole. He throws them down into the deep dark hole never to be heard of again, and if you listen carefully in the gale, you can hear the lost souls of his victims screaming in the wind…And tonight, it's your turn, to be devoured and torn apart, and thrown to the bottom of the blowhole. Well, enjoy your night, and if you need anything, just ask. I'll be here."

Stretching my legs out in my sleeping bag, I watched the night sky for a while and wondered how my foot would be in the morning. Hopefully the swelling would have gone down, and I could make it back to the village. From there I would catch a bus to Penmaen and get to Maggie's cottage. My plan of attack to pass the night was to get to sleep as quickly as I could before it got completely dark, just like in the old days at Bacon Hole, and hopefully when I woke up, it would be morning.

I closed my eyes and thought of God, and I said to Fear: "I'm trusting God to take care of me and I'm not going to be afraid. I've asked Him to give me his peace, and a good night's sleep, and to heal my ankle while I rest. So leave me alone, Fear. I trust myself to God's care, and I resist you, and you will flee from me," and God answered my prayers and gave me his peace. I was able to go to sleep meditating quietly on something I had read in my Bible.

Peace I leave with you. My peace I give to you. Not as the world gives do I give unto you.

What was that? Where am I? I thought, as I awoke in the howling wind. Suddenly Fear was back in full force, and now Doubt and Confusion were here to visit as well. What was going on? I faithfully said my prayers and put my trust in God to look after me, and now I've woken up in a storm. The wind was so strong, I dared not stand up. I rolled on my side with my heart racing.

The Rock at the End of the World

"What is going on, Lord?" I cried out in a frightened voice. The gusts of wind were so strong that I dug my hands into the long grass to make sure I wasn't moving and in danger of being swept off the cliff, and what was that frightening noise? The winds were now howling like a 1000 voices around what was now the "terrifying rock at the end of the world." Lightning flashed and thunder clapped. When the lightning stopped, it was black all around, apart from lightships that stared like demon eyes far out to sea. I could hear between the clashes of thunder the most haunting sound. It was the sound of the blowhole with its strange, hollow booming sound.

Fear whispered in my ears, "The Devil has started his walk, and there is nowhere to hide." Lightning flashed overhead now, lighting up the sea below me. The waves were as big as houses, snarling with their white frothy teeth attacking the rocks. Fear held me captive now in full force. I cried out to God, and asked him to calm the storm. "Please take it away, God, I'm afraid." Quickly I found my Bible, and there was still some light in my flashlight, even though I had left it on. I turned to the story where the disciples were out in the middle of the Sea of Galilee and they became afraid, and Jesus stood up in the boat and calmed the storm.

As I read his words amidst the storm, I heard him speak to me within my heart. "Kingsley. Are you going to trust me in this storm? Or are you going to allow fear to consume you?"

"Dear God, I believe your words to be true, and that you calmed the Sea of Galilee, that even the wind and waves obeyed you. Now I ask you to please do the same for me, oh Lord, calm the storm." Closing my Bible, I waited for God to act. For a little while the storm seemed to be going away. The lightning flashes were getting further apart, and the clashes of thunder were moving out across the Bay. Then suddenly it was back with a vengeance.

Lightning flashed right over my head and a loud clap of thunder shouted, "It's true. The Devil is on his way and he is after you."

"God is *not* going to calm the storm." Fear whispered close to my ear. "In the Bible, it says that Jesus raised his hands and said 'peace, be still,' and the wind and waves calmed instantly. Look around you, Kingsley, and listen to the storm. He has not calmed it for you, has he? He hasn't even heard your prayer, because he's not even real, that's why. The storm is getting worse."

And with Fear's words, the rain started to pelt down on my face. "Where are you, God?" I shouted. "Didn't you hear my prayers? I'm trying to trust you, that you will do the same for me and calm the storm. Are you sleeping, Lord? If you are, wake up and help me."

"Kingsley. Kingsley." a quiet, strong voice spoke within my heart. "Do not let your heart be troubled or be afraid, for I am with you. It is I, the Lord your God."

I picked up my Bible which I had dropped in my fear. It was lying on the ground and open and with the light of my flashlight I started to read. It read:

[I have chosen you and have not rejected you. So do not fear, for I am with you, do not be dismayed, for I am your God. I will strengthen you and help you, I will uphold you with my righteous right hand.]

As I read God's words to me, I became full of joy because a feeling of peace suddenly surrounded me, and I became as bold as a lion. Wow, what an amazing feeling, to meet me here, right where I'm at, in the middle of this storm, and tell me those wonderful things about what you think of me, and give me promises from your heart to help me in my distress.

[All the rage against you will surely be ashamed and disgraced, those who oppose you will be as nothing and perish. Though you search for your enemies, you will not find them. Those who wage war against you will be nothing at all.]

"Did you hear that, Fear?" I shouted out to the storm. "All who wage war against me will be as nothing at all and will perish. So be gone with you, Fear. I am not afraid."

God did not answer my prayers in the way I'd asked him. He chose not to take away the storm, but to allow it to blow in all its fury, all around me all night long. Through the storm though, he taught me a wonderful lesson, and gave me a gift of understanding that would surely become a part of my life for always. "God quiets the storms within our hearts." Fear would always be around the corner if He had just stopped the storm. Instead he was building me into a strong ship that could withstand the waves of life, no matter how big they got.

In the morning, as I lay safe and secure in my sleeping bag, the Tempest now calmed and God's work performed in my heart, it was time to greet the new day. I wrote this morning poem as I was so touched by my experience. It touched my heart in such a wonderful way through his words.

Cave Days

IN THE SECRET OF HIS PRESENCE

In the secret of his presence,
all my darkness disappears,
For at my cry he comes walking
upon the waters,
And as a sun that knows no setting,
he throws a rainbow on my tears.
Above the sound of the Tempest,
his tender ear hears.
So my day grows ever lighter,
broadening to the perfect noon,
So my day grows ever brighter,
here he comes, near and soon,
And as for my fears there is simply
no room.
In the secret of his presence,
never more can my foes alarm.
In the shadow of the highest,
I can meet them with a psalm,
For his strong pavilion hides me,
and I am safe all the day long.
And I know,
whatever betides me,
all I have to do is sing his song.
Kingsley, I died so you could live,
and I want you to be my song.
© *Kingsley Ross Hill*

"I hope you like it, Lord."

And I know he did.

Rolling up my sleeping bag, I stood up on my twisted foot. It still hurt as I put weight on it, but the swelling had gone down, and I hobbled down from the inner head to the Shipway, which was already half exposed by the outgoing tide. I was quite thankful that the tide was still going out, because I hobbled along the shipway about as fast as the tortoise in the story of the race between the tortoise and the hare; "darn slow,", if you haven't heard the story.

It gave me lots of time to think and meditate. And I couldn't help thinking of God's wonderful words to me. They weren't just words that you can read and then forget about them.

I couldn't get over how God had "chosen me." It took me back to old Pennard primary school, where at each playtime, or recess as they call it here in British Columbia, Canada, I stood in line with about 10 or 12 other boys, hoping to be picked by one of the two captains of the school football team. Slowly, the two captains would look us boys up and down and begin to pick who they thought the best players would be, and of course they picked their friends first. All our hands went up as we shouted, "pick me, pick me." One by one, the line grew smaller as the captains picked their teams.

For me, it wasn't a matter of being picked first or even which team I ended up on. What mattered to me was not being the last to be picked. Oh the hurt and embarrassment of being one of the last two boys standing there, while all the other boys, having already been picked, shouted to the captains, "pick George or Michael, not Kingsley. We don't want him on our team," and most often I would be standing there alone. To make my rejection worse, sometimes the captains would argue about who was going to take me at all. If the teams already picked had even numbers, then both captains would say, "sorry, Kingsley.'" No, they didn't even call me 'Kingsley.' They would say, "sorry, Queensley, it's odd numbers today so you don't get to play, but you can play with the girls if you like." As I turned my back, the laughter stung more than a kick, and I thought, God, why did you bother making me? Why did you allow me to be born to be rejected and feel this pain? The *saddest* thing was that I was a great footballer, and I so rarely got the chance to show it. It's hard being rejected when you're only eight or nine; you tend to carry it with you through your life. That is, until someone chases you and tells you that you're "a Prince."

So I say: for God, the greatest captain of all, to choose me and not reject me is amazing. I couldn't get my head around it.

My mind went back to my first few years of high school, when I became the best football player in the school. I found myself as the favoured captain standing in front of about 30 boys with their hands in the air shouting, "pick me. pick me." My assistant captain stood with me and we collaborated on picking a team together. As the chosen boys stood at our side, I noticed one boy with his hands down and not shouting at all.

"Who is that?" I asked my assistant.

"Oh that's George Matthews. Don't pick him, he's always last. He can't play for toffee, and he comes from Sandy Lane, the poor area of Pennard."

So I picked him. "Why on earth did you pick him?" my assistant protested, "I told you he's a loser."

"I know what it's like to be picked last." I replied. "Now, don't argue, or I'll pick another assistant."

I'll never forget the pride on George Matthews' face, and the wonder and joy in his eyes as he walked forward to join the Gowerton Grammar School Football Team. I think he must have thanked me about ten times during our first practice meet, for picking him and giving him a chance. That's how God made me feel when he said, "I have chosen you, Kingsley, and not rejected you."

Later on that year, George Matthews, having inspired the whole team to work very hard, became the new captain of the Football Team. The assistant captain often said to me, "How did you know what he was really like, that he would become such a great player?" My answer, of course, was: "I didn't. I picked him because I knew how it felt to be last." God sees in us what we can't see ourselves, and we are immeasurably valuable to him. God believes in us and knows what we can become.

I continued my way across the shipway, stopping every so often to soak my foot in the cold water of the rock pools. Even though I still had pain, it helped to keep the swelling down. As I continued on, I could feel how crisp and clear the atmosphere was after the storm. Everything seemed fresh and new again.

One of the lovely things I have experienced living on the cliffs, is "clear shining after the rain." After a heavy shower, or a continued rainy season, the Sun shines again, and there is a delightful cleanness and freshness in the air that we do not experience at other times. Perhaps the brightest weather is just after the rain has ceased, when the wind has driven away the clouds, and the Tempest has stilled, and the Sun appears from his chambers to gladden the Earth with his smiles.

I managed to make it to the end of the Shipway and then hobbled up the Cliff path to the village. My foot was swollen again and too painful to walk any further. I made it to the bench at the bus stop and waited for the Rhossili 18 bus, which would take me back to Penmaen, and then it was just a short walk to Maggie's cottage. Thank you, God! I'd made it. And oh, what a blessing to see that green bus come around the corner. My mother had told me that 'beach' was my first word and then it was 'bus', and as that bus came around the corner I said it three times: "bus bus bus."

"Yes, that's right, it's a bus." said an old lady who was also sitting on the bench, and she smiled and looked at me like I was a two-year-old.

"Yes, a bus." I laughed. "I'm just so happy to see it."

"Where on Earth do you come from to be so excited about a bus? You can't be from around here."

"No ma'am, I'm not."

"Well, where do you live then?"

"Oh here and there, and last night I slept out on the Worms Head."

"The Worms Head," she said, dropping her walking stick and shaking her head. "I've never heard of anyone mad enough to sleep out on the Worms Head." And those were the last words she spoke to me as she gracefully shuffled over on the bench.

As the bus travelled through the narrow lanes of Rhossili, I thought of the comfort that awaited me at Maggie's cottage. There would be food, warmth and rest, and even a roof over my head—an appropriate welcome for a man who travelled "around the world in five days."

The bus arrived at Penmaen village at 3:15 sharp, and there were five sheep waiting to greet me, as well as one lost cow and three escaped chickens. What a welcome. I should have worn my white gloves and waved from the bus as I arrived. And where was the red carpet? There were cow poo patties along the road—nice welcome, you guys. And the sheep "baaahd." It must be the way I'm walking, I thought. They must think I'm a bit odd.

When I reached the store, I could hardly take another step. Maggie pulled out a chair. "What have you done to your foot?" she asked. "You're limping badly."

"Oh, I twisted it out on the Worms Head."

"You were out on the Worms Head?!" she exclaimed. "How did you make it all the way back on your injured foot?"

"Oh little by little, Maggie. It's a long story."

"Well, you will have to tell me all about it when I close the store at five. I'm glad that you didn't leave it any later, Kingsley, as I've got lots to show you before I leave in the morning."

In between customers, I told Maggie of my adventures and experiences with God.

"I'm so glad that you're using your Bible, Kingsley, and that you're back safe. He sure has his hand on your life."

"Yes, I know he does, Maggie, and he's revealed himself to me in so many ways, and taught me so many wonderful things in my journey around the Gower."

"And you even found your horse family, Kingsley, that's wonderful. You see how faithful God is."

"Yes I do, beyond what I could have dreamed or imagined possible."

Maggie closed the store and helped me down the road to the cottage. "Now you can sit on the couch and rest your foot up on this stool," she said. "If you rest it all evening, and have a good night's sleep, it should be a lot better tomorrow." She made me a lovely home-made supper, and I had a custard trifle for dessert.

"Oh, thank you, Maggie. I am as hungry as a hunter, and trifle with custard is my favourite dessert."

"I knew it was, so I've made enough to last you at least for the first week I'm away. And then after that there's some home-made pies left over from the summer in the freezer."

I felt so blessed that Maggie had gone out of her way to prepare for my stay, and I thanked God in my heart for bringing Maggie into my life.

After supper she showed me my chores, including the food portions for the animals. "And don't forget the chickens, Kingsley. There should be fresh eggs for breakfast each morning if you want them, and the rest just put in the cartons in the fridge. Oh, and there's £15 on the table for anything else you need, and what you don't use you can keep. You can catch me another fish when I get back. Well, I'm off to bed now. I've got an early start in the morning. The bus leaves for Swansea at 6:45 so I probably won't see you before I go. I will call you mid-week to see how you're doing. I'm so thrilled that you're experiencing the Lord. You keep trusting him and he will continue to bless you greatly in your life."

"Thank you Maggie, he already is, and thank you for trusting me to look after your cottage while you're away."

"God bless you, Kingsley, and I'll see you when I get back."

"Good night, Maggie, I'll talk to you in the week."

"Goodnight, Kingsley."

Chapter Twenty-one

The Song of the Morning

To wake up in the most comfortable bed and hear the sound of the birds outside my window, and just lie here, is wonderful. And not having to be doing anything or going anywhere in particular was something I got used to living on the cliffs, but it felt wonderfully strange this morning here in Maggie's home that I had all to myself along with all its comforts. There was such a presence of peace in the cottage, unlike at my father and brother's house. There was a sense of sadness and loneliness there. Even when we were all together it still felt lonely. On more than one occasion I had asked Maggie if she liked living alone, and she said, "Why I don't live alone! I have the Holy Spirit with me! He is in my heart and around the house." Maggie, I now understand what you were saying: "Where God makes his home, there is peace!"

What should I do? I thought, still lying in bed. Maybe nothing, just lie here in this comfortable bed and listen to the birds sing their morning songs. The clock on the wall read eight o'clock. Maggie had left before seven. With one more stretch,

I decided to start my day with a bath. Yes, a real bath! The last time I had taken a bath was well over a month ago at my father's house when I was visiting Fraser. It was sure going to beat the Killy Willy River and a bar of soap.

With the bathwater running I looked at myself in the mirror. Well Kings, a shave wouldn't hurt you either, old boy, and to wash your hair in warm water again is going to be a real treat.

Stepping into the warm bath felt *so good*, like the warm kiss of lying in the sand dunes at the end of the summer. My sore foot felt a lot better this morning as I stretched out my legs in the hot water.

Well, what was next? Breakfast, yes breakfast. I would go out to the chicken coop and bring in some eggs, which I will have on Maggie's home-made bread with strawberry jam. My mouth was watering already.

After making tea in Maggie's old stainless steel teapot, and dressing it with a tea cosy, I went to say good morning to the chickens. Maggie had five hens, four of which had each laid a large brown egg. The rooster had lost his head months ago, Maggie had said, and was chilling out in the freezer. "I don't mind being woken up at 7 a.m. in the winter time, but 3 a.m. in the summer months was getting a trifle early."

I decided to name the larger hen Hatty, and as I reached gently under her feathers for the egg she gently pecked my hand and said something in chicken, and even though I speak fluent rock dove, I didn't understand what Hatty was saying, at least not yet. I decided she was saying good morning, so I said good morning back and thanks for the egg and for being so gentle. After filling the food trays with fresh grain, I went back to the

The Song of the Morning

cottage for breakfast. And as I poured my Yorkshire tea with goat's milk and one sugar, there was only one thing missing between my bites of toast, and that was Coronation Street. I would have to wait for Monday night for that. Maybe Hatty would like to join me?

For the rest of the day I just relaxed and enjoyed having this wonderful cottage to myself. As I looked around, Maggie had pictures of the family everywhere, and they told the story of a good mother and wife. A life well lived and still blessing others! There were pictures of her late husband who had died 10 years ago. I had wondered why she hadn't married again. She said she had found the love of her lifetime and that she was looking forward to going to heaven so she could be together again with her husband. I hoped that I too would one day find a love that would last a lifetime.

My mind flashed back to Gay for a few minutes. Was she the love of my life and now she was gone? No, there had to be someone in this world for me, and I remembered Maggie's words after I'd shared with her that Gay was moving away. "God has someone special for you, Kingsley," she had said. "Even though it seems now that there could be no one else but Gay for you, God has got someone picked out for you, and He will bring her into your life at the perfect time."

The day went by quickly considering I didn't do much, apart from lounging around the cottage. My foot was continuing to get better and I felt no pain in it now as I walked to the bedroom for an early night. I was still tired from my adventures around Gower. I found my horse family, I reminded myself, but it didn't feel the same with Thunder Child roaming the Rhossili hills. He was far away from my beloved Pobbles and Three Cliffs valley. I wondered if he'd ever come back to the beach and his cave. "He will find you, boy!" Yes Sir, I hope so, Sir.

On Wednesday morning, Maggie called to see how things were going. She seemed so happy to talk to me, and she told me what a blessing it was for her to have me looking after things, which made me feel good. "Don't forget to help yourself to anything Kingsley, and there's more food in the other fridge in the pantry."

Wow! This is the life for me, I thought. Two fridges full of food!

"I'm doing great, Maggie, and really enjoying staying at the cottage…. And yes, thanks, my foot is doing a lot better."

"You continue to rest it now, and don't go chasing horses for a while."

"It's okay, I won't."

She also told me that she was thinking of staying another week and asked if I'd be interested in staying longer. Of course I said yes. I could get used to this cottage comfort.

I had another great sleep in my comfortable bed and woke up Thursday morning to the sound of torrential rain outside my window. As I lay in my warm bed, I thought of God's perfect timing and provision for me. Outside, the winds and rain of November grey were blowing and I was cosy and warm here in the cottage. He has given me food, warmth and shelter, even friendship and fellowship, through Maggie.

After my Bible reading and time of fellowship with God, I did my morning chores and had breakfast. For the next week the heavy rains continued, making me appreciate my time at the cottage even more. Outside every window was the face of November grey. What an incredible journey I had been on

The Song of the Morning

since my first experience at Bacon Hole. It was over a year now since I'd come to live in the wild, and today it felt like lifetimes had passed. They have, I guess, if I behold what I have learned and experienced out here.

But what now? Was it time for me to go back and take my place in the community? I've been feeling like it is for a while. It feels like I know in my soul that I've learned what I needed to learn and my life has been changed forever.

Yes, it was time to go back. But to what? I am not the same any more, and society will seem such a different place now, not that I ever felt like I had been a part of it before. That's why I'd come to the cliffs to live, to try and find some meaning and purpose to this life after all. And I found out here what I wasn't looking for. I found something so wonderful and great that I could never have comprehended finding it in a lifetime.

For a while, I grieved at the thought of having to leave the cliffs and go wherever I was going, but then came the accompanying words from God that I read in my Bible this morning.

You are with me all the days of my life, and you have already gone before me into my tomorrows and laid out a path for me to follow.

Towards the end of my second week at the cottage, November grey changed to sunshine and I ventured out into the world again, visiting my beloved places along the cliffs and on the beaches. My world of the Gower Peninsula seemed to be smaller, as I in my inner man had become bigger.

I never thought I would ever say this, but on this sunny Saturday morning, Kingsley Ross Hill, Prince and Knight of Gower, had outgrown his territory.

There was only one thing left to do now and that was to ride the Thunder Child, but how? He was still roaming Rhossili Downs and I was here. Maybe he had outgrown his territory too? Was that why he had taken off to the hills? Maybe he wasn't coming back.

"What are you talking about, boy? Of course he's coming back! You went looking for him and of course he's not going to let you catch him up there. He will come looking for you, boy, when he's ready. Don't you remember what I told you?" Yes Sir, I do! "Then just trust and wait and he'll come back."

I made the most of the blue sky days, and every morning after feeding the animals and having breakfast, I headed down to Three Cliffs and Pobbles, hoping that Thunder Child had come back.

One morning I decided to walk along the banks of the Killy Willy River towards Pennard Castle, to see if there was any skate in the river, and there was. In the same slow-moving turn in the river where I had speared my first skate, there was another one. My heart raced at the sight of it, but I didn't have my spear with me. It was still in my cave, unless I had more visitors and someone had stolen it. I would have to go and get my saddle soon too, where I had hidden it in one of the crevices up on the Tor.

Now what was I going to do about this beautiful skate? I didn't need to sell fish anymore because Maggie had said she was going to pay me for looking after the cottage, even though I told her that having a place to stay was payment enough. It would be nice to have a skate all prepared in the freezer for her when she got back, though. I knew she loved eating fish. That was all the excuse I needed. I had my Bowie knife with me and somehow I was going to catch that fish.

As I looked down over the bank, the skate's whole body was on top of the sand now and his fins were moving like he was ready to swim away. Quickly I stripped to my underpants and jumped into the river, knife first, right on top of the skate. Taking a deep breath of cold, I lifted the fish up to the surface and waded back to the bank. What a sight I must have looked, up to my waist in the frigid water of the Killy Willy in just my underpants, with the top half of my body covered with mud, blood and scales. No wonder the sparrow hawk just flew overhead without a sound. He just moved his head from side to side and thought, "There's that crazy Kingsley Hill!"

Oh well, it was worth it, I said to myself, chattering with the cold and trying to pull my jeans up over my wet legs. I fell over in the process. The sparrow hawk flew back in my direction, and when he was overhead, he squawked. I didn't have to know fluent sparrow hawk to know what he said, and I shouted back in agreement: "Yes, Mr. Sparrow Hawk, I am a bloody idiot, but you must admit it's a beautiful skate I caught!" I think he agreed.

By the time I gutted the skate in the river and carried it up to the Burrows, I was warmed up again. The blue sky remained and I felt the warmth of the sun on my shoulders as I walked along the Cliff path to Maggie's.

How nice it was to reach the cottage and close the door behind me, and have my own dwelling place where no one could enter uninvited. When you live in a cave, there is always an open door to your dwelling place, and boundaries are only within your mind, wherein you wrestle with fear and uncertainty, or sit down with peace. When you know Jesus, there is always a choice regarding whom you dine with.

As I was saying, in a cave the "entrance is always open," and intruders can come in. In the cottage, you can close the door behind you and let in only whom you please. It is so with the human heart. We can let in whom we please, and often it is the impostor we let into our lives, unless we have discernment and protection from God within our hearts. What a respected guest He is in this world of people barging in, who, like the devil, come to destroy. Once you invite him in, you don't want him to leave. Have you ever met a guest like that? Someone you can be your real self with all of the time? Someone who will sit down with you and help you? Someone who can help carry your heavy burdens, and love you enough to be completely honest with you when you're wrong, and not judge and condemn you, but help you overcome your problems and then strengthen you so that you can do what is right?

I know that someone, and I'm so glad that I opened the door of my heart and let him in. He is the most wonderful guest that I've ever dined with, and I don't want him to ever leave. When I first heard him knocking on the door of my heart, I felt intimidated and afraid to let him in, for my house was in such a mess, but once I let him in, he started to clean out all my rooms and he threw out all the garbage. It was such a wonderful feeling, to feel clean and pure. When I looked at all the garbage that had been thrown out, things that I once regarded as valuable, my eyes were opened and I could see it for what it really was, garbage!

As I closed the cottage door behind me, I felt good about the secure walls around me and the comforts that had been absent from my everyday life for so long, and my bed – oh yes, my comfortable bed. Surely this was another sign that I was getting ready to leave the wild.

I cut the skate into portions for one or two people, so Maggie could have enough for herself or invite a friend over to share a larger portion. After putting the skate in the freezer, it was time to put my feet up on the couch and turn on the television, and see what people saw through this window into the outside world, or what was portrayed to be the real world outside. All seemed loud and strange compared to my simple quiet world on the Gower Peninsula. Here, in the wild, if I wanted adventure and excitement, I lived it, I didn't just watch it. Would I ever get used to the busyness of life again? Or indeed, did I ever want to? I thought that in time, I eventually would, but I wasn't quite ready yet.

Turning off the TV and the lights, I ended my day as the sun went down behind Cefn Bryn, and my soul stilled to the fading natural light of the setting sun. In my bedroom I lit a candle and watched its gentle light dance, as I had every night at the cottage. Its light flickered shadows upon the walls, but the faces were friendly ones, unlike the large frightening figures reflected from my fires at Bacon Hole. This is a good transition for me, I think, going from cave fire to candlelight, although Fear had lost his power over me now since I'd met the light.

Tomorrow I would go and visit Dad and Fraser, I thought, as I watched the candle's last flicker. "Why does a candle shine so brightly just before it goes out? I asked the candle.

"We all have a story to tell," it replied. The flame of a candle is much like a person's life. How brightly we shine out our light on others determines whether people will stop and take notice that our life is different and that it shines out light in a dark world. The flicker of light just before we burn out is a reminder that we only have a little time here on this earth to shine our light in the world and reflect the great light of God within us to others. Once our flame has burned out, it's too late to shine in this world. The candle finished reading me my story, and I too would burn again tomorrow.

The sparrows chirped a good morning and I opened my eyes. It was time to feed the chickens, and the cat needed some attention as she brushed me back and forth with her tail.

"Yes, Tilly! I know how you feel, I really do. Just like you miss your Maggie, I miss my Gay." I opened up her favourite can of food, and she purred loudly. "Gay used to purr too," I said when I rubbed my fingers through her hair. "Oh Tilly. Why do I still dream of her, when I have tried so hard to get her out of my heart?"

"When Love comes, it doesn't always leave," purred Tilly.

"You're right there, old girl," and I went out to see Hatty and the other chickens to get my breakfast. "Good morning, ladies. I trust that you had a good egg-laying night. You did! Thank you very much for the lovely brown eggs."

After breakfast, I slowly made my way to my father's house, taking my time across the Burrows, and stopping in at my cave on the way. As I approached, I had an uneasy feeling that I'd had visitors while I'd been away. I had! All my clothes were gone, including my two best winter jackets, and they had stolen my collection of glass fishing floats. I walked to the back of the cave, and there upon the ledge was my rabbit fur robe, along with my spear and knives. They'd missed those.

The Song of the Morning

I was sure glad that I'd moved my saddle and fishing gear to a secluded crevice on the other side of the Cliff, and they were still there. I would take them back to Maggie's when I returned from visiting Dad and Fraser. Wait a minute, where's my message in a bottle? Oh, that's right, I'd already taken that over to Maggie's to show her. My message in a bottle from God, and my saddle from Gay were my most treasured possessions, and I still had them both.

I had a feeling of violation as I thought about who would have come into my cave and stolen my clothes. My glass fishing floats were rare and worth a fair bit of money. Could it have been those hikers that I'd chased away with my spear? It could have been anyone out on a walk and exploring. Oh well, they were gone now and that was that.

After climbing down from the Burrows, I walked across Three Cliffs Bay to the Killy Willy as the tide was out, and then I turned inland to the Valley. Maybe Thunder Child would be back? As I turned the corner from the pebble stones and looked up the Valley, I could see two horses in the distance. My heart raced as I saw that one looked like a foal. "Little Thunder!" I called out. Right away the larger horse lifted up its head and turned in my direction "Thunder Spring!" I called out with excitement in my voice, and the two horses started walking towards me. Could it be?

It had to be. They recognised my voice and they're coming towards me. I could see now that it was them, and I looked around to see if Thunder Child was watching nearby. Thunder Spring and Little Thunder came right up to me, and I made a big fuss of them.

"Thunder Spring, it's great to see you, old girl, and look at you, Little Thunder. Look how much you have grown." I kept looking around, expecting Thunder Child to show up, and I'm sure that Thunder Spring and Little Thunder were waiting for him too. "Don't worry, you two. He'll be back soon and we'll all be together again."

I stayed about an hour with Thunder Spring and Little Thunder in the Valley and watched Little Thunder play.

From the Valley, I climbed up the steep and sandy path to my great friend Pennard Castle, who keeps my secrets, and I stood in one of his arch windows that are too old now to tell the time, and I looked down at the Valley below where Thunder Spring and Little Thunder were now taking a drink from the river, as the tilting sun sparkled orange upon Killy Willy as he shouted out "the day's last call." And oh, such a silent song he sang to the waiting sea.

Cefn Bryn, who had learned to sing, looked down from his throne on high as a lonely wood pigeon was listening to his own song echoing through the still Valley, and Cefn Bryn began to cry, and so did I when the sun climbed down from the jealous sky.

When I arrived at the house, Dad and Fraser were sitting down for supper. Fraser saw me peering in through the window before I had a chance to ring the doorbell.

"Good to see you, Kings. Come on in. Dad will be happy to see you."

"Hope so," I said sheepishly. I felt guilty for not having visited them for so long.

"Sit yourself down, Kings," Dad said. "You're just in time for supper. Fraser and I have already started, but there's plenty left on the stove if you're hungry, old son."

The Song of the Morning

"That's great, Dad, thanks. I'm pretty hungry alright."

"Well, tell us what you have been up to. You're not still living out in the wild, are you?"

"Not in this weather. It's been so wet, apart from the last few days. I was staying at a friend's place in Penmaen, Dad, house-sitting for a few weeks."

"So you're warm and dry then?"

"Yes, it's really nice, and I'm feeding the animals and I have freshly laid eggs for breakfast, which is a nice change from fish and rabbit."

"I'm sure it is, and having the luxury of being warm and dry has hopefully made you want to live indoors, at least for the winter, hasn't it?"

"True enough, Dad. It's pretty miserable in the rain, but I've had a wonderful time, and I've learned so much. There is something I want to talk to you about. I'm not just here for a visit. I want to come home soon and give things a try at living at the house again. As soon as my friend Maggie gets back and I'm finished looking after her cottage, I'd like to come home, Dad, if it's alright with you? I'm not sure about going to Grandma and Grandpa's to live though."

"Come home, Kings, until you know what you want to do. Fraser and I would be happy for you to come home and give things a try again, wouldn't we Fraser."

"Yes, Kings, it would be great to have you back."

"Thanks, it means a lot to have your support."

"Are you sure you're not coming back because the police are chasing you, old son?"

"Well, they haven't caught me yet, and I don't plan on getting caught either."

Cave Days

We all roared with laughter at my words.

"Did James ever catch up with you?" asked Fraser. "He came looking for you a month or so ago here at the house."

"No, he never caught up with me."

"I guess you feel you paid him back a bit for your magpie, eh Kings?" asked Dad.

"It did feel like that for a while, Dad, but I don't steal any more. I know you may find this hard to believe, but I found God over the time I've been living on the cliffs, and I asked him to come into my heart and life, and he did. I'm trusting him to direct my future."

Dad and Fraser were silent, surprised by my words, and waiting for me to crack a smile and for the whole thing to be a joke. They were used to the rebellious son and brother, the outlaw Kingsley Hill, not this new creation. Their silence remained, and the smile on my face never came.

For the next hour and a half, I shared with them the message in a bottle, and my near drowning, and how God had saved my life through Thunder Spring in the cave. "And just the other night I was stuck out on the Worms Head with a sprained ankle and a storm blew up. I was so scared, but God came and comforted me and gave me his peace. I could write a book about my experiences. In fact, I think I will write a book one day telling of the great things he has done!"

Dad and Fraser didn't say a thing, they just listened. Who was this new person? My brother's eyes asked.

"That's good news, old son," Dad said as I finished.

"It sounds like you have had some wonderful revelations."

"I have, Dad. Everything is different now. I'm so excited about the future."

As I stood up from the table, I knew that it was going to take more than words for them to see the difference in my life. I knew in my heart that God was pleased that I'd shared with Dad and Fraser my experiences of him in my life.

For the remainder of the evening, we enjoyed good family time together, and I didn't feel like a stranger any more. I felt God was affirming to me that the next step for me to take in my life was to come home, at least for now. I'd spend the night at the house and head back to Maggie's in the morning.

"If you get up early enough in the morning, Kings, I'll give you a ride back to Penmaen before work."

"That would be great, Fraser, I'll see you in the morning."

"Good night, Kings."

Chapter Twenty-two

Great Thunder

As Fraser and I rode through the narrow lanes towards Penmaen, the sun shone brightly in the sky, thrilling my soul as I anticipated enjoying another beautiful day. I sang from the back of Fraser's motorcycle that wonderful John Denver song 'Sunshine', and I felt the warm sun on my shoulders as we rode along. I would start my day with a large breakfast, I thought, and then go for a walk along the beach and head up to the Three Cliffs Valley to visit Thunder Spring and Little Thunder, and of course the Sunshine almost always makes me happy.

"Bye, Fraser and thanks for the ride."

"Bye, Kings, you take care alright?"

Eggs, toast, and a large glass of Maggie's homemade apple juice was the order of the day, and one of the eggs was a double yoker too, courtesy of Hatty the hen. "Thank you, Hatty, my dear! Now you lay me another for the morning, old girl."

After feeding the animals, I headed out to enjoy the sunshine. It was about half tide as I walked along the Sands, which are always golden under the sun. The autumn season was cool and crisp around me as if announcing its arrival with

Great Thunder

every breath. I crossed the Killy Willy and headed up the beach to the archway of the Three Cliffs. There is always a coolness and stillness as one stands in the archway, and it feels much like a cave that has two entrances. Sometimes during the winter months, a haunting wind howls through it like a restless demon and you want to run through as fast as you can and escape from the screaming wind. My father once said you have to cover your ears and run, lest you hear the terrible things the voices in the wind will tell you, and you will never return there again.

"It is where the winter lives!" My mother once told me when I was dawdling my way through the archway as she waited on the other side. At her words, the wind started to howl, and I came running through the archway. "I heard the Winter, Mum, and he howled at me!"

Above the archway, the slightly higher middle Cliff looks out with its brothers. They are like three knights, guarding the sacred valley behind them. As you walk through the archway, you come to the Emerald pool, a beautiful sandy pool in a rock basin. After a storm, depending on what direction the winds and currents are moving, the pool changes like it has its own magic. It does, boy! Yes Sir, I know it does.

Sometimes the waves wash out the sand, leaving the pool deep and more mysterious. It is said that if you enter the pool just as the last waves are receding from the archway, its waters impart a special wisdom and strength. Thus the mermaids come and sit and retain their mystery, and are able to steal away into the waves at the first intrusion of mankind.

If you find the pool shallow and full of sand, it is said that you have become shallow and vain, and you need the depths of the sea to wash through your soul. I have found an easier remedy for when my soul has felt empty and needing. I climb to the top of the Three Cliffs and look out over what God has made.

Today the pool was deep and Emerald, and I climbed around it by the slippery rocks to its right side. Many times, since I was a boy, I have slipped and fallen into the pool, and I don't think it made me any wiser, because I fell in the same way the next day! I'm sure God in his heaven laughed and said to all his hosts: "I'm sure that comparing people with sheep was the right idea. Look he's fallen in again today, and his socks aren't even dry from yesterday!"

Falling into the pool, however, always changes my day. Falling in the winter time is a rude awakening from the deepest of daydreams, but in the summer, it's a cool refreshing bath. I passed without falling in today, and headed up towards the Valley. After crossing the pebbles at the top of Three Cliffs beach, I turned the corner and could see up the valley.

There looked to be two herds of horses, one each side of the river. As I got closer, I could see Thunder Spring and Little Thunder grazing alone just down river from one of the herds. There was no sign of Thunder Child or any other stallion, just mares and their foals.

Suddenly I heard the sound of hooves from behind me. There were two large horses a distance away and it looked like one was giving chase to the other. They galloped closer and closer until I could hear them snorting and grunting. They were coming right for me!

I ran to the trees at the edge of the Valley. It was Thunder Child, and he was in pursuit of the other stallion. They

Great Thunder

thundered past me and on up to the top of the Valley underneath Pennard Castle.

Waiting and watching, I wondered if they would come back this way. Things seemed quiet again for a few minutes. Dare I cross the river to the other side of the Valley? It would give me a better view if I did. I would chance it and move quickly across.

Taking my shoes and socks off, I stepped into the river. Suddenly they were on their way back, having crossed the river, and on the same side that I was crossing to. The safest place was surely to stand in the river and not risk stepping out in front of them, or should I make a mad dash back to the other side again to the shelter of the trees? It looked like they were going to pass me, but the other stallion stopped and turned, and up on his hind legs he went. Thunder Child didn't slow down and ploughed right into him like a freight train, knocking him to the ground. Now it was Thunder Child up on his back legs and slamming his hooves on top of the other stallion, who made an awful screaming noise! Thunder Child turned and went around to the other side of his rival, which gave the other stallion time to scramble to his feet. Thunder Child knocked him down again, but fell down himself in the process.

Was this a good time for me to make a run for it, back to the cover of the trees? No, to move and run in the open would be too much of a risk. What if the other stallion ran and trampled me? So I stayed in the river and stood still. Now the other stallion climbed to his feet first and slammed his hooves into Thunder Child, who screamed and grunted in pain. Rearing up, the enemy stallion thrashed his hooves at the King. What could I do? My stomach knotted, as I looked around the river bed for a stick.

Then Thunder Child was up on his feet again, and both stallions were screaming and grunting and charging. Thunder Spring and Little Thunder had moved down the Valley and now stood opposite the battle on the other side of the river. This was a family battle now, so I raced back from the river and stood with my horse family. Thunder Spring made noises I'd never heard before, obviously due to her concern for the King. Having picked up a stick and waving it in my arms, I shouted. "Come on, Thunder Child! You must win! Come on, Thunder Child, you're the King around here!"

It was hard to see who was winning as one thrashed into the other. One minute one was standing, the next they were both on the ground kicking and biting. Surely the horse with the most heart and stamina would win this battle. They both seemed equal in brutal strength. Thunder Spring stood silent now, and I put down my stick, anticipating one of them being injured or killed. The fighting continued and the sounds of screams and grunts filled the Valley, and I wondered, would both of them die? A buzzard circled high above as if waiting for the weakest to fall. Slowly the sounds of battle ceased, and both horses remained on the ground. I felt faint inside, thinking that Thunder Child might be dead, for I could see no movement from where I stood.

Leaving my shoes and my horse family, I picked up my stick and slowly crossed the river. As I reached the other side, I could see both horses moving. One of them trying to lift his head. As I got closer, I could see that it was Thunder Child trying to get up.

Great Thunder

"Come on, Old Thunder," I called. "Come on, old boy, stand up!" But he just raised his head and lowered it down again. The other stallion lay flat on his side, his body just twitching like a fish that had been hit on the head, it's nerves making it move.

I stood right over them now, and oh, what a terrible sight. Both were bleeding from open wounds, and I couldn't tell whose blood belonged to whom. Sick to my stomach, I almost gagged. The only movement now from the other stallion was his tummy, which slowly rose and fell to his shallow breathing. I noticed a massive gash to his head where I could see part of his skull.

Thunder Child looked weak, and knowing that I was there, continued to try and lift his head up. "Oh God," I cried. "Please don't let him die."

I stood beside Thunder Child. "Come on. Thunder! Come on, old boy. You have to stand up, otherwise you won't get up again!"

Thunder Spring and Little Thunder had now crossed the river and they stood nearby. "Come on, Thunder!" I continued, "We are all here! You can't die now. You have your family and a whole life ahead of you. If you stand up now, you will be King of the Gower. You have won this great battle."

Was I saying this for myself? No, it was for both of us, for I identified with this horse like no other animal I had ever known in my life before. It wasn't just that our paths had crossed at this time in history; he was a wonderful kindred spirit in a way that I far from fully understood. As I stood over Thunder Child's bruised and broken body, my heart told me that our experience together was not going to end here.

I looked closely again at the other stallion. I could see that his breathing had stopped. He was dead. Oh, my gosh! What about Thunder? Would he die of his wounds? No, I had to have faith! I prayed again, asking God to not let my great friend die.

I knelt down in a pool of blood and pushed on Thunder Child's side. Grunting and groaning, he lifted his head again, and this time he moved his legs trying to get up.

"That's it, Thunder! You can do it, old boy, just keep trying!"

Suddenly Thunder Spring made a noise in horse language, and Thunder Child tried his hardest to stand. Was she speaking to him and willing him to stand up? She called again and Little Thunder came trotting to his father's side. Up came Thunder Child's head and he pushed with his legs. For a few moments, it seemed that the whole valley was silent, standing with us and watching; every bird, every creature, quiet in anticipation, and hoping against hope that he would stand up!

With one more try he was up. "Thunder Child is standing!" I shouted. My voice echoed across the Valley like a knight of long ago announcing a great victory. I shouted and danced, and the birds sang, and the Killy Willy roared. Pennard Castle shouted, and life continued again.

But what now? The King was standing, but he was wobbly and weak, and he staggered badly as he tried to walk. Where would he go so badly injured? He walked for short distances and then stopped, and then he'd start again. A few times it looked like he was going to fall down, but somehow he found the strength to stay on his feet. Thunder Spring and Little

Great Thunder

Thunder started walking ahead, back down the Valley towards the beach. Thunder Child hobbled behind, and I walked behind him wondering what I could do....

Come on, Kings, think! There's a dead stallion lying in the Valley covered with blood and there's a big gash on his head. It's only a matter of time before someone finds him and reports what happened, and then we will have all sorts of people looking around. What will happen when they see Thunder Child limping around wounded? They will take him away, that's what they'll do, and he will probably never return to the wild, at least not around here.

There was only one place to take him, and that was to his cave. We could hide out in there until he was healed. I could bring him food and water like Gay and I had done with Thunder Spring when she wasabout to give birth.

Thunder Child staggered now and let himself down to the sand, his legs almost buckling underneath him, and I feared he would not get up again. His family came and stood beside him as the afternoon Sun sank lower in the sky. How was I going to get him to the cave? I would have to get him in there while it was still light.

Wait a minute! There was some thick rope in Maggie's chicken shed. I could make a lead rope as Gay had taught me to do for her horse, and I could lead him to the cave with that. I looked at the sun again, and it was beginning to go down behind the horizon. I didn't have much time before dark.

After running most of the way to Maggie's cottage, I found the rope in the chicken shed and then went into the cottage to get some bandages and disinfectant from Maggie's first aid box.

With the light fading fast, I ran all the way back to the Valley. I was surprised to see my horse family right at the entrance of the Valley. Not only had Thunder Child managed to get up again; he had also walked a good distance. I'd had visions of having to heave him up by the rope.

"Well done, old boy." I said, "and you guys too. Well done, Thunder Spring and Little Thunder, well done. We only have a short distance to walk now until we reach the cave."

I waited until Thunder Child stopped walking again, and then eased the loop of the rope that I'd made over his head. He was too weak to resist, and I pulled gently, taking up the slack until I felt it snug on his neck. Come on, Thunder Child," I said, pulling firmly on the rope. "I'm taking you back to your cave so you can get well."

To my surprise, he responded. What a wonderful feeling to be leading the King of the Gower. "Well done, boy! Lead him on, he is yours now." "Yes Sir, he is."

I led him around Three Cliffs Point, and on to the golden Sand, where he stopped. I pulled for him to keep going, as he'd only rested a few minutes before. "What is it, old boy?" I asked, continuing to pull on the rope, but the king stood fast and would not move.

Suddenly a breath of wind stirred my hair, and then blew around us. There was no wind. Where had it come from? Thunder Spring, who had been walking about 50 feet in front of us, also stopped and lifted her head, as did Little Thunder. "What is it?" I shouted back. "What is it that you can feel?" And with the next breath of wind, I found myself looking deep into the brown eyes of the King. Oh, what feelings and emotions caressed my soul, as in his eyes I could see that he knew

Great Thunder

me and regarded me as his friend, and I knew him. We stared at each other face to face for what seemed like years. He had come back and found me, just like the old man had said, only this is not the way I'd thought he would find me, needing me to help him, the King of Gower.

Was this the way I was going to be able to ride him? Help him back to strength and then put the saddle on his back? When he was healing in the cave, it would be a good time for him to get used to it. Gay had said you walk him first with just the saddle on, and once he is used to it, then you can try and ride him.

Thunder Child now staggered and nearly fell, waking me from my daydream. He was a long, long way from being ridden. Now if I could only get him into the cave, for the next time he rested it would surely be for the night. As we approached the cave, Thunder Spring and Little Thunder went on ahead of us inside, and I wondered if they had known all along that this was my plan, or did I need to understand that this had been *their* plan?

"Did you guys know? You did, didn't you. When you lifted up your heads, it was God's spirit in the wind that led us on." Thunder Child and I now entered the cave, and when we reached the place where Thunder Spring had given birth, his legs gave out and he lowered himself quickly to the ground. As Thunder Spring and Little Thunder stood at the King's side, I could see that it was too dark in the cave for me to bathe and bandage Thunder Child's wounds. I would have to do that tomorrow when there was more light. I would bring food and water with me too. It was time for me to head back to the cottage for the night. At least I knew that Thunder Child was safe now and that Thunder Spring and Little Thunder were at his side.

It was almost completely dark when I arrived back at the cottage, and I lay on the couch exhausted. I contemplated getting up and making some supper, but I was too spent, and I drifted off to sleep thinking about riding Thunder Child across the Sands.

I started the new day with a bath, washing the dried blood of Thunder Child's battle off my skin. The water turned red as I washed my knees, and in my mind's eye I saw the other stallion lying dead in the bloodstained grass. Would he still be there, or would someone have found him already? He had been Thunder Child's enemy, but I would not gloat over the death of such a wonderful animal. Nor would I celebrate Thunder Child's victory yet, for I didn't know if he would fully recover from his wounds and run again like the dancing winds across the Sands. Anything less would not be a true victory.

After my morning prayers, I believed that God would help him make a full recovery and that he would be even greater than he had been before the battle. I decided to change Thunder Child's name to 'Great Thunder' as a sign of my faith in God's promise.

I went out to the chicken coop. Hatty had laid two eggs this morning, and along with a large amount of bacon and two pieces of Maggie's home-made bread, I had a wonderful breakfast. It was time to head off to the cave and see how my patient was doing. Would he be able to stand up this morning and walk, I wondered? And what about the large gash on his hind leg? I would wash his wounds with seawater, which is both a

Great Thunder

cleanser and healer. It had always worked for me when I'd cut myself on the rocks, although it stung like the dickens.

Taking Maggie's bucket from the shed, I filled it half full with apples and carrots. And once Great Thunder had been fed, I could carry the sea water to the cave in it. I was sure Maggie wouldn't mind me borrowing the bucket as long as I brought it back.

Closing the door behind me, I headed off. The tide was high this morning and there wasn't much beach left for me to cross in front of the Three Cliffs Point and on up to the cave at Pobbles. I hurried along, switching hands with the heavy bucket and hoping that great Thunder would be all right. I stopped a few times to rest and collect grass along the way. A King could not live on apples alone.

When I arrived, Thunder Spring and Little Thunder were still there. "Well done, you two." I said, "That's what family is all about, sticking together." It looked like they had been there all night and not ventured out of the cave. There was a lot of fresh horse manure in the cave, and I hadn't seen any fresh hoof prints outside.

The King was sitting like he hadn't moved all night, but he looked alert. "Here you are, old boy," I said, feeding him an apple. He was hungry too. He ate two apples and several carrots. It felt like feeding time at Paignton Zoo when all the animals crowd around you, only there you had the added thrill of a big gorilla throwing shit at you. I can remember it hitting my grandmother in the face and Fraser and I peeing ourselves with laughter.

"Come on, you guys, you're crowding me in. The apples are for Great Thunder, not for you two." I fed him another apple and then moved onto the grass. I think he liked the apples better.

Thunder Spring and Little Thunder each had an apple and some carrots, and I hid the rest up on a ledge at the back of the cave for later. Taking the bucket to the sea, I filled it with the salt water and brought it back to Great Thunder. No sooner had I put the bucket down, than Little Thunder had his head in it. He quickly lifted up his head and sputtered water all over.

I laughed. "It doesn't taste very good, does it?" Thunder Spring made a noise as if she was laughing and nodded her head in agreement.

"It's good to start the day with some humour," I said. "Now you guys back off and give me some room here."

Taking a cloth that I had brought from Maggie's, I dipped it into the salt water and began to bathe the stallion's wounds. It obviously stung as he jolted and pushed his leg out, and then made a loud noise as I washed the deep gash on his hind leg. "Keep still, old boy. I'm not going to harm you. I've got to do this or your wounds will get infected."

The rest of the family watched for a while and then left the cave, leaving us alone. After I had finished wrapping his leg with the bandages, I left the cave and headed towards the Killy Willy to get some fresh water. It looked like Thunder Spring and Little Thunder had stopped for a drink and then headed up the Valley according to the fresh hoof marks in the sand.

I must go up the Valley and check if the dead stallion is still there, I thought, as I filled up the bucket. I stayed with the King for about an hour, making sure he had a good drink and some more apples and carrots before I headed off. "Well, old boy, I'm going to let you rest for a while now, and I'll come

Great Thunder

back in the afternoon to see how you're doing. We will see if you can stand up and maybe go for a walk then." I would have to find something to clean out the cave so his wound would stay clean as well, but that could wait for later.

When I arrived at the Valley, I could see in the distance a tractor and two men. They were right at the place where the dead stallion was, and I watched them from the cover of Three Cliffs Woods. They seemed to have the stallion wrapped up in a harness, and they were attempting to lift him up with a tractor into a wagon to take him away.

Coming out from my cover in the trees, I went to investigate. "Good morning gentlemen," I said. "What's happened?"

"We are moving a dead horse," one of them replied. "Looks like it was killed by another horse."

"Probably that wild stallion that's been chasing people up on Rhossili Downs," the other man added. "Have you seen that wild horse around anywhere, lad?"

"No sir, I haven't. Just the usual mares and the younger horses."

"Well, if you do see him, be careful. He's liable to chase you."

"I'll be careful," I said.

I returned home to the cottage for lunch and the phone rang. It was Maggie saying that she would be home on Tuesday. That would give me three more days to have this place to myself, and then I'd have to make my journey to the cave from Dad's house.

In the afternoon, I went to the great Tor to get my saddle that I'd hidden in a crevice on the north side. It sure was heavy as I carried it down the Burrows and across the beach to the cave. I remembered Gay's words again. "I want you to have this saddle, Kingsley. It's the best gift that I have to give you. You can ride the Thunder Child with this."

"His name isn't Thunder Child any more, Gay.!" I said aloud. "His name is 'Great Thunder,' and I am going to thunder across the Sands on his back like the fury of the wind. I wonder how you're doing at university, girl? They can't teach you what I'm learning out here."

Dropping the saddle next to Great Thunder, I sat down to rest and to see how he was doing. He was still alert, and to my surprise he tried to stand up. "Steady on, old boy," I said, as he pushed on his leg several times. On the fourth try, he was up. "Well done, old boy. Do you want to go for a walk then? Wait a minute. We had better make sure those two farmers have left the Valley with your dead enemy. They are looking for you, old boy, and they know about your antics, chasing people on Rhossili Downs. You're getting as bad as I am, you know that?" He nodded in agreement. "Well, we better lie low for a while until folk aren't looking for you anymore. I'll give you these apples and carrots to eat, and then I'll go and check that all is clear in the Valley. You stay here, old boy, and I'll be back soon."

I climbed the dunes to the cliff top that overlooks the Valley, and I could see that the men and the tractor had gone, and they'd taken the stallion with them. Good, that was a relief. Now I could take my stallion for a walk. As I walked back I looked for a flat piece of driftwood I could use to scoop the manure out of the cave. It took me a few minutes of backtracking before I found a piece sufficient for the work.

"Well done, old boy. You're still standing up and all ready for a walk, are you? Let's go for a walk along the beach." I led

Great Thunder

him out of the cave and we walked down the beach towards the sea. He seemed to be walking fairly well, considering his wounds, and he was obviously stronger than he had been yesterday, but the limp in his left hind leg was bad, and he continued to stop and rest about every 50 feet.

"You are still in a lot of pain, aren't you, old boy," I said, gently encouraging him on. "We will soon reach the sea." It was a great thrill for me to be leading the King of Gower across the Sand

We reached the sea and I took my shoes and socks off and stood in the waves. Gosh it was cold, but clear and cleansing, and it would be good for his wounds to have the salt water swirling around them. I pulled on the rope for him to follow me into the waves, but he stood fast. "Come on, old boy," I said, shivering. "I'm doing this for you," and I pulled an apple out of my pocket. For a few moments he just stood there with his head down looking like he'd lost his last shilling, or in horse language, his last carrot, and then I accidentally dropped the apple in the tide. Well, he wouldn't come in now, I thought. "An apple in the hand was worth a horse in the sea." I said aloud. "But no apple in my hand and he's laughing at me."

I pulled hard on the rope, and to my surprise he followed me into the waves. The larger waves crashed about his knees, but they were up to my waist, and I urged him back closer to the shore, fearing that I would soon be swimming.

We walked along in the waves until we reached where the Killy Willy came into the sea at Three Cliffs Point. That was as far as I could go, as my legs were numb and I couldn't feel my toes. "Well done, old boy, you made it all the way to the point." I shouted excitedly. "I never expected you to make it this far."

As we walked back to the cave at the edge of the surf, I dreamed again of the day when I would put the saddle on his back and ride him across the beach. Once we were back inside the cave, he lay down on his side to rest. I made quick work of removing the manure and making sure the cave was reasonably clean, then I made one last trip back to the river to fill his bucket with fresh water.

"Well, old boy, I'm off back to the cottage to have something to eat, and I will see you in the morning!" Before I left, I remembered the apples and carrots that I'd hidden up on the back ledge of the cave. I gave him one apple and a handful of carrots. He still had some grass left over from what I had picked earlier. "That should last you until the morning," I said.

On my way back to the cottage, I detoured up to the Valley to see how Thunder Spring and Little Thunder were doing. I stood again at the place of the great battle. The grass was still stained with blood. Great Thunders victory had come with a price. He'd had to do battle with an enemy, and shed his own blood. Winning the battle had set him free from the bondage and oppression of the other stallions influence on his life. Never again would he have to be chased away and defeated. The victory was won, and he could now be all that he was meant to be, the leader of the Three Cliffs Herd. The parallels between our lives did not go unnoticed, and I too felt I had won a great Victory.

∽

Over the next several days, I continued to care for Great Thunder. I walked him in the waves and across the Sands

Great Thunder

westwards, following the same route where he used to gallop all the way to Oxwich. We went only as far as the Killy Willy at Three Cliffs Point and back. It had been over a week now since the great battle, but still his limp remained, and I wondered if he had torn a ligament or even fractured the bone in his back leg.

When Maggie got home, I shared with her all that happened. "I don't know what to tell you, Kingsley," she said. "He is a wild horse, and if his leg is damaged, he might need a vet."

"Yes, Maggie, but if I get a vet, they will take him away for sure, especially after the trouble he got up to on Rhossili Downs, and besides he is my horse now."

"He is indeed, Kingsley, he is indeed. You have probably saved his life with all the love and care you have given him."

"Thanks Maggie, he is a wonderful horse, and I just want him to live a happy life, wild and free, just like he's meant to be."

"I know you do, and so do I."

Maggie was happy to see how well I'd looked after the cottage and taken care of the animals. She said that as I was still taking care of Great Thunder, I could come and stay at the cottage on weekends. "It will save you coming all the way from your dad's house each morning."

"Thanks Maggie! That will be a great help."

So I stayed at Maggie's Friday, Saturday, and Sunday nights. I found that besides being close to Great Thunder on weekends, it also gave me a good transition time going back to my father's house. Dad was also happy that I'd made friends with Maggie and that she was having such a positive influence in my life.

Maggie remained my confidante, and through her God taught me many lessons. I was encouraged that I was meeting a need for Maggie as well. Maggie shared with me how wonderful it was to be able to share her faith with someone, and to be able to pray and see how God was working in my life. She said that God was teaching her things as well through me.

On Tuesday morning, Maggie and I had special prayer time together and we prayed for Great Thunder. We asked God to heal his leg and to bring him back to full strength again. After breakfast I headed off to see him. He was standing outside the cave when I arrived.

"Well done, old boy," I said, patting his neck. "You're all ready to go, aren't you." Just as I was about to take the rope and lead him, he started to walk, and we walked like two friends down the beach to the surf.

Excitement filled my heart as we grew in our friendship, and as we reached the waves he walked into the sea without me having to lead or coax him to come in. It was as if he knew this morning that walking in the waves was good for him. We followed our usual route westwards as we did each morning, but today he kept going all the way to Oxwich Bay. By the time we reached the Killy Willy, I had to come out of the water, as my feet were numb with cold, but he kept walking in the waves. "What are you doing, old boy?" I shouted. "I'm impressed. Are you going to swim to Ireland then?"

His limp was still there, but it was only slight now, and I could see his renewed strength and energy. I stopped and gave thanks for his healing. As we started on our way back, I reached for the rope to lead him and he let me lead the way. I didn't want him to run wild again, not without me on his back.

Great Thunder

When we crossed the Killy Willy, I stopped to put my shoes on again, and he pushed me over with his nose.

"Are you wanting to play?" I asked, as I tied my shoelace, and all the way back to Pobbles, we played a game. I walked in front of him, and each time I stopped, he pushed me with his nose as if to say "get going buddy." I would turn around fast, not wanting him to push me over, and he would show me his teeth, and I would say, "Are you laughing at me, old boy?" He would nod his head and make a noise as if saying, "Yes, I am. Now get moving."

Just before we got back to the cave, I noticed a glass ball from a fishing net half buried in the sand, so I knelt down to pick it up. Suddenly I felt his warm breath and soft nose on the back of my neck and as he gave me a strong but gentle push, I fell flat on my face in the sand. I turned over on my back spitting the sand out of my mouth, only to see him lower his head inches from my face and sniff me with his warm, wet nostrils. "What is it, old boy? You're really checking me out, aren't you. Are you trying to tell me that I need a bath? Because if you are, it's rude to tell a gentleman that he smells, or is that a lady? Anyway I'll make you a deal. You lift that wet nose off my face and I'll give you an apple."

It was a deal. I was able to get up and he got an apple.

We reached the cave and I took the rope to lead him inside. But he would not come. "Come on," I said, pulling harder on the rope. "We have to lie low for another week or so, because they are probably still looking for you," but the King remained stubborn, and as far as I know from that day forth he never entered the cave again. I wondered why? Surely it had been a good dwelling place for him, and for the birthplace of his son.

Cave Days

"I'm sure you have a good reason for not going inside your cave, old boy, but I wish you would tell me what it is. I regard our cave as sacred. It is the place of my miracle, when God kept me alive on the warm belly of your mare Thunder Spring, and in so many ways it's our family home. What is it, old boy? Am I a sentimental old fool, or a young dreamer? I don't like either of those titles, do you? Come on, you can tell me," and I looked into his big brown eyes, and he looked back at me, and then I understood. "It's because you are wild and free, isn't it?" I pointed towards Oxwich Bay and the horizon, and I said, "Your heartland is wherever you want it to be, as you roam free around Gower, isn't it." He nodded his head in agreement.

"Well, my boy, I love you. You are so much like me. Tomorrow we will try you with the saddle, and you can start getting used to it."

I was too excited to wait till Friday to tell Maggie how well he was doing, so before going home to Dad and Fraser, I ran to the village and told Maggie of my wonderful day, and how God had answered our prayers.

"That's wonderful, Kingsley. He really does hear and answer our prayers, doesn't he?"

After a cup of tea and a snack, I left for my father's house.

"See you on Friday, Kingsley. The Lord will watch over your stallion, and one day I'm sure he will allow you to ride him."

"Thanks Maggie, I'll see you on Friday."

Chapter Twenty-three

Thou Art Mine

It was late by the time I got home to my father's house, and well past midnight by the time I'd shared all my news with Fraser. Dad was away for a few days on a business trip, and Fraser and I woke up late. Late as in 8 a.m. Sleeping indoors again, between Maggie's cottage and my father's house, was already having an effect on my inner alarm clock. I always woke up between 4 and 5 a.m. sleeping in my cave, and there always seemed to be time to lie still and listen to the sounds of the new morning before getting up and greeting the world. It had been my time to think about whether the dreams I'd had in the night were revelations of warnings and guidings, or just visions that made no sense. In a house, the stillness of one's soul can be more easily interrupted. That is if one's soul is even still at all.

My Tuesday morning started with the loud intrusion of my brother's alarm clock.

"Well, Kings, I must be off to work. I'm sorry I can't give you a ride to Penmaen this morning, otherwise I'd be late."

"No worries, Fraser, you have a good day at work."

"You have a good day with your stallion, and I'll see you tonight."

"Thanks, Fraser, and bye for now." As he closed the door behind him, I felt like shouting out, "Wait, what about the birds and their song, can you hear them?"

Of course he couldn't, he was hurrying off to work and I respected that. Not everyone has the time to be still and listen to the song of the morning, though I would not want my day to start without a song.

After cereal and toast, and listening to the chorus of the song thrush in the front garden, I walked two miles from where we lived on Brown's Drive to Pennard Cliffs, and then another quarter of a mile to Pobbles. It was sure closer to walk down to the beach from Maggie's cottage, but I was beginning to feel comfortable at home again now, and that made the long walk from Dad's worthwhile.

When I arrived at the beach, I could see my stallion standing outside the cave, and I wondered if he'd been there all night.

"Hello, old boy. How are you this morning? Are you ready to try the saddle on your back? Just give me a minute and I'll go inside the cave and get it."

As I came back with the saddle, Great Thunder had already started walking down the beach towards the surf, just like we did each morning. "Just a moment, old boy. Wait up and I'll be right there."

"Stop!" I shouted. I was still carrying the saddle, and my feet were sinking into the fresh wet sand. "Man, this thing is heavy. Stop, Great Thunder, stop. We need to put this saddle on your back."

Thou Art Mine

But he just kept going, and wasn't going to stop for anything. So I abandoned the idea of trying to put the saddle on him until we got back from our walk, and I walked back to the cave to drop off the saddle.

Running to catch him up, I took his rope and he allowed me to lead him across the sand. He was walking faster this morning, and I had to walk as fast as I could to keep pace. If I walked too slowly, he nudged me on the shoulder with his nose. "Are you wanting to play another game?" I asked, looking back at his big hooves. I didn't want to get caught under one of those. The faster I walked, the more he picked up the pace, and by the time we reached the Killy Willy I needed a rest.

"This isn't a fun game, Great Thunder, unless you're a horse that is. That's funny, isn't it? Get it? Unless you're a horse. Anyway, old boy, I'm not a horse and I'm not playing anymore."

I let go of the rope and walked by his side. After another 10 minutes, he slowed to his regular walking speed. "That's better, now I'm not having to run to keep up with you." We walked side-by-side until we reached the far end of Oxwich beach, where he decided to stop and rest.

"So this is where you come on your gallops across the Sands, is it? Well, you must bring me here on your back one of these days. I must say you do have a beautiful view from here, looking back to the Three Cliffs and Pobbles beach in the distance." Just as I finished talking about the view, Great Thunder started to walk again. We walked side-by-side all the way back to the cave, only stopping once on the way for him to drink at the river.

With my stallion standing outside his cave again, and hopefully tired from the walk, I went back inside to get the saddle, and also the last of the apples and carrots, which I hoped to distract him with while I put the saddle on his back. I dropped the apples and carrots in front of him, and he lowered his head. This was it, and with both hands I attempted to thrust the saddle onto his back. His back was higher than I had the strength to reach, and he moved out of the way thinking I was pushing him, and the saddle fell to the sand.

As it turned out, he wasn't scared off by my failed attempt, either that or he couldn't resist another juicy apple. He lowered his head again to the ground. This time I went to the left side of him which seemed to favour my right arm. Either way it was a heavy saddle to lift so high, and it would require all my strength to sling it onto his back. Then I remembered what Gay had said at the stables. When you're putting a saddle on a big horse, you gently push it against his side and *slide* it on. Yes, Gay, but this wild beast is not tied up in a stall where he is confined and can be climbed up to on steps. One wrong move and he's gone like the wind.

"Well, let's try and slide it onto your back, old boy. You stand still for me and let me get this on your back and I'll buy you a whole bag of apples. Here goes," and it seemed we had struck a bargain.

He stood almost completely still as I eased the saddle up his side and onto his back.

"It's on, it's on, old boy! Now keep still and let me buckle up the straps, and please don't kick me while I'm under your belly. Remember those apples now. They are only yours if you keep still and behave." I just about had one side of the straps buckled up when he started to move.

"Stop. It's no deal if you walk. You have to stand still," but he was on his way to the surf and there wasn't anything I could do about it except follow him and hope the saddle wouldn't fall off. He walked slowly, so the saddle stayed on his back, at least for now. I grabbed the girth which was hanging down and gently flipped it upside down resting it on the saddle. I walked along beside him and hoped he wouldn't walk too far, or pick up speed. My legs were tired. "Aren't you tired? Will you stop just for a minute so I can buckle up the rest of your straps?" But he kept walking and walking, and we soon reached the Killy Willy again.

"Hey, Great Thunder, aren't you going to stop for a drink? Come on, old boy, the water tastes good. Dag nab it, I thought you had a limp leg. This is not funny, do you hear me? Why can't you just stop for two lousy minutes so I can buckle up the saddle?" What could I do? I couldn't give up. What about my saddle? If it fell off his back, I'd never be able to carry it back all the way to the cave. I was exhausted.

My only hope, I said to myself, is that he will stop at the far end of Oxwich beach again, and I can try again there. Finally we reached the end of the beach and he stopped. Now come on, Kings, you can do this, you just have to buckle those two straps on the other side of his belly without him moving. Here goes.

I tried not to look at his big hooves as I bent under his belly and grabbed the girth. As I did one of the straps up and cinched it until it was snug against his skin, and not too tight. That's it, Kings, now just push the strap into the buckle….

There! It was in. Now one more…. Come on, Great Thunder, just one more to do up and it's all done, but it was too much to ask. He moved his legs and off he went, back along the beach to Pobbles. Oh well, at least I had the saddle on his back and three of the straps done up, and I'd try one more time today when we got back to his cave.

As we walked along to Pobbles, my legs felt like lead as my feet sank deep into the fresh sand, still wet from the falling tide. I was so hungry, not having packed a lunch. What I wouldn't give for a Cornish pasty. I thought of going to Maggie's for something to eat. It would be a lot closer than walking the 3 miles, no, it was probably 4 miles from here to Dad's, and we hadn't even reached the Killy Willy yet.

Now I mustn't overuse my welcome at Maggie's. I know she would be happy to see me and make me something nice to eat, but I need to make it back to Dad's, and once Great Thunder is back at his cave I'll try the other strap and then head home. We reached the river, but instead of continuing on to Pobbles, Great Thunder turned inland and started making his way up to the Valley. I tried to stand in his way and I held my arms up in front of him, for I felt the local farmers would still be on the lookout for him. They would be suspicious of him walking around with a saddle on his back and no rider. That didn't spell normal, I'm sure. "Come on, old boy! Don't go up the Valley, they may be looking for you."

But he wasn't having any of my persuasion and he kept going. Oh well, there was nothing else to do but follow him up the Valley. Too tired now to keep pace, I was soon a fair distance behind him. "Thanks for waiting," I shouted, as he turned the corner. "That's real considerate of you, and don't ask me for any more apples." Finally I caught up with him grazing beneath Pennard Castle. And as he munched on the grass, I looked around for any signs of the two men who had been moving the dead stallion the other day. I wish I'd brought my spear with me, I thought, as I pulled my Bowie knife from its sheath to inspect the blade. It was still good and sharp, and if push came to shove, I was sure I could scare them away... and get arrested too. I heard Gay's words of caution call out to me again.

"No one is going to take my stallion away from me." I shouted out like a caveman, waving my knife in the air. I needn't have felt threatened as the Valley was empty. Not one person was walking their dog or bird watching. Only the sounds of the wood pigeons deep in Three Cliffs Woods echoed through the still air. Maybe everyone had heard there was a caveman on the loose. "What do you think, old boy? What? A mad man? I'm not a mad man. I just look a bit like one today, that's all."

Great Thunder lifted his head to see Thunder Spring and Little Thunder on the other side of the river, and we were off again, crossing the river to join them. Once across, he stopped to sniff and smell the grass at the very spot of his great battle. He seemed consumed for several minutes, just wanting to sniff and smell, maybe reminiscing about his great feat. I managed to get the other saddle strap buckled up while he was distracted. "What are you thinking?" I asked, as he continued to inspect the bloodstained grass. "Can you still smell your enemy there? Is his blood calling out and saying something? Or is your blood calling out to him and shouting out the cry of victory!" He lifted his head and made several nods. "I'll take that as yes, you've won a great victory here."

Thunder Spring and Little Thunder soon arrived at his side, and Little Thunder ran around and played while his parents grazed. I felt a great sense of satisfaction knowing that we were all together again, after having been apart in three different areas of the Gower Peninsula only a short time ago. As Little Thunder ran and galloped around his father, I noticed that Great Thunder still had his limp. He looked like he wanted to run and play with his son, but he only walked after him, not even trying to trot. Little Thunder continued to dart around, trying to coax his father to join in the fun, but obviously his father wasn't ready.

As I continued to spend time with my family, I wondered how I was going to be able to climb up on his back and into the saddle? Gay had made it look so easy with her horse Blaze, but I had visions of my stallion taking off fast and furious with me being dragged behind with my foot caught in the stirrup.

There was no stepladder out here for a beginner like me, as there was in the stables, and how about reins and a bit? There was no way I was going to get a bit in his mouth, Gay had said. "He is a wild horse, Kingsley, and you will have to hold onto his mane. Even Blaze doesn't like a bit being put in his mouth, yet alone your wild stallion."

I'd wait until Friday and talk to Maggie. Maybe she would have some ideas. That will give him some more time to get stronger before he has the weight of a rider on his back.

Each day we walked across the Sands to Oxwich. I wanted him to remember how he used to thunder across the Sands, not that he would ever forget. I think it was me that needed to remember, or should I say, believe that he could do it again, for I wanted to see him gallop as fast as the wind blows.

As the days went by, we played our games together, he pushing me with his nose, and lowering his face to mine. When

I fell and lay still on the sand, he would start to nibble my long hair, which was something new, and he was always smelling me, even after I'd had a nice bath at my father's house. "What is it you smell, old boy? It is just me. I'm so glad you like the way I smell." I think it was his way of showing affection. A wet nose kiss on my face, and a good sniff, and I'd say "love you too, Great Thunder."

Friday arrived, and not once during the week had he tried to trot, yet alone gallop. Was he emotionally scarred as well as physically? Would he ever be the horse he was before the great fight? Or was I being impatient? Only time would tell.

"Bye Dad, bye Fraser, I'll see you on Monday night," and I headed over to Maggie's. Maggie had made a lovely supper, and was excited to see me as always. "So tell me Kingsley, how is Great Thunder doing? Did you get a saddle on him yet?"

"Yes Maggie, I got it on him, but he is not even trotting yet, and I'm wondering if he will ever be the same again, the way he was before he had the fight with the other stallion."

She said nothing for a while, and then she said, "Give him time. You mustn't forget that it was a fierce battle he fought, bad enough to kill the other stallion. As far as trying to ride him, the fact that he is still injured may be giving you the only opportunity you will have to climb on his back and ride him. There would be no way that he would have allowed anyone to ride him the way he was before. He would throw you off his back in seconds and not allow you near him again."

"I remember a time up in the stables when a man tried breaking in one of the wild horses," continued Maggie. "That horse bucked him off his back I don't know how many times. Even with Mrs. Griffith's help—and she is an expert on horses—they weren't able to train him. Try to look at his injury as an opportunity for you, Kingsley. Remember, God is in this, and he allows things to happen for a reason. It sounds like you have already built a trust with him, in feeding him and taking him for a walk every day."

"I hadn't thought of things that way, Maggie, thank you."

"You're welcome, Kingsley, now why don't you sit down and have your supper, and tomorrow I will come with you to the stables and we can talk to Mrs. Griffith and see if she has any ideas. She knows a lot more about horses than I do."

"Thanks, Maggie, that would be great."

In the morning, Maggie sent me out to the chicken shed, and Hattie had laid another lovely brown egg. She gently pecked the top of my hand again as I felt under her warm feathers. Each of the other hens had laid an egg too, and we had brown eggs and toast for breakfast. And this morning Maggie brought out her home-made blackberry jam.

"Oh Maggie, your jam is the best I've ever tasted."

"I'm glad you like it, Kingsley. I made it at the end of August this year. I'll give you a jar to take home to your father and brother if you like."

"Thanks Maggie, I know they will love it."

Maggie then asked me how things were going at home.

"They are going well," I said, even though I felt in my heart more at home here with Maggie than I did with Dad and Fraser. Things were going well with Dad and Fraser, as well as I could expect, but without my mother there, the home was broken, and I felt her absence every time I went there.

"Family is important," Maggie continued, "even when there are challenging times for you all to go through. Next to

God, your family is the most important thing that you should devote your time and love to."

"You're right, Maggie. I've learned a lot about that since coming to the cliffs to live, but I've also learned that being away from home and living in the wild teaches you many wonderful things that you could not learn at home."

We talked more and then we went to the stables to see Mrs. Griffith. As we approached the riding field, such sweet memories flooded my mind, and my heart longed again for Gay.

"You still miss her, don't you," Maggie said.

"Is it that obvious?" I asked sadly.

"Yes it is, Kingsley, but God will bring someone else into your life when the time is right."

While she was still talking, something happened that I wasn't prepared for. There, coming across the field towards us, was Blaze, Gays horse. She said she had sold him, but she hadn't told me that she had sold him to someone local.

"Hello Maggie," a voice called out. It was Mrs. Griffith calling from the barn. "What can I do for you?"

We walked over to the barn. "This is Kingsley, Mrs. Griffith," said Maggie. "He has some questions about riding one of the wild horses."

"A wild horse," Mrs. Griffith echoed back.

"Yes, a wild horse," I replied. "I've already got a saddle on one of the wild horses in the Valley, and I want to know the best way to climb up onto the saddle and ride him."

"Oh, I remember you, Kingsley," she said. "You came up here a few times with Gay and you rode Blaze, didn't you?"

"Yes, that's right, Mrs. Griffith, I did. It's nice to see you again."

Cave Days

As I looked around the horse shed, I could hardly hear what Mrs. Griffith and Maggie were talking about, for I was surrounded by Gay, and my heart interacted with our memories. There on the table was the brush that she had taught me to use on Blaze's coat, and I remember her warm hand on mine, and her voice saying, "You brush firm like this, and you use long strokes. That's how Blaze likes it." And there was her new saddle that we'd treated and polished together. She had sold the new saddle with Blaze. There were her riding hat and boots still hanging on the horseshoe hangers, which had the horse owner's name on a plaque above it. I read the name Gay Tripp. Mrs. Griffith hadn't taken her name down yet.

"Kingsley," Maggie called out, waking me from my daydream. "Mrs. Griffith is talking to you."

"Sorry, Mrs. Griffith, I'm listening now."

"I think it's a waste of time trying to ride a wild horse. Maggie has told me it is a stallion too. You would sooner turn back the sea than ride a wild stallion."

So that was where Gay got those words, I thought: "sooner turn back the sea."

Mrs. Griffith continued: "...and you'd never get a bridle over his head and a bit in his mouth. But I'll tell you what, if you're that determined, you're welcome to use anything here that belongs to me, apart from a saddle, but you already have one of those, don't you? How on earth did you get it onto a wild horse's back, and where did you get the saddle from if you don't own a horse? They are very expensive, you know."

"Gay gave me her old one, before she moved away."

Mrs. Griffith looked at both Maggie and I again, and said, "As I say, you're welcome to use anything I have here except a saddle," and then she carried on with her work out in the field.

"Let's go back to the cottage," Maggie said. "It sounds like Mrs. Griffith doesn't hold out much hope of you being successful in riding Great Thunder, but remember, she doesn't know him like you do, or understand the bond you have with each other. Plus you have God on your side."

"Thanks Maggie for reminding me, I appreciate you so much."

"Are you alright, Kingsley? You didn't do a very good job of hiding how you were feeling. As soon as you saw Blaze, and Gay's name still up on the equipment wall, you went into a trance and were miles away, or should I say you were back in time. I understand more now just how much you loved her, and still love her. It was written all over your face. I wish I could change things for you, Kingsley."

At Maggie's words, I wept. It was like she was right inside my heart, knowing exactly how I felt. She hugged me tightly and she said, "Kingsley, I do know this! If you put God first in your life, he will give you the desires of your heart, including a young lady when the time is right. Now how about some lunch, and then I must go and open the store."

"And I'll go and visit my stallion, Maggie, and meet you back at the cottage at supper time"

We finished lunch and I headed off to find Great Thunder. He was standing outside his cave with the saddle still on his back. I felt encouraged by Maggie's words. I was determined to prove Mrs. Griffith wrong and make my dream come true. Her words wrestled in my heart again: "You would sooner try to hold back the sea than tame your wild stallion."

Cave Days

I prayed and asked God to help me ride my stallion across the beach, and suddenly as I was looking where Great Thunder was standing in relation to the rocks behind him, I had an idea. I pulled on his rope and turned him so he was facing sideways, almost against the rocks. If I can keep him in this position, I can climb the rocks behind him and lower myself down onto the saddle. Yes, it might just work, if he just stays still.

Feeling nervous and excited, I put an apple and some carrots in front of him, and made sure he was standing as close to the rocks as I could get him. "You stay there," I said, and he lowered his head to eat the apple. Quickly I climbed the rocks, and once above him I spoke gently saying "Be still, old boy, stay still now," and slowly I lowered myself down on top of him.

First I pushed my right leg out over the saddle, and then holding onto the front of it with both hands, I pushed my left leg off the rocks and pushed again on the saddle to straighten up. Up came his head and off we went with a jolt. I grabbed his mane with one hand and put my other half way round his neck for balance. For a minute or two I felt I was falling off, and I leaned forward holding tightly to his mane and the rope with my left hand and the top of the saddle with my right. We were heading for the sea. Not galloping, thank God, but trotting quickly down the sand. My heart raced and my body bumped to his trot and I held on for dear life. It was a long way to fall into the sand from up here. We reached the sea and I shouted, "Yahoo, I'm still on your back. Good boy, Great Thunder. Thank you for not bucking me off. Now can we walk some more?"

Reaching into my pocket I pulled out another carrot and then leaned over his side to give it to him. I missed his mouth and it fell to the sand. As he leaned his head down and began crunching it, I was jolted forward and almost fell off. After leaning back and readjusting myself in the saddle, I began to relax as he seemed more interested in eating his carrot than being concerned about me on his back.

After he lifted his head, we were off again, and now he walked our usual route to Oxwich Bay, and I shouted out in excitement again. "Yes, yes, I'm riding Great Thunder. Come on boy, let's go all the way to Oxwich."

He walked until we reached the Killy Willy, and then he lowered his head to drink. "Come on, Thunder," I said after a few minutes, "you're going to drink the river dry." Up came his head and we were on our way again. As we walked along, I felt so honoured that my great friend had trusted me riding on his back, and I wanted to gain his complete trust. On we walked until we reached the top of Oxwich Bay, where he stopped and stood still. I sat up straight in the saddle and felt my feet pushing against the stirrups. How I wished I had some reins to hold onto, but I didn't, only his mane, neck and the rope still tied around him.

On our return to the cave, I would try to pat his neck and gently dig my heels into his side as I'd seen Gay do with Blaze, and hopefully he would trot for me again. What if he gallops? I thought. Well, I will hold on for dear life, and if I fall off, at least it's sand and not concrete I'll be falling on.

I waited until we crossed the Killy Willy again, and then called out, "Hey, boy. Let's go!" I patted his neck firmly and gently pushed my heels against his side. To my surprise, off we went, faster this time. Was it a canter or a slow gallop? All I knew is that we were going faster, and I bounced up and down on the saddle, my bum and back feeling like a shock absorber.

"You have to sit up straight in the saddle and keep your back straight," Gay had said. Easy for you to say. I've got nothing to hold onto except his mane. How I wish I'd listened to her more and watched Blaze, rather than just wanting to look into her eyes and beautiful face.

Come on Kings, you're just running scared on the back of a horse; of course you would do the same if you saw her again. You would look at her lovely curves, not the horse. Suddenly Great Thunder surged forward, picking up stride. "Wow," I shouted, "this is definitely a canter or even a gallop." I leaned forward with my head against his neck, grasping a fistful of his mane in each hand. He thundered now, faster and faster.

"Not so fast, Great Thunder!" I shouted. "I thought you had a bad leg, old boy. Wow, yahoo, and great Scot. You must be healed. You're running like the wind."

What a rush. I felt the adrenaline running through my veins. All I could do was hold on and hope for the best, as the great King of Gower thundered and snorted lightning across the Sands.

Somehow I was still on his back as he slowed down on our approach to the cave. "That was a gallop, old boy, wasn't it." I said, my body still shaking. As he came to a trot again and then stopped outside his cave, I shouted "Yes, yes, I rode the Great Thunder" at the top of my lungs. I'm sure they could hear me miles away in the village.

Now how to get off a horse? I hadn't thought of that. I mean I never expected to still be sitting here on his back. Well, there was only one way to do it as far as I could see, and that was to climb out of the saddle and slide off his back to the sand, hopefully landing on my feet.

I managed to get my feet out of the stirrups, and then one leg out over the saddle, and the rest was all down horse so to speak. I got my other leg over the saddle and slid off his side to the sand in one awkward movement.

…And up went the judges marks! Zero point one for presentation, and one point three in the skills section, but I scored a 10 in the entertainment category, and I landed on my feet to boot, so I took a bow and carried on. "Did you see that, old boy? Are you impressed? Not only did I stay on your back, but I landed on my feet coming off."

He said nothing, and he did nothing, but the look on his face said, "I've seen some things in my life, but you getting off a horse is something else." He was a good sport about it though and he didn't rub it in. I stood in front of him so full of excitement.

I didn't know what to do next, so I ran to Maggie's store to tell her the good news. Bursting through the door, I shouted: "I rode him, Maggie. I rode Great Thunder!"

There were two elderly ladies in the store wondering what the heck I was talking about, but Maggie spoke up and said "That's wonderful, Kingsley. I'm so happy for you. If you wait until I've finished serving Mrs. Jones and Mrs. Evans, I'll close the store and you can tell me all about it over a cup of tea."

When Maggie had closed up the store, she said, "This deserves a celebration. I'm going to cook a special meal this evening." I followed her back to the cottage.

She cooked us a lamb dinner with roast potatoes and carrots, and her own homemade gravy and a mint sauce. "And I'm going to let you try some of my homemade pear cider," she said. "I was saving it for a special occasion, and this is a special occasion!"

Through dinner I shared with her every detail of my great adventure, and we toasted my stallion several times. "Oh this tastes so good. Lamb is my favourite meal, and I really like your pear cider."

"Thank you, Kingsley, you better not have too much or you will fall off your stallion." We both roared with laughter.

Maggie asked, "What's next for your adventures?"

"Well, I want to learn to ride him better, and find out about some of the equipment I could use. Mrs. Griffith said I could use anything she has at the stables."

"Yes, she did, didn't she, and that reminds me, did you take the saddle off him yet?"

"No, I'm afraid that I'd never get it back on him if I took it off."

We both laughed, but when I thought of the time and effort I had spent trying to get it on, it wasn't really funny.

"You will have to take it off for the health of his skin tomorrow, plus he's a target for people to report to the authorities if they see a saddled horse with no rider. They will think there's been an accident or the horse has run away from one of the riding schools."

"You're right, I do need to take it off, but I was hoping to ride him a few more times first so that he can get used to me."

"Right you are, Kingsley, that does sound like a good idea, considering how hard it was to get it on him. Watch he doesn't get sore or uncomfortable or you may never get it on him in the future if he has a bad experience. There is one thing that I would really do if I were you."

"What's that?"

"Well, I would go and talk to Mrs. Griffith again at the stables. I know she comes across as a bit grumpy and a know-it-all, but when it comes to horses she knows more than most people, and she's a wonderful lady when you get to know her. She will teach you about the equipment and how to use it."

"I'll go and talk to her again tomorrow, Maggie."

"Good idea, Kingsley."

Maggie and I finished our celebration meal and then sat in the living room for a cup of tea.

"Now Kingsley, do you remember what I shared with you about God being involved in you being able to ride the stallion at this particular time in his life?"

"Yes, I remember, and I thought about it a lot. I know that if he hadn't been injured in the fight, and I hadn't had the chance to take care of him, there is no way he would have let me ride him or even put the saddle on his back. I can see how God worked things out through the circumstances of his injury. He used that to answer my prayers, didn't he?"

"Yes, he did, Kingsley, and if you trust him with the circumstances in your life, he will work things out for the very best all through your life!"

God had given Maggie a wonderful ability to share his truth in relation to the circumstances and experiences of every day life, and for that I was so thankful.

Maggie and I ended our evening with a time of prayer together, and I thanked God again for making my dreams of riding Great Thunder come true!

In the morning I went over to see Mrs. Griffith at the stables.

"Well Kingsley, how did you get on with your wild horse?"

"It went really well, Mrs. Griffith, I actually got to ride him. I want to ask you about some of the gear I need to use in order to ride him properly."

"What do you have at present? You obviously have a saddle of sorts. Oh, that's right, you have Gay Tripps old one, don't you. That's an excellent saddle; she used it here on Blaze. Now what else do you have?"

"That's it, just the saddle."

"How on earth are you staying on his back and keeping control?"

"I'm just holding on to his mane, leaning forward when he gallops, and holding on for dear life."

"Well I've never! Who do you think you are, Tonto? It's amazing to me that you even got the saddle on him."

"Yes, Mrs. Griffith, I was surprised too."

"Will you please stop calling me Mrs. Griffith. Heather would be just fine."

"Yes, Mrs.—I mean Heather."

"That's better. Mrs. Griffith makes me sound old, plus I had a headmistress called Mrs. Griffith and she was a miserable cow."

I couldn't help but laugh, and Heather said, "You wouldn't be laughing if you'd had to contend with her while you were at school."

"I'm sure I wouldn't," I replied, pinching myself to stop laughing.

"Well, Kingsley, I've got riding lessons to give this morning, but you come back at about 1 o'clock this afternoon and we'll see what we can do".

"Thanks, Heather, I'll see you this afternoon then."

I went into the store to tell Maggie how things had gone. "You're right, Maggie, Mrs. Griffith is a really nice lady once you get past her brazen exterior. She even asked me to call her Heather. She's got a sense of humour alright." Maggie smiled with a knowing sparkle in her eyes. "She wants me to come back and see her this afternoon," I said. "I don't know what to tell her, or what not to tell her, about Great Thunder…"

"I wouldn't worry about it, Kingsley, just go back and see her this afternoon. Your secrets will be safe with her. She knows you are staying with me, and I have told her how you have nursed that stallion back to health. She has a special place in her heart for people who love animals, and especially horses."

After lunch I went back over to the stables. The clock in the barn read a quarter after one, and she hadn't come. Maybe she was still giving a lesson, though I hadn't seen anyone riding in the field.

"Sorry I'm late," came a voice from behind the equipment shed. "I'm in here, Kingsley," she shouted out. "Come on in and I'll show you what you need."

On the wall were riding hats and jackets, and whips—which I'm sure had another name, and in the corner was an anvil and horseshoes. Maybe she was a jack of all trades?

"We need this and that," she said, handing me what looked like a type of harness and two long leather straps attached to it. "I'll carry this blanket and lead rope."

"Where are we going?" I asked.

"Take me to your horse," she said, "and we'll see what we can do."

Swallowing fast, I repeated what she had said under my breath: "Take me to your horse."

"That's right. Take me to your horse, or as they say on Star Trek, take me to your leader."

I chuckled and started to relax. "That's great," I said. "He's down on Pobbles Beach."

We talked along the way, over the Burrows and down through the dunes to the beach.

"Have you always lived on Gower?" I asked.

"Yes, I was born in Port Eynon, and my mother and father had the farm. I married and moved to Penmaen farm with my husband."

I wanted to ask what had happened to her husband, but I remained silent.

"It's alright, I can tell you," she said out of the blue. "I lost my husband five years ago and I couldn't keep up the farm by myself, so I opened a riding school and stables, and that's how I help pay the bills. As you know, Maggie comes and helps me when she can."

"I'm sorry to hear about your loss," I replied, "but I think it's a great idea having started a riding school and stables."

"Yes, thank you, it is. I board six horses and I have five riding students, and you know Blaze. He's a good horse to learn on, and of course you have been on him, haven't you, when you spent time with Gay. I'm sure you miss her a lot. She's a lovely girl and very pretty."

"Yes," I said, speaking up, "and don't remind me," I murmured.

"Now where's this wild animal of yours?"

Thou Art Mine

"There he is over there, standing outside his cave."

"Good golly, Kingsley, he's a monster. Look at the size of him."

Great Thunder was pleased to see me and he came trotting towards us.

"He looks like he's happy to see you," said Heather.

"You are, aren't you, my boy." Great Thunder lowered his nose to my hand and I patted his neck. "Now this is Heather and she's come to see you."

"My, you're a beauty," Heather said as she inspected him from back to front. "And look at this scar on his hind leg. It's very deep. Someone has taken great care to keep it clean so that it could heal."

"I walked him into the waves every day to try and keep the wound clean and disinfected by the salt water," I said, "and it's healing up quite well, I think."

"Well, you saved his life, there's no doubt about that. A wound like that unattended would have diseased and festered, and he'd have died a cruel death out here in the wild. You're to be commended, and there's no reason why he won't regain full mobility in that leg."

"Thanks for saying so, Heather. I'm relieved to hear that."

"Now I'll tell you what we're going to do. Do you have any treats to give him?"

"No, I gave him the last apple before I rode him."

Heather laughed. "I still can't believe you rode him with only a saddle, and it's not on properly either." Heather unbuckled the saddle and slid it off gently. Great Thunder didn't even flinch. I saw he was very sweaty from the saddle and now understood how he could get sores. Maggie was right again and it was good I had Heather to help.

"This is an English saddle and is much lighter than a western saddle. That may be why he let you put it on his back without too much fuss. After he cools off a bit we will put it on right and see how he does. I thought he was a bit wilder than this."

"Oh you haven't seen him really run, he is as wild as Thunder!"

"I will trust you on that," Heather said, rubbing his back to help him cool off faster. "Why don't you go and get some water and by the time you get back he should have cooled down enough to try again."

"I'm not sure how he will act if I am gone to be honest," I said hesitating.

"Well then we will both go and get the water and he will see we are friends. It will help with his trust when I help put the saddle back on." And off we went to the river.

When we returned, Thunder was still standing in the same spot, probably enjoying the coolness blowing in from the sea. After he had a nice drink we decided it was now or never. Heather held up the small blanket for him to sniff. He seemed curious if anything. The rope was still around his neck and Heather took it off and replaced it with the lead rope. Once around his neck, she handed it back to me.

"I'm going to try and place the blanket on him now and see how he reacts." He turned his head and swung it from side to side recognising the different texture on his back. "Okay, try walking him around a bit and let him get used to the different feel," Heather said. I walked him forward and circled back a few times before Heather told me to stop. "Now we will try the saddle again. You hold the lead rope and rub the side of his neck." I did what she said and talked to him reassuringly. Heather slid the saddle up on his back the same way that Gay had showed me, so at least I did that part right I thought.

"Now these straps are called billets and they buckle into the girth. It is important to get the right placement so the horse is comfortable. Too far forward and it will hit the back of his front leg and too far back it will be around his stomach and if the saddle moves forward at all it will loosen up and shift to the side. Feel under here, Kingsley, there is a flat part about 4 inches from his leg. Can you feel it?" I put my hand where she had showed me and it felt like a natural place for the girth to sit. "You had it almost right, but it was too far forward. This will be much more comfortable for him."

As she did up the billets, Thunder turned his head and snorted. I patted the side of his neck again waiting for him to move at any minute. He didn't, at least not yet I thought. Now comes the hard part that, putting on the bridal. How on earth would Heather accomplish that? No doubt Great Thunder would not accept something on his head, Heather herself said it might be impossible. I waited to see what would happen.

"Kingsley, start rubbing his nose and gently work your way up to his ears." I rubbed his nose as she said and moved my way up to his forehead. His ears flicked a few times and he looked at me a bit confused at what I was trying to do. "That's good, just talk to him gently. He can feel your energy and if you are anxious then he will be too." This must be why we were so in tune with each other. Great Thunder could feel what I was feeling and even though inside I knew it to be true it surprised me to hear her say that he could also feel my anxiety. Our connection was so great we were like one. I relaxed more now, proudly understanding my horse more through my own emotions. As I relaxed he did too and Heather moved to stand on the opposite side of his head than I was and gently ran her own fingers down his nose and when she brought her hand back up she had the bridal and had slipped it over his nose. She moved her fingers up to his forehead and around his ears it went. She buckled it on the side and all was done.

"You don't have to ride a horse with a bit," she said, "although it does give you more control. Even though he is calm now, I think this is as far as you should go with him. He trusts you and you trust him. You can attach reins to the rings on the bridal and you can turn his head just by gently pulling on one rein or the other. When you pull on the right rein his head will turn right, and if you pull on the left, he will turn left. This is called plow reining. You can also turn him by leaning and pushing your thigh against one side of his torso and having no pressure on the other side. He will be able to feel the pressure against his side and turn naturally. This is the kindest and gentlest way to ride a horse if you are in tune with it and just wanting to ride for the pleasure of it." Wow, she sure knew a lot about horses I thought. Who says I'm not in school!

"As for stopping, I think the best way would be for you to voice train him."

"Voice train him?"

"Yes. I will give you a few things you can do to practise and it will help with this as well as keep him entertained. Horses get bored too, you know." Yes, I knew. I think that was why Great Thunder would do his run everyday. I did the same as I walked up and down the beach every morning. I am not sure it was out of boredom so much as just biding the time and enjoying God's creation, but it did keep me entertained as she had said.

"Now the last thing I will show you is the voice command. Take the lead rope from around his neck and attach it to the bridal. Now I want you to take him for a walk and try and walk beside him. Once you are walking beside each other I want you to stop and say STOP in a commanding voice. Then, wait a minute until he stops and then start walking again. Do the same thing then stop and say STOP again. By doing this it will reinforce the word with the motion, then once you are on his back you can practice using the word stop again. Go ahead and give it a try."

I did as Heather told me and to my surprise after the second try, Thunder stopped when I did. I tried again, this time saying the word STOP when I stopped. Wow this was really working!

"Now take the lead rope off and do the same thing without it on." I did and he stopped when I stopped again. "Try walking beside him then turn and take a wide circle."

"Hey, he's doing what I'm doing! Wow, you should give lessons," I stated and we both laughed. As we ended our session I thanked Heather for all she had taught me and I vowed to keep practising. I felt I could take his saddle off now and that he would allow me to put it back on as we had grown so much in our understanding of one another.

Heather gave him a pat and he nuzzled her hand looking for an apple. Thunder was so much more comfortable with Heather sensing her experience and expertise. He was far more wild with me. "You're not living up to your name old boy," I muttered under my breath. "Heather is going to think I'm a liar."

Just then with the saddle and bridal off and free at last it was as if he knew it was time to be wild again and off he went, doing his run.

"Look at him go! You were right Kingsley, he is still as wild as the west wind!" I looked on as proud as a man could be, watching this beautiful creature do what he was meant to do, Thunder across the Sands as fast as the wind blows.

∽

Over the next few weeks I practised putting the saddle on and taking it off. It took a lot more time for him to get used to the bridal, however, being put over his head but we persevered together. As Thunder could read my emotions so well I learned the importance of being stern and deliberate while fitting the saddle and bridal.. It looked so easy when Heather did it, but it was getting easier every day. A few treats here and there obliged his willingness I'm sure.

Heather was coming today to meet me again and give me another lesson. I had looked forward to it all week and was anxious to show her what we had learned. "We have graduated from primary school now, haven't we old boy."

"Hello, are you down there?" Heather shouted from on top of the dunes.

"Over here," I yelled back waving my arms so she could see us.

"I will be right there." I watched as she got closer and closer. Great Thunder seemed excited as well. Maybe he was just expecting more treats. That would get me excited too, although I would much rather have a pasty and a refresher.

"I see you have him already saddled," she said.

"Yes and we are excited to show you what we know." I walked with Thunder back and forth starting and stopping and turning in a circle and he followed beside me mirroring my movements. Then I walked forward, stopped and started walking backwards. Great Thunder did the same.

"Well done you too, that was an advanced move and you can tell he trusts you."

"Yes, Great Thunder does trust me," I said. "We have quite a history."

"Well Kingsley, he's all ready for you to climb up onto the saddle now. So let's give it a try. How on earth did you manage to climb onto the saddle before?"

"I lowered myself onto his back from the rocks."

She laughed loudly and said, "You're as wild as the stallion yourself. Now here's what you do. You put your left foot in the stirrup and pull yourself onto his back by pulling with both hands on the top of the saddle. I'll hold onto his lead rope and reins until you're sitting in the saddle."

It took me three attempts to mount him, and once I was sitting in the saddle, she made me dismount and do it again. It took me another three times before I was in the saddle again.

"Don't be discouraged," she said. "He is a large horse and you're mounting him from the sand. The more you practise, the easier it will become. Now I want you to dismount one more time, and I'm going to show you how to make sure the saddle is ready for riding. When you put a saddle on a horse they sometimes tense up. After you walk him around a bit, he will relax and you may have to cinch the billets up a notch or two tighter. You may have to check up to three times before you actually ride a horse to make sure the saddle is secure."

Sure enough, the saddle needed to be tightened. I don't know how it didn't shift when I rode him the first time but I was thankful to not have fallen off.

We went over how to use the reins for a few minutes, and also leg pressure and positioning. "Well done, Kingsley." she said. "And now it's time for you to take him for a ride."

"Really? Right now?," I said, feeling nervous because she was watching. I wanted to show her I could ride well.

"Of course, ride him now. I didn't come all this way to teach you what you have learned and not have you practise it!"

"What I'm concerned about, Heather, is that he is used to taking me for a ride, not me taking him."

"Well, that's about to change, isn't it. The whole idea of learning riding skills is so you can ride the horse and take him where you want to go. Now off you go and show me what you have learned."

I mounted correctly the first time and was off to a good start.

"See, it comes with practice, doesn't it," said Heather. "Now, don't forget what I told you about pulling on the reins to turn, and when to queue him with your leg. Be stern with him and you'll do fine."

And off we went. We started with a walk and then went into a trot. Heather shouted out a few more instructions before her voice faded away behind us.

So far we had ridden only in a straight line. It was time to try a turn and Heather's instructions echoed in my mind: "Now hold one rein in each hand." Okay, I'm doing that already. I need to have my hands an inch or two forward of the saddle and several inches above, so my fists are at a 30-degree angle. Okay, Kings, you're doing what she said.

Great Thunder continued to trot in a straight line, obviously heading for Oxwich Bay.

I heard Heather's words again: "To queue the horse to walk forward, you keep a gentle elastic-like contact between your hand and the horse's mouth; the reins should be taut but not too tight. Apply a gentle pressure bringing his head up to slow him down. It worked!

"Well done, old boy," I said calmly as we slowed to a walk. As I cued him with the left rein, I continued to keep contact on the right rein. Again, I remembered Heather's words.

"...that will control the amount of bend he takes when turning. Don't let it go slack, and don't hold it too tightly. Remember Kings, everything slow and gentle.... Now for how you use your leg. At the same time that you cue with the reins, apply pressure with your left leg on the horse's side, so the horse is turning around your leg."

"My gosh, it's working!" I shouted, as Great Thunder made a slow wide turn towards the sea. What a great feeling it was to have him respond to my cues. I hadn't expected to have such control over a wild stallion.

I turned my head around in search of Heather, hoping she could see me using my skills, but she was too far behind us. Now what's next? Oh, that's right, as the horse obeys the cue, I stop the pressure of my hand and leg. "Wow, I've done it, I've made a turn."

I tried then to turn him to the right, and it worked. "Kings, you're learning to ride!" I shouted out excitedly.

We practised slowing to a stop and speeding up again, and he obeyed, and I shouted to Heather, who was gaining ground behind us. "I'm taking him for a walk now, instead of him taking me."

We reached the Killy Willy and he lowered his head to drink. In the distance, Heather continued to follow. "Dare we go for a gallop, old boy? What do you think?"

Thunder lifted his head and nodded a few times.

"I'll take that as a yes, old boy. Off we go then. Yahoo!"

We were on our way, thundering across the Sands. I could hardly believe it, this was fantastic. My confidence was growing by the minute as we passed the great Tor. Two girls stopped in their tracks on the beach to watch as we thundered by.

"This is one of the greatest days of my life, God!" I shouted. "I'm riding the King of Gower!"

We reached the end of Oxwich beach and I slowed him to a canter and turned him towards the sea. Then slowing to a trot, we splashed in the waves, and the cold water from his hooves splashed up over my face. The first time I had ridden Great Thunder I felt like I was bouncing around, but now I felt my movement was in unison with his and I didn't feel like I was going to fall off. We had found a rhythm together.

Turning him inland, I was doing well with the reins. We picked up the pace to a canter and I shouted, "yah yah, let's go." and Thunder exploded into his fastest gallop. We passed the girls, who stopped again, and then thundered past Heather, who clapped her hands and shouted "Well done, Kingsley, well done!"

Thou Art Mine

Before we reached Pobbles Beach, I slowed my wild stallion to a trot, and then made a wide turn and headed back towards Heather. On our approach, I turned him to the left and then to the right to show her how well I was doing.

"Excellent, Kingsley!" She called out. "Keep it up, and remember, nice and easy on the reins."

We reached the girls now, who waved their arms for us to come over.

"They sure look pretty, old boy," I said to Thunder. "Let's go and meet them."

"Wow, what a beautiful horse," the fair-haired girl said, "and he's so fast."

"Thanks," I said. "His name is Great Thunder, and he's a wild stallion."

"Is he yours?" The other one asked.

"Yes, he is, and I'm just learning to ride him."

"Well, you're doing really well."

"Thank you. I'm Kingsley, by the way. Nice to meet you both."

"I'm Jane," the fair-haired girl replied, "and this is my best friend Sky."

"Pleased to meet you both."

All the time we were talking, Sky kept looking into my face and smiling. She reminded me of Gay, and I guess that's why I came over to talk to them. Sometimes I still look for her.

Maggie once told me that God had a bigger plan for both of us. Sometimes I wished I knew what that plan was.

"Are you on holiday, or do you live around here?" I asked.

"We both live in England," Sky said, "and Jane and I are down here for a week visiting my grandmother who lives in Pennard."

"Pennard," I echoed. "I've lived there most of my life. Do you girls know your way around Gower?"

"No, this is our first time visiting," Jane said.

"Would you like me to show you around?" I asked. "I have some time tomorrow."

"That would be great," they both said excitedly. "Where shall we meet you?"

"Do you know Pobbles Beach? It's the first sandy cove behind us on the left. I could meet you there tomorrow at about 11 o'clock."

"That would be great, Kingsley, thanks a lot."

"I'll see you tomorrow then," I said with a smile, and Great Thunder and I headed off to catch up with Heather. When we reached Heather, I dismounted.

"That was excellent riding," she exclaimed, and we walked the remainder of the beach to the dunes. "Some people take a while to find their horse's rhythm but you have already found it and that is going to help you alot in these early stages of learning to ride."

"Yes I felt connected to him, if that makes any sense."

"It makes absolute sense," she said. "You should feel as if you are one."

"I did."

"What are you going to do with your stallion?" Heather asked.

"I don't know, but I know that I need to come up with a plan real soon."

Thou Art Mine

"Let's get his saddle off," said Heather. "How do you get it back and forth? It is a long walk to anywhere. Maggie didn't mention where you kept your saddle."

"I kept it at my cave in Leather's Hole, and then moved it to a crevice in the rocks so it wouldn't be stolen."

"Well, you are a wild one, aren't you, Kingsley," she said with a smile.

I didn't know how much Maggie had told her about me, so I didn't say anything back, just smiled.

Heather said goodbye to Great Thunder and I and started climbing up the dunes to the Burrows. I thought she would have waited and helped me get the gear off him. Maybe she was just giving me the practice. I quickly took the saddle off and ran it up to my secret crevice in the rocks and covered it with the blanket. I then ran to catch up with her, almost tripping on the lead rope and bridal I had in my hand. Nice of you to wait for me, I said under my breath. Finally I caught her up.

As we walked to the village, Heather asked me if I'd like to keep the riding gear. "Keep it? Did I hear you right? That would be wonderful, but I don't have the money to buy it off you."

"I am saying you can have it, Kingsley, as long as you look after it."

"Thank you so much, Heather and I will take care of it."

We reached Maggie's cottage and I said goodbye and went inside. Maggie was getting dinner ready and asked how things went.

"You should have seen us, Maggie. Heather taught me how to use the gear, and I can use the reins now, turning him left and right, and we galloped like the wind from Pobbles to Oxwich and back, and guess what?"

"What?"

"Heather said I can keep the riding gear. She sure is a kind lady, Maggie."

Just then the doorbell rang. "Can you get it, Kingsley," asked Maggie, "I have to get this meat out of the oven."

I was surprised to see Heather at the door.

"Hello Kingsley. Maggie asked me over for dinner tonight."

"Sit down at the table, you two," Maggie shouted from the kitchen. "Dinner is ready and I'm bringing it out." Maggie had made roast beef and Yorkshire pudding, roast potatoes and carrots. "And I've made bread pudding and custard for after," she announced.

"It's not Sunday, so what's the occasion?" I asked.

"It's just because," Maggie replied. "Now pass me your plate."

"Kingsley did very well with his riding today, Maggie," announced Heather.

"That's what I've heard," said Maggie.

My face began to beam as I couldn't hide the joy inside my heart. "It's my dream come true to ride Great Thunder, and thank you both so much for helping me."

"I'm happy for you, Kingsley," Maggie said, "and God answered our prayers, didn't he?"

"Yes, he did," I exclaimed, "It's amazing how he worked out every detail, and that includes meeting you, Heather."

"I've done very little, Kingsley, just given you the basic instruction you need to ride, you've done all the rest yourself."

Thou Art Mine

I felt a great sense of accomplishment and pride as I heard Heather tell Maggie that I'd saved my stallion's life by attending to the wound on his leg.

"We are both very proud of you," Maggie added, "and we have a proposition for you. You've shared with me that you have decided to go and live with your grandparents in Devonshire sometime within the next few months…"

"Yes, that's right."

"Well, Heather has offered to have Great Thunder come and stay with her at the stables while you're away."

I turned to Heather, who smiled and said, "I know he's a wild horse, and in some ways he will always be wild, but to have him roaming free while you're away will put him in danger of being captured by the authorities and taken away. Do you remember when he left the Valley in the autumn, and you found him running wild up on Rhossili Down?"

"Yes, I remember. I won't forget that in a hurry."

"Kingsley, while he was up there he chased a number of people, almost injuring them, including Mr. Rees Jones of the National Trust organisation here on Gower! Great Thunder chased him and his wife and children, and frightened them. After the dead stallion was found and reported by two farmers, Mr. Rees Jones asked that your stallion be captured and removed from the Gower Peninsula."

For a few minutes I felt like Great Thunder and I were being read our rights, and I looked sadly at Maggie.

"It's true, Kingsley, but Heather and I have come up with a plan that we think will work. It's up to you, of course; no one is going to force you into anything, but this is a proposition for you to consider…."

Cave Days

I turned back to Heather…."If you agree to Great Thunder coming to the stables," said Heather, "he will always remain your horse, and while you are away in Devonshire, I will work with him and help train him. This way he won't be taken away, because as far as his *status* goes, he will be privately owned by you, Kingsley, and stabled here with me in Penmaen."

"Yes, but what about him being able to father another foal with Thunder Spring, and being able to be with the family he already has – with his son, Little Thunder? I know what it's like to come from a broken family, and I want my horse family to be together."

"Maggie has already explained this to me Kingsley," replied Heather, "and we have an idea. During the spring and summer months, I am planning to take my riding students to practise their skills down on the Sands, and on those days, Great Thunder can roam free and visit his family in the Valley. If we leave a saddle on him with an ownership tag – which I can put on him – then even if he does take off to the Downs, we can get him back."

"Maggie looked at me and then looked at Heather, and then she said, "Kingsley, I think you have found a partner in crime." She started to laugh and soon we were all laughing hysterically.

Heather said, "I never thought I'd meet a real Jesse James until I met you, Kingsley Ross Hill. You're quite famous around Gower as the wild caveman of the Cliffs."

"I have two partners in crime." I said happily. "How blessed can I be?"

"If you decide this is a good plan, you can bring your stallion to the stables a few times a week right away if you like," said Heather. "That way, he will be used to coming here before you leave for Devonshire."

"I don't need any more time to think about your proposal," I said gratefully. "I can't risk losing him, and nor can Thunder Spring and Little Thunder. We are his family, so I accept your proposition, and thank you both so much for giving Great Thunder and I this opportunity. I do have another question though. How about his food and keep, Heather? That's expensive."

"I'll let Maggie tell you about that," said Heather.

"I've agreed, on the condition of you accepting our offer, Kingsley, to pay Heather a year's supply of food for your horse in payment for you having taken care of my cottage for me."

"And your boarding is free for a year, Kingsley." Heather added. "Until you have a job in Devonshire and can afford to give me something towards it." Tears filled my eyes as my heart overflowed with joy!

"Now how about some Bird's custard and some of my home-made bread pudding," Maggie said.

"And let's drink to a great proposition and a plan worked out," added Heather.

After a few toasts of celebration and several helpings of Maggie's wonderful bread pudding and custard, Heather went home, and Maggie and I shared a time of prayer and Thanksgiving for God's goodness in my life, and then I retired for the evening.

Chapter Twenty-four

High Tide

After breakfast, I headed out for the day.

"Bye Maggie, see you in a few weeks."

"Bye Kingsley, have a nice time with your father and brother. Don't forget I'll be praying for you as you tell them of your plans to go and live in Devonshire."

I had decided that I would spend the next two weeks with Dad and Fraser as I wanted to spend some quality time with them before I left.

As planned, I met up with Jane and Sky at Pobbles, and then spent most of the day showing them around. They liked climbing and exploring, so I took them to Bacon Hole and Leathers Hole.

"Did you really live in the cave?" Sky asked.

"Wait here," I said, disappearing into my chamber of Leathers Hole. I came out wearing my rabbit pelt robe, and I had my spear in my hand. Both girls looked at me with shock and excitement – thinking either I was completely mad or a real caveman.

I chose to be a caveman again that day. I taught them how to spear skate in the Killy Willy, and I trapped rabbits with my snares, and I introduced them to my horse family in the Valley. As I saw them react and respond to what I shared of my life here on the cliffs and beaches, I was reminded of the many gifts and revelations that God had given to me in my life, which was now so full of such wonderful meaning and purpose.

In the late afternoon, I took the girls for a walk with Great Thunder. What a hero I was in their eyes as we watched him thunder across the Sands to Oxwich and gallop through the waves. It felt so good to hear their screams and laughter, and their words of wonder as he raced with the wind.

∽

Over the next several weeks, I took Great Thunder to the stables at least three times a week. He soon got used to his time there with Heather, and he enjoyed the other horses. One Friday evening, when I went over to the cottage to visit Maggie, she said, "Come with me over to the stables. Heather and I have something to show you."

I followed her into the barn, and there proudly hanging on the gate of the horse shed was a plaque, which read "Great Thunder, owned by Kingsley Hill." Heather came into the barn and said, "Here you are, Kingsley, I think these must belong to you," and she handed me some sheets of paper and a certificate.

As I read them, I saw that they were registration and ownership papers for Great Thunder in my name. I was so excited I didn't know whether to dance or shout, so I did both!

"A dancing caveman," Heather exclaimed, laughing.

"He's all mine now," I shouted, "legally mine, and no one can take him away!"

"That's right," Maggie echoed

"Thank you, Maggie. Thank you, Heather. Thank you both so much."

"You're welcome, Kingsley, we are glad you're happy."

And I thanked God in my heart for showering me with such a blessing.

Each time I brought my stallion to the stables, Heather gave me lessons, and my skills got better and better. Great Thunder and I roamed around most of the Gower Peninsula.

On the days I wasn't at the stables, and when we had finished our adventures for the day, I took his saddle off at the head of the Valley, so he could run free with his family. In the mornings our meeting place was always at his cave, which he guarded as our family's most sacred place, for I think he understood that our cave was the place of God's great miracle in saving my life, and of course the birthplace of his son, Little Thunder.

Each morning I brought him apples and carrots, and my friendship, but he gave to me more discovery and adventures that I could write in a hundred books. There is only time to write one book for you, dear reader. I hope that in these pages you will see God through all of these events and people, and especially through a family of horses that changed my life forever.

Some mornings I would just climb onto Great Thunder's back and allow him to take me wherever he wanted to go. We covered so many miles together, and he took me to secret places that I could never have found without him, places where I would never think of going.

High Tide

There is a marsh behind Oxwich Bay that is known mostly by birdwatchers and some locals from the village, but there in the long grasses in front of the steep woods is the "place of the stallions." When I was a little boy I would ask my mother and father where the stallions went when they weren't running with the herd.

"Nobody knows," my mother said. "It is a secret place!"

"They are somewhere watching you from their hideout in the trees," my father said when he didn't want me playing too close to the horses. I would slowly look around, scared, and my mother would say, "Don't frighten the boy!"

The first time Great Thunder led me through the marsh where the reeds and grasses are ten feet tall, all of a sudden it opened up to a secret meadow, and I counted seven stallions grazing together. They lifted their heads as we approached, but they looked unsurprised. Great Thunder ran to greet them, and they greeted him while I rode high on his back like a knight. As I looked around at the other stallions, I held on tight to Thunder's mane. They were different ages and colours, and I could see that my stallion was the biggest and strongest of all, and there was no question among the other stallions who was the bravest, for they all knew where the bloodstained grass does grow!

One day we walked all the way along the banks of the Killy Willy, while I shot my arrows off his back at the skate. I put the skate in an old potato sack and carried them to the village where I sold them, and we traded one for a bag of apples, which was part of our deal. We climbed back down the Burrows and on to the Valley where we rested below Pennard Castle, and I polished his saddle. I was an expert now at getting

Cave Days

it on and off his back, and once it was off, that was his cue to run and charge about like the wild stallion that he was, but he always came back to pick me up, and away we would go on another adventure.

From Three Cliffs Valley, we climbed a path and travelled through Park Mill Woods, a place where I've always felt a sense of mystery, as if I was in another time. Even when the yellow leaves have fallen, you can hear the oak and the sycamore cry out. They tell their stories to the other trees, who answer back, their voices calling in the morning mists. There are foxes and badgers, and cackling magpies, and a strange little horse that lives here all alone. I've only ever seen the back of it, but it is said to have a horn!

From Park Mill Woods we cross the road, and then walk across the stone bridge to old Park Mill School where I first kissed a girl, or should I say she kissed me. I'd kissed three now, but Gay's kisses were the best.

From the bridge we enter the Ilston Coombes, where I still catch eels and trout to eat. 'How many today, boy?' Two eels and a trout, Sir! 'The same as last time, boy.' Yes Sir, but this time it's a rainbow trout. 'Well done boy!' Thank you, Sir.

I make a fire and cook my fish, while Great Thunder stands and dreams. What are you dreaming about, old boy? Is she beautiful? This is the same place where I dreamed as a boy. I didn't know what to say to her at nine years old. I had these feelings and desires for her that I didn't understand. In the end I asked her, "Do you have a horse?" And then I kissed her. She said, "no, I don't have a horse," and she kissed me back. I know you're supposed to keep your eyes closed, but I opened mine and I saw hers were closed, so I quickly closed mine again.

High Tide

It is here on the banks of Ilston Stream where we have most of our conversation time. Man to horse and horse to man, and we understand each other, you see.

Last week we rode through the Fir Woods, which rarely has heard a bird sing, and as you walk the path of pine needles, which are like soft cushions under your feet, if you listen through the tops of the trees, silence rings her bells. It's the place where Gay and I first heard the melody of our hearts. It is here too, where silence sings to the birds, that I told Great Thunder my most intimate secret, how Gay had left and taken half of my heart with her. A man can tell a horse, but not his father and brother.

"And the ache won't go, away old boy! Have you ever felt like that? Did Thunder Spring ever steal away your heart?"

"No, she never took away my heart where I felt pain. I only knew I didn't want to be without her. I did meet the most beautiful mare once, and she wanted a foal, but I was only a yearling then, and the dominant stallion took her away from me, but then look what I've got now, a beautiful mare and Little Thunder. I believe things happen for a reason, and what I have was worth waiting for!"

"You're right, old boy! I don't believe in coincidence. God is teaching me that things happen for a reason, and when I look at your life with Thunder Spring and Little Thunder, I've asked God to give me the same things in my life one day, a loving wife and children. Yes, old boy, look at you now. You have a lot to be thankful for."

At the top of Ilston Coombes is old Ilston Church, where the tombstones still have no names. I lay flat on a gravestone, wondering "What is it that man leaves behind?" Here, that's all that's important, isn't it, old boy? What a man has done in his life, and what he's left behind. I want to leave good deeds behind me now that I know God, and be rewarded for the good things I do, and forgiven for the bad.

Suddenly what looked like a crazy man in a woman's cloak came running toward us shouting, "Get that horse out of the church yard." I jumped up from the stone and onto Great Thunder's back, and we raced through the church yard dodging the stones, and with a brown cloak behind us we didn't look back.

"If that's the priest, old boy, no wonder church attendance is dropping off."

Great Thunder neighed with laughter, and as we turned the corner we separated a woman and her dog.

"You idiots!" she shouted.

And I shouted back "Top of the morning to you, madam." It was three in the afternoon. My word, time really does fly when you're having fun.

"Oh, our time is an adventure, old boy. You have filled my soul with such joy and wonder for all time. Riding on your back and knowing you are mine has made me a rich man. I am a Prince, a Knight, and a King, and when they throw me in that hole, I'll remind them that I died a rich man, for both you and God are mine."

You were so right, old man. The stallion did come and find me, but do you know that he helped me to understand that all my blessings come from God's own hand?

༄

Our times went on, and so came the spring. "It is time for me to go, old boy, and follow the path that God has laid out before me. This is his plan, and I know you understand."

High Tide

Before I left my beloved horse family, I got to watch Little Thunder grow up, and even win his first fight. "The other horse was about twice his size, wasn't he, Great Thunder."

"No, he was at least three times his size." Anyway we changed his name that day from Little Thunder to Clashing Thunder!

I noticed that Thunder Spring was pregnant again. "My gosh, old boy, when did you do that? I only went away for three days when I visited Grandma and Grandpa in early spring. Well done, old boy, and congratulations. We must drink a toast to you with Maggie's cider."

Before I took my saddle off the King for the last time, he took me for a ride from Pobbles to Oxwich. We galloped so fast and we caught the wind. Like warrior poets, we crossed the Sands, for we were not divided in our plans. He is the King of Stallions, and high on Gower Hills he stands.

"Where are you going to say goodbye to him?" Maggie asked.

"Outside our family home, of course, our cave."

"I think they should name that cave after the two of you – the Kingsley and Thunder cave."

"Then that's what we will call it, Maggie."

When I told Dad and Fraser that I was going to accept Grandma and Grandpa's invitation to go and live with them in Devonshire, Dad was happy about my decision and he said how proud he was of me. How affirming and healing those words of my father were to me that day. To know I had pleased him made me grow two feet on the inside.

Maggie remained my confidante and continued to encourage me spiritually. "Promise you will write to me,

Cave Days

Kingsley, and let me know how things are going. Your grandparents are blessed to have you. I know that I have been very blessed to have you in my life, to see you learn and grow in the faith has been a great encouragement to me, and you have grown into a wonderful young man who I am proud to know."

"Thank you, Maggie," I said in tears. "Thank you for being such a blessing in my life too. God has taught me so many wonderful things through you."

"And remember, Kingsley, God will be with you and go before you wherever you go."

∽

My last weekend at Maggie's arrived, and then on Sunday I would spend one more night with Dad and Fraser before leaving for Devonshire on Monday morning.

I arrived at Maggie's late on Friday night, after going out with Fraser for a goodbye dinner and drink at the local pub in Pennard. My friend Mitch and his parents had been there too.

"Well, you're leaving Gower as a legend." Mitch said.

"Yes, you and that stallion of yours," his mother added. "You're famous throughout the land."

We all lifted a glass to Great Thunder and my adventures, and my mind flashed back to that lonely night when I'd come into the pub seeking companionship and warmth – anything that would help ease that season of great loneliness.

Look at my life now, I thought. It didn't bother me anymore that my best friend Mitch was at university and I wasn't. It didn't matter what anyone else was doing or how

High Tide

successful they seemed to be in their lives. My life was full of meaning and purpose, and my soul overflowed with a joy that I had never known before. I had God in my life, and I wouldn't trade what he had given me in my relationship with him for anything in the world.

Fraser gave me a ride to Maggie's after our Sunday dinner, and I said goodbye to him as I got off his bike. He would be leaving for work early on Monday, and I wouldn't see him again before I left.

"Good-bye Fraser, I love you," I said. "I'm glad you're my brother."

"Love you too, Kings, and don't leave it too long before you come and visit."

"I won't Fraser, and look out for the horses for me. They're in the Three Cliffs Valley."

"I will, Kings."

On Saturday morning, Maggie had a special going away meal for me. "Thank you, Maggie," I said, holding back my tears. I wanted to tell her how much I loved her, though in my heart I knew that she already knew. I'd wait until tomorrow and say "I love you!" as I was saying goodbye.

After our usual great breakfast and a peck on the hand from Hattie, I headed off to the beach to say goodbye to my horse family. Maggie gave me a bag of apples and some carrots to feed them. First I headed up the Valley to find Thunder Spring and Clashing Thunder. As I walked beside the Killy Willy, the water flowed brown and clouded, which meant there were horses drinking or crossing ahead, and there under Pennard Castle were the two of them standing in the river.

Cave Days

"I knew it was you guys," I said, holding the apples behind my back. Thunder Spring came running to see me, and then came Clashing Thunder as he saw the bag. "Steady on," I said, pushing him back. "Is that the only reason you have come to see me then, so you can have an apple or carrot? Is it?" I repeated, rubbing his neck. "I felt you when you were in your mother's tummy. Your hoof woke me up the morning after I'd fallen into the sea. Yes, it did," I said, giving him an apple. "And look at you now. You're almost grown up."

"And look at you, old girl. Your tummy is getting big again. Are you having another stallion like Clashing Thunder? Or is it a girl this time?" And I rubbed her tummy. "Well, I think it's a girl this time, because she's not kicking me like Clashing Thunder did."

After giving them a few more apples, I prayed for them, asking God to keep them safe and to give Thunder Spring a healthy baby foal.

It was time to head over to Pobbles to see Great Thunder, and there he was, larger than life and proud as punch.

"How are you, old boy, or should I say 'Your Majesty' as you stand there as proud as a lion, with your head up high."

Great Thunder ran around me in a circle, excited to see me, and then he stopped and lowered his nose to my face. "My, that's a nice welcome, old boy," I said, rubbing the side of his head. "Here you are, I've brought you some apples and carrots. He munched the apples like there was no tomorrow and then nibbled on my hair. "My gosh, old boy, you eat apples like I eat Cornish pasties, and you're as messy as I am when I'm having breakfast. Maggie tells me to slow down. She says that even if I turn around and back again the food will still be there. I'm sure she's right, old boy, but I just kept wolfing it down anyway. Us men and our food, we sure like it, don't we."

Rubbing his nose, I said, "Well, my boy, this is it! I had this great speech as to what I was going to say to you, but here I am with tears in my eyes, and feeling like I'm going to cry. I'll try not to, old boy, but if I do, I know you'll understand."

"Through you, I have learned so much about being myself, and being a man, about what it really means to live wild and free. That's right, my boy," I said, my eyes flowing with tears. "It was through you that God taught me that I could just be me, and to not have to try and be anything I wasn't. I love who I am, Great Thunder. Heather said it would be easier to hold back the sea than to ride you, old boy. She was wrong about that one wasn't she."

THE GREAT THUNDER

You ran as wild and free as the wind. I was just a boy when I first heard your thunder. You thundered across the sand and the surf, and the wind could not catch you! From the very first time I saw you, I wanted to be just like you: wild and free, running with the wind always chasing behind me, and the rising Sun before me. As I grew from a boy to a young man somewhere between the golden sunrises and the sunsets upon the western sky, I realised that you were much like me. You never fitted in with the other horses, and I was never accepted by the crowd. But as the tides of our time came in and went out, we knew we had so much more! To hold the wind and ride the sea, and climb the mountain and be truly free. Thank you, my great friend, the Great Thunder, for helping me to see that this is the way it was meant to be, for you and for me. I see!

© *Kingsley Ross Hill*

"Now you take care of yourself, old boy, and look after Thunder Spring and Clashing Thunder while I'm away, and be good for Heather and Maggie. I'll come and visit you as soon as I can. Now go on, old boy, off you go!"

As he galloped away across the Sands. I watched until he became a dark spot in the distance and then headed back to Maggie's.

Well, my last day on the Gower arrived, and God gave me sunshine. Maggie made me a lunch to take with me to the beach before we said goodbye and Heather walked down from the stables to wish me all the best.

"Thank you, Heather, for all you have done, and especially for teaching me to ride. It's a gift I will have all my life."

"It was my privilege, Kingsley, and do come and see me soon. I've got some good plans for your stallion. He's fitting in at the stables quite well."

Heather left to give a riding lesson, leaving Maggie and I alone.

"Well, Kingsley, goodbye," she said, starting to cry, "and please know how much I love you!"

"I love you too, Maggie, and thank you for everything. I thank my God for you."

High Tide

And with smiles and tears, and what words could not say, we turned and walked away.

"Don't forget to write, and eat your lunch, and no riding wild horses up in Devon."

I laughed and shouted back, "I will write soon, but I don't know if I can promise anything about not riding any wild horses. Asking me to do that would be like trying to hold back the sea."

When I arrived at the beach, I just stood there for a few minutes. I had said all my goodbyes to man and beast. There was only "hello" to say now to the future. As I walked again along the tide lines high up on the beach, I was leaving behind months and years, and even lifetimes it seemed, of friends and adventures, and experiences that had changed my life forever, and I would miss them all.

I walked to the top of Pobbles beach and climbed the sharp limestone rocks, where there is a natural arch bridge. As a boy, I would carry a sharp rock to the bridge and smash off pieces of the precious crystal stone that formed on the underside of the arch. I would take them home as treasure, or give them to the pretty girl who lived on our street, who made jewellery out of the stones.

Below the arch bridge is my favourite rock pool in the world. It is nothing special to look at, at first glance, except maybe for the red seaweed and the light green moss-like plant that makes the pool look ancient. You have to look into its mysteries carefully, and listen to the little creatures who live in it because they will speak to you.

It was my secret place, where I rarely brought another boy or girl to peer into its mirror of secrets, unless I wanted to

Cave Days

share what I had discovered with them. Today I would spend my last hours on Pobbles beach remembering the secrets of the rock pool. I lay on my stomach on the bridge and peered over the edge into the glistening water. The warm Sun shone upon my back and the fresh smell of the incoming tide rode the sea breeze and swirled gently around me. Suddenly I was back in the summer of yesteryear, peering again into my mirror of secrets through the eyes of that young boy....

My secret pool lies far up in the dry rocks, and it hears the tide and knows that its refreshment and replenishment is coming. The little shrimps and crabs are starting to move around the pool in anticipation. Oh, how I am like those little shrimps and crabs, as I wait excitedly for the sea to come in so I can jump and swim in the waves with my friends. I hear God's voice speaking, and he says wait, be patient, my sea is coming. The other pools nearer the surf meet the sea first, and I hear my friends leaping and laughing in the waves, but I must wait patiently though I am so excited. My pool knows the tide will not turn back till it has reached us. For can God go back on his word? Of course not. The sea rises and falls to his command. Even the smallest shrimp knows he is not forgotten. By and by the blessed moment comes. The last height of rock is washed by the sea. The stream pours in, at first just a trickle pushed by the effort of the largest wave, but by and by the great sea in all her fullness comes crashing into my waiting pool and I am satisfied. I dive off the rocks and swim and play with my friends....

It is not so different for me today as I look into the pool as a young man. Only I wait for God to pour himself into me. For he is my supply, and I wait patiently for him. He will come

High Tide

as the crashing tide and satisfy my thirsty soul. Come now, Lord and lead me on to walk upon your paths. I want to walk by your side, though I know you may lead me through some of life's most dangerous tides. But with you in my heart, Holy Spirit my guide, I know that as you lead me across the swelling tide, and though close to the treacherous rocks we abide, I don't have to run and hide, for you oh God, are with me, my pilot and friend at my side.

On Monday morning, Dad drove me to Swansea docks, where I boarded the good ship "Waverley," on which I crossed the heaving tide to Devonshire.

"My word King!" Grandma said, as I arrived. "What have you brought this saddle for? There aren't any horses around where we live. Only the "wild horses" up on the moors. You won't be needing a saddle." And I smiled.

Introducing: Gower of the Hills

*Book Two of
the Gower Peninsula Series*

My plane landed at Heathrow Airport at ten twenty-five in the morning, local time. I'd taken a night flight, leaving Vancouver, Canada at 11:45 p.m., and I didn't get much sleep, maybe forty winks here and there. But all said, it was a good flight with very little turbulence, and the flight crew did their best to take care of our needs.

Going through Customs looked more like the Berlin Airlift during World War II than checking in baggage. People were running around everywhere, and trying to find someone who spoke British amongst all the confusion was rather a tall order.

"No, I don't want a flight to Delhi! Just the way out, please! Oh It's that way, is it?"

Finally, I got out of the terminal, and stepped into the cool misty air of the London morning. It had been so hot in Vancouver, and I welcomed a cooler day.

Now, where was the bus? There was a sign that read 'Oxfordshire and South Wales, Stand 3,' and a bus pulled up almost immediately.

"Excuse me, Sir?" I asked the driver. "Is this the right stop for Swansea, South Wales?"

"Next one over, stand 4," he replied.

Coming home to the Gower I lugged my heavy suitcase and saddle over to the sign, and read: 'Newport-Cardiff-Swansea, via Bristol and Oxfordshire'.

"Oh, I'm so happy to have arrived in England, I could kiss a sheep!" I said to a middle-aged lady wearing a fur coat. She hurried away at my words, and I was tempted to shout, "Don't worry Madam, I won't kiss you, even if you do look like a sheep!"

I was just so happy to know that there were no more plane rides and oceans between my beloved Wales and me.

Once I crossed the Severn Bridge into Newport, I would be on Welsh soil again! As much as I enjoyed my life on Vancouver Island, Canada, the Gower Peninsula of South Wales would always be my home!

And there at the bus stop was a lovely girl wearing a T-shirt that read: "You may be able to take the girl out of Wales, but you will never take Wales out of the girl!"

About the Author

Kingsley Ross Hill was born in Mount Pleasant Hospital, near the city of Swansea, in Glamorganshire, South Wales. He presently lives in Creston British Columbia, Canada, with his wife Janais Hill. He is a full time writer and adventurer and enjoys time in the outdoors camping, fishing, and exploring new places. His inspiration comes from his childhood heritage and memories in his beautiful home country that he endeavours to honour in every book. We hope you enjoy these books as much as he has in writing them.

Kingsley is also the author of the Gower Peninsula Adventure Series in which Cave Days is the first, Jerry the Magpie series, and The Mermaids Of Mumbles series.

www.ingramcontent.com/pod-product-compliance
Lightning Source LLC
LaVergne TN
LVHW010252260326
834688LV00044B/1246